Taking the Wheel
For
Disciple-making

Volume Two

Herb Hodges

Taking the Wheel For Disciple-making

Volume Two

©2012 Herb Hodges

ALL RIGHTS RESERVED

No part of this publication may be reproduced, stored in a retrieval system, or transmitted in any form without prior written permission.

Spiritual Life Ministries
2916 Old Elm Lane
Germantown, TN 38138
Herb Hodges -- Executive Director

Web site: herbhodges.com
E-mail – herbslm@mindspring.com

Table of Contents

A FEW LESSONS BEFORE TAKING THE WHEEL 5

AT WHAT LEVEL DO YOU LISTEN
TO THE LORD? 17

CHRISTIANITY CONDENSED 37

THE PRACTICAL VALUE OF THE
WORD OF GOD 55

PRAYER THAT PREVAILS 79

WANTED: MEN WHO WILL
MODEL CHRIST 93

HIS LAST WORDS, HIS LAST WILL 113

DOES OBEDIENCE PRODUCE
SLAVERY OR FREEDOM? 129

THE DANGER OF LOSING
SIGHT OF JESUS 151

FROM THRONE TO THRONE BY
WAY OF THE EARTH 167

THE BIBLE AND DISCIPLE-MAKING 193

THE INFINITE IMPORTANCE
OF ILLUMINATION 207

THE CHURCH - THE BODY OF CHRIST 229

WHAT DOES A GENUINE SALVATION
EXPERIENCE LOOK LIKE? 241

WANTED - PEOPLE WHO KNOW
THE ROPES 257

THE CHRISTIAN RACE 275

ADDENDUM 295

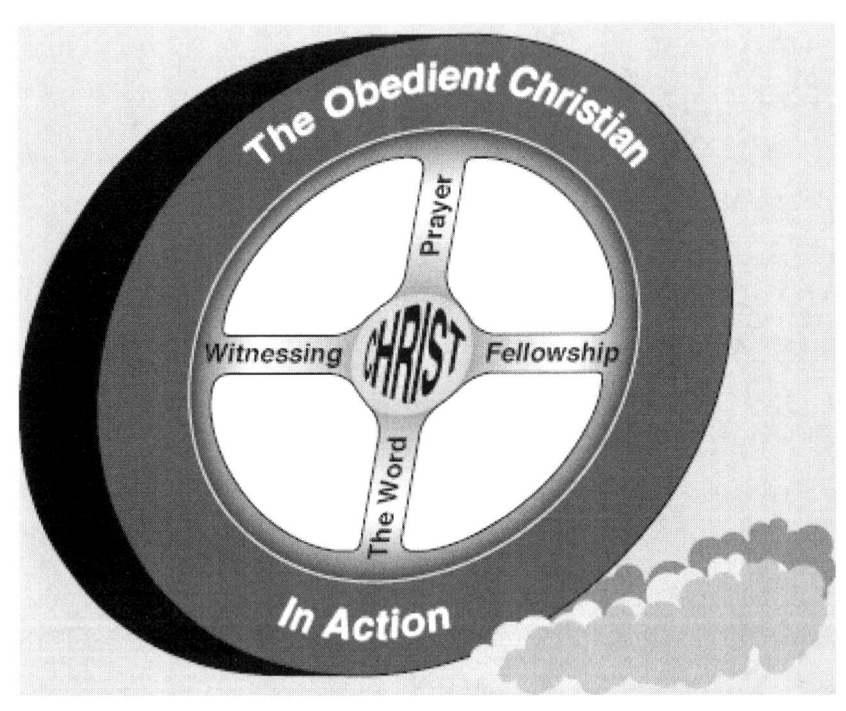

A Few Lessons before Taking the Wheel

We are assuming that you have finished volume one on <u>Taking the Wheel for Disciple-making</u>, and are ready to embark on volume two. Before you zoom off on this second trip using the Navigator's wheel, we want to set forth a few roadway advisory signs.

Many of you have already started making disciples using the curriculum of volume one. Others are ready to start making disciples. Or perhaps you have already had spurious starts, like the false firings of an automobile engine, and you are still willing to gear up for "one last try." I wish you knew how many times I have seen excited, motivated, hot-hearted, emotionally charged believers get a sampling of disciple-making by hearing one or two or three solid sessions of teaching on it and then rush out ready to take on the world, thinking "this will be a breeze." A short time later, they withdraw into silence, or into loneliness, wanting to blame a shortcoming in the concept rather than a deficiency in their understanding and execution. Or they begin to "produce," but the product is pitifully inferior when compared to the promise that is inherent in the process. "I tried that, and it didn't work," one pastor said, and his tone was one of finality. When I asked him to explain what he did in the "trial," his answer reflected little or no real understanding of true disciple-making as it is presented in the New Testament.

I will risk the telling of an actual account, withholding names to protect the guilty. Some years ago, I spent a Monday-Friday week on a college campus, teaching disciple-making for four and one-half hours a day to about 125 people, many of whom were pastors. Admittedly, this was not the ideal setting. The size of the crowd precluded proper give-and-take and adequate communication of the concept, though it was a wonderfully live time each day. On the last day, a pastor came to me in tears and said, "You have saved my life in the ministry this week." I sympathetically said, "What do you mean?" He said, "My church has just experienced a down-the-middle split, and I have my resignation written out on my office desk at home. I was intending to read it this Sunday to the church. I am here this week only because I wanted to get away from it all. My only standard of success in the ministry has been numerical growth, and this split has absolutely devastated me. But you have shown me an entirely different standard of ministry this week – and I can do it! So I'm going home and getting a group of men together, and will begin discipling them as soon as possible." I said nothing about this show of enthusiasm, and simply encouraged him in his new-found thrust.

About one month later, I received a phone call one afternoon from this pastor. After we greeted each other, he said wistfully, "I have a problem." I answered, "Yes, I know, and I know what it is." He said, "How could you know what it is?" "Well, I do know what it is," I replied. "Then what do you think it is?" I insisted, "I know what it is. Your problem is that you don't know how to do it; you heard the entire week of teaching on disciple-making, and then discovered as you attempted it that you don't know how to do it." He said, "Well, you're right; I thought I understood it, but when I started, I found that I didn't know what to do." I said, "That's not surprising. You see, the teaching only gave the foundational idea; it did not present the technique. So what can I do?" "Can we get together sometime soon?" he asked. I answered, "I would be delighted to meet with you." So we met shortly thereafter in an informal restaurant setting. After we had visited for a couple of hours, he asked, "Can we get together again?" I said, "Sure. When?" He answered inquisitively, "Once a week?" That was the beginning of a small group of pastors meeting once a week (when I was in town) for seven and a half years!! And we did nothing but read aloud to each other great devotional and strategy literature!! I chose the literature, alternating from devotional classics to great strategy books, and we read them page after page to each other-with no discussion! You see, preachers do all of their thinking between their nose and their chin (remember that I *am* one, and this is an "inside" confession), and they "think" all the time (!); if they ever start discussing, they will never cover the subject matter. So we (only) read for one hour at each meeting, then we reserved thirty minutes afterward for discussion of what we had read.

Only eternity will reveal the radical revolutions in our lives and in their churches during that time!!! Both of their churches turned completely around. The man who had "written out his resignation" seven and one-half years before was now one of the happiest and most fulfilled pastors I have ever met, remaining many more years as pastor of the same church. For seven and one-half years, we read and talked disciple-making and all of the "filler" dimensions. Learning steadily about how to do it, he practiced it in an enlarging way, and the changes were incredible and dramatic. It would take far too long to tell of advances in the other man's life and church, but again, the results were remarkable. Before I leave this paragraph, let me caution you not to think that such a long time (7 1/2 years) is at all necessary to learn the procedure of disciple-making. I have seen some run with it productively to the ends of the earth after only a few *hours* of teaching.

So how does an aspiring disciple-maker start? My motto is, If he truly *sees* it (the full concept of disciple-making), he will do it. So, when anyone asks me, How do you do it? I always ask, Have you really *seen* what it is? Are you sure you have seen the New Testament Mandate and Model of disciple-making? Nonetheless, let me offer a few "rules for the road" as many of you prepare to hit the discipleship road.

START SMART

Start smart, but not with *my* worthless "smart," or *yours*, but with *God's*. The Bible calls it "wisdom," and it indicates that God has an exclusive market on this wisdom, and that He is not reluctant to give it to hungry men – but it never comes except by a top-drawer, Class A, heavyweight championship miracle. This miracle is called "illumination," and it is a miracle of God – as great a miracle as the New Birth, or the Creation of the world, or the Resurrection of Christ! Yes, I mean exactly that!

My motto verse at this point was written by the Apostle Paul to his younger disciple, Timothy. Paul said, "Consider what I say, and the Lord give you understanding in all things" (II Timothy 2:7). Remind yourself that this verse is recorded in one of the greatest chapters on disciple-making in the entire Bible. Paul is pouring out one picture after another of disciples and disciple-makers when he suddenly "interrupts" with this statement. Note two things about the statement: Divine illumination may follow human communication. Human communication almost invariably begins the illuminating process. This means that human intelligence must be "brought to the table" when truth is spoken (after all, what do we have to *begin* with except human intelligence?). So human communication by the speaker or writer must be greeted by human intelligence in the reception of the listener. Hopefully, the Holy Spirit has already directed the speaker in choosing and presenting the truth, and hopefully, the recipient (listener) is already filled with the Spirit and walking in the Spirit when the moment of communication arrives. Then, while the communicator is speaking or writing, and the auditor/reader is listening or reading, God the Holy Spirit turns on the lights inside the recipient. I repeat: this is a first-class miracle of God!

The Lord give you understanding in all things." When this occurs, the teacher is the Holy Spirit, and He improves/overwhelms the human communication with Divine authority and power (and the human communicator may not even know it is happening, because it is occurring within the recipient). James said, "If any of you lack wisdom, let him ask of God, who gives to all men liberally and will not rebuke them for asking" (James 1:5). Ask God for the miracle of illumination, and let it become the overwhelming and desperate request of your daily prayer times. You will begin to live and walk "with the lights on," and God Himself will explain the dimensions of the disciple-making process to you. You will realize that you should never "force-feed" anybody the disciple-making concept. "Slam dunks" do not work in this process. Keep a record of all the lessons God teaches you and retain them for future use. Start with God's "smart."

START SMALL

Start small! In fact, don't be disturbed if your disciple-making never takes on the dimensions of "Madison Avenue `Big'" One Timothy, one Silas, one Barnabas, one Titus, one Epaphras, one Epaphroditus, may set in motion the multiplication process that will *impact the entire world.* Of course, you likely don't believe that, or you can't even comprehend it, or you question it. But you don't know what I know, what any long-tenure, productive disciple-maker whose vision agrees with God, knows. I have seen this with my eyes, and many times. I said to a brother recently, "I can't believe that God has let me live long enough to see this kind of productivity, and it has to be a miracle, because I stumbled along in the process, learning by trial and error, even doing things He seemed to spell out when I wasn't even certain about what I was doing." I can introduce you to a large network of disciples who are consumed with the process, building disciples regularly, witnessing for Christ consistently, and being blessed by great productivity as they engage in The Process.

Start small. Everything big starts little. A massive oak tree began as a tiny acorn. A 260 pound man began with the union of a tiny female egg and a tiny male cell. Jesus trusted the strategy and the process which He modeled in His ministry and commanded in the Great Commission. By this process, the Christian movement was initiated and implemented, and it was His intention that the movement maintain this process throughout the remainder of history. His original model is evident. While personally ministering to masses of people as opportunity arose, His entire "basket" had only twelve eggs in it (and one of them was a "rotten egg" in the dozen!). Jesus was smart enough to start small, but we are usually stupid enough to try to start big. You can't have two disciples until you have one, so begin by asking God for one, for a bona fide, genuine, solid gold, God-pursuing, teachable disciple.

If you have my book <u>Fox Fever</u>, go back to the study on Colossians one and read the acrostic for the word "faithful," and ask God for that kind of man. Also in the book, go back and read the study on Psalm One, and ask God for that kind of man. Go back and read the chapter on multiplication, and ask God for that kind of man. And remember that any man you meet may be that man. Bury your life in this kind of man, trust God to let him see the Fox, watch him catch Fox Fever, and then stand back amazed as you see him return from one "Fox hunt" after another. He will have the hoarseness of the "Tally Ho" cry in his throat and "fox hair in his teeth" (disciple Roy Campbell's graphic phrase). Movements of disciple-making will begin to spring up all over the world; in fact, if that is not happening, some-one needs to look for the deficiency. I would like to be able to summon any one of fifty or more "fox hunters" before you, and let them testify. Their ministries will not die when *they* do. Their influence will compound through generations because of their skill and motivation in making disciples. Nonetheless, at the beginning, start small.

START HERE

Start here! Don't wait for the ideal environment or the perfect spot. Any golfer knows that you don't choose your lie after you have hit the ball, nor can you "improve" it in the normal course of a normal game. You hit the ball where it lies. When a football is fumbled in a game, you don't recover it where you *wish* it had been fumbled; you recover it where it falls on the field. Start where you stand. Don't wait until you (!) and your situation are "perfect." A Chinese proverb says, "Even the longest journey still begins with the first step." Start where you are and take the first step. Engage in on-the-job discipling, and God will give you on-the-job training. Continue trusting for the wisdom of God, even when you stand baffled at a crossroad. When Jesus said, "As you are going, turn people into disciples," He meant, among other things, that you are not to take one more step without beginning to make disciples. Be sure you are a student in Christ's school of discipleship, attending "class" regularly, fulfilling all assignments and studying for the daily "pop quizzes." Then invite someone to enroll in the same school you are attending. While Jesus is your teacher in the "private class" every day, you are to be a personal tutor, echoing His truth and His strategy to your enlistee. Start where you are at this moment.

START NOW

Start now! Though this rule merely echoes and re-enforces the last one, it deserves to be high-lighted in a separate treatment. Procrastination is the thief of productivity, and drift will cancel your efficiency. "A procrastinator is a person who will not take *now* for an answer." In order to guard against the peril of procrastination and the deadly danger of drift, begin now and trust God to keep you up-to-date.

STAY STEADY

Stay steady! Sometime ago, the daily news told of a ninety year old woman who walked a long distance from a city in Florida to a town in the upper eastern part of the United States. When asked how she had done it, she simply replied, "I took one step at a time." Dear Christian, do not stop taking the necessary steps! Keep growing in your understanding of disciple-making, keep contact with other disciple-makers, keep praying for your disciples, keep pouring Jesus' truth and strategy into their lives, keep trusting for multi-generation multiplication in their lives, and don't allow anything to deter you. A young guy said to an old man, "How did you live to be one hundred and one years old?" The old man replied, "I didn't drink, smoke, overeat or carouse around." The questioner said, "I had an uncle who lived by all of those rules – and he died at fifty-seven. How do you explain that?" The old man retorted, "His problem was that he just didn't keep it up long enough!" The shores of eternity will be lined with the sterile lives of Christians who never faithfully and steadily pursued the impulses of the Spirit, with potential disciple-makers who respected the strategy but never applied themselves with steady sub-mission to Jesus in the disciple-making process. A disciple-maker who wants to be used of God to impact the world by fulfilling the mandate of Jesus must determine to "put his hand to the plow and not look back" (Luke 9:62).

The late great NFL football player, Walter Peyton, who for some time was renowned as the leading ground-gainer as a ball-carrier in NFL history, was playing his final game for the Chicago Bears on the NFL "Monday night game of the week." The two play-by-play announcers were reciting Peyton's statistical accomplishments with great approval and appreciation. One said, "It is downright hard to believe that this relatively small man carried the football in National Football League competition for over nine miles!" The other replied, "Maybe so, but I find something else to be even harder to believe, and that is that on an average of every 3.8 yards, he was knocked down violently by one, or two, or even three men, men who were usually twice as big as Walter is!" Then the commentator added, "The test was not how well he ran in the open field; the test was in how he went back to the huddle and prepared to take the ball again after he had been run over again and again by something twice as big as he is."

I am thinking of one disciple who had been around the disciple-making process for a long time before he ever saw the full truth of it. He was at my house one morning at 6 a.m. with a group of regular weekly attendants who came at that early hour at least once a week. He was sitting innocently in a chair as I taught and we discussed disciple-making. Suddenly he went rigid in his chair, turned his face upward toward the ceiling, and exclaimed, "I see it! I see it!" He repeated this over and over. When someone asked him, "What do you see?" He exclaimed loudly, "Multiplication! Multiplication! Multiplication!" That night, he called two men and invited them to begin the disciple-making process with him. Many years later, one of those two men (a layman, an electrical engineer) has traveled all over the world on many training trips, training pastors and leaders in "how to fulfill the Great Commission of Jesus by building world-visionary disciples who will reproduce others of the same kind and thus will impact the world to the ends of the earth and until the end of time." That disciple, the electrical engineer, told me when I inquired recently that he can teach nearly three hundred Biblical strategy sessions and curriculum sessions on disciple-making! This is an example of the motivation I have seen arise in men who have truly seen The Standard. His discipler, the man who "saw" it in my home that morning, is one of the most visionary and productive disciple-makers I have ever met. But what if we had given up when he didn't "see" it at first exposure? What if he had dropped out of The Process? What if I had discontinued teaching it? He and everyone around him in The Process stayed steady, and this allowed God to work more completely than before. The boxer known as "Gentleman Jim" Corbett was the reigning heavyweight champion of the world for five years before the turn of the twentieth century. Corbett once relayed this advice to aspiring boxers: "Fight one more round. When your feet are so tired that you have to shuffle back to the center of the ring, fight one more round. When your arms are so tired that you can hardly lift your hands to come on guard, fight one more round. When your nose is bleeding and your eyes are black and you are so tired that you wish your opponent would crack you on the jaw and put you to sleep, fight one more round – remembering that the man who fights one more round is never whipped." Christian, when you are opposed by the enemy *beneath you,* the *infernal* enemy called the Devil, and by the enemy *around you,* the *external* enemy called the world, and by the enemy *within you,* the *internal* enemy called the flesh, and when these enemies are uniting to tell you to give it all up, *fight one more round.*

Max Dupree, a renowned teacher of leadership principles, once said, "I do not want to be a world champion in the 95-yard dash. The first 95 yards will have no meaning and no record in the track record books if I am not able or willing to make it through the final five yards." Disciple-maker, stay steady! The next trophy you win by steadfastness may be a discipler who will win and train multitudes of disciples."Be ye steadfast, unmovable, always abounding in the work of the Lord, forasmuch as you know that your labor is not in vain in the Lord" (I Corinthians 15:58). When you stand at the Judgment Seat of Christ and He deliberately turns you around to see who is in your train, what will you want to see? When He asks about your down-line of disciples, what will you want to report? When He mentions multiplication as the normal result of the right use of His Strategy, how many generations of disciples/disciplers will walk in your wake?

AT WHAT LEVEL DO YOU LISTEN TO THE LORD?

Matthew 13:3-9:

"And he spake many things unto them in parables, saying, Behold, a sower went forth to sow; And when he sowed, some seeds fell by the wayside, and the fowls came and devoured them up: Some fell upon stony places, where they had not much earth: and forthwith they sprung up, because they had no deepness of earth: And when the sun was up, they were scorched; and because they had no root, they withered away. And some fell among thorns, and the thorns sprung up, and choked them: But other fell into good ground, and brought forth fruit, some a hundredfold, some sixtyfold, some thirtyfold. Who hath ears to hear, let him hear."

     A parable is a handle which Jesus puts into our hands to enable us to pick up a truth and take it home with us. We normally call this story "the parable of the sower," and this title probably is used mainly as one of convenience (see Matthew 13:18). The parable seems to be told as an analysis of the soil-types more than an assessment of the sower. So it could easily be called "the parable of the soils." Verse nine gives us an excellent key for interpreting the parable. "Who hath ears (there is a person's capacity to hear) to hear (there is a person's opportunity to hear), let him hear (there is a person's responsibility to hear)." This is a parable about hearing. Sixteen times in some eleven verses in the text and context, Jesus referred to hearing (read this sentence again and ponder it carefully).

What people hear when confronted with the truth of God, "the word of the kingdom" (Matthew 13:19), is determined by the spiritual sensitivity of their heart. The word "kingdom" is a key word in understanding the thirteenth chapter of Matthew and the parables it contains. What distinguishes a kingdom? Is it not the presence and reign of a king? The kingdom of God is an absolute monarchy with a benevolent "despot" (Greek, *despotes*), King Jesus, on the throne. This means that all rules are established by Him, and any revolt or disobedience is a serious offence. But be very careful to note the word "benevolent" in our definition of this Kingdom. King Jesus is only and always good, and His reign is good for all of His subjects. However, this parable admits that not all listeners in the Realm give full cooperation to the King. It tells us that we set up "rival kingdoms" of self-interest and self-dominion. If you are absorbed with your own kingdom, the truth of the Kingdom of God, the "word of the kingdom," will be diverted from your heart.

Let me "traffic the text" for awhile, interpreting a few of its main points. Note that the parable opens with the word "behold." This is not a mere wasted word, used as an introductory device. It seems to be used in the Bible to suggest that what follows is very important, and can only be known by Divine revelation and illumination. No Divine revelation and illumination are required to see farmers sowing their fields in the springtime; no, it is the spiritual message of the parable that requires Divine revelation and illumination.

AT WHAT LEVEL DO YOU LISTEN TO THE LORD?

Note, too, that there are four different "levels" at which the seed penetrated the various kinds of soils in the story. These four levels of penetration and production represent different levels of listening to the Lord, or they represent different levels of cooperation with the truth heard. In the first case, the seed was on the soil, but not in it. In the second case, the seed was on the soil, and in it, but it could not get down. In the third case, the seed was on, in and down, but it could not get back up. In the final case, the seed was on, in, down, **up and out.**

Keep the word *out* stored in the forefront of your mind. It pictures the desired result with regard to Gospel penetration. Always *out*! The kind of Christianity that exclusively (or even primarily) implodes into a place and a gathering is highly suspect as a version of New Testament Christianity. Jesus mandated the outward, outgoing procedure many, many times in the Gospels. The entire book of Acts is either a record of the outward movement of the Gospel, or a record of the struggle to overcome the provincial, parochial, in-turned tendency of Christians who settle for attractive human substitutes for the strategy of the Gospel.

In the story, the human heart is like soil, and the message of the Kingdom is like seed. Each listener discriminates in his listening, filtering the truth that is "sown" on the soil of his heart by his preconceptions and his preoccupations. The first kind of hearing is represented by much-trodden wayside soil. This person's heart is closed and hardened to the extent that there is zero penetration of the Gospel of the Kingdom. The auditors in this category are completely self-absorbed. When the seed strikes the soil, it cannot penetrate, so it lies vulnerable on the surface until birds detect it and devour it. This type of soil represents the listener who really thinks the Gospel is "for the birds"! His heart has been hardened by much traffic on it, and some of the traffic has been comprised of the very feet that sow the Gospel seed. So it is dangerous for a man to attend church, treat the truth he hears with glib indifference, and make no serious response to the demands of that truth. With every such trip, he is hardening his heart through the circumstance of this kind of listening. The Bible gives stringent and frightful warnings about hardening the heart against God and His truth (see Hebrews 3, as an example).

The second kind of listening is symbolized in the story by shallow soil. Jesus is describing a terrain in which a sub-surface shelf of rock is covered by a thin layer of topsoil. The seed had "no depth of earth," and thus could not subsist beyond a show of life. "When the sun was up, the new plants were scorched; and because they had no root, they withered away." This listener is very enthusiastic and receptive *at first*. However, when the real terms of the Kingdom begin to fully dawn on him, and persecution and trouble are thrown into the mix, he quickly turns back to his old self-centered ways.

The third kind of listening is symbolized by thorn-infested soil. The plant would bear fruit, but it is choked by the thick thorns that infest the soil as the plant tries to emerge from the earth. These thorns, according to Jesus, represent "the cares of this world, the deceitfulness of riches, and the lusts of other things entering in," and those competing interests choke the word, and it becomes unfruitful.

The fourth kind of listening is symbolized by the good soil. This kind of listener bears fruit unto God (Romans 7:4), yet even here there are varying degrees of cooperation with the kingdom and thus, varying degrees of productivity as well. The degree of cooperation with the King and commitment to the Kingdom will determine the exact amount of productivity.

AT WHAT LEVEL DO YOU LISTEN TO THE LORD?

In verses 18 through 24 of Matthew 13, Jesus interpreted His own parable. It would neither be fair nor safe for us to ignore His interpretation of His own parable. In verse 18, Jesus struck the keynote again: "Hear ye the parable of the sower." He seemed to teach and caution constantly about hearing.

"When any one heareth the word of the kingdom, and understandeth it not, then cometh the wicked one, and catcheth away that which was sown in his heart. This is he which received seed by the wayside." The term "wicked one" bears major emphasis in the verse. Satan is emphasized in the verse. The devil knows the value of the truth! And Jesus indicated that Satan has a great "follow-up program" after the word of the kingdom is presented. Satan attends church! More than you do! More than I do! And he easily capitalizes the hard heart. With each hearing of the Word, the unresponsive, unproductive heart gets harder. So deadly forces are in work within him and upon him when he hears the truth without proper response. The Word is caught away, and he is left in chilling silence, subject to his own selfish devices.

"But he that received the seed into stony places, the same is he that heareth the word, and anon with joy receiveth it; Yet hath he not root in himself, but dureth for a while: for when tribulation or persecution ariseth because of the word, by and by he is offended." Two terms bear major emphasis in this statement. One is the word "joy," which makes this response sound so hopeful. The other is the term, "for a while," which removes the hope that had been excited. The response of this listener is like a straw fire — quickly kindled, brightly flashing for a moment, and then gone. Actually, the word "joy" should have created suspicion in us from the beginning. Joy is a part of the emotions. The emotions are the shallowest part of human nature. God would never suspend His deepest work in the shallowest part of our nature. As important as the emotions are as a vital part of true humanity, they are not solid enough to be foundational for any eternal work. This listener's response is one-dimensional only. Jesus said "he hath not root in himself." His roots are in the accident of the moment, so he only endures as long as the moment sustains him. When the demands of the King are fully known, "by and by he is offended (made to stumble)." He stumbles over the high cost of following the King, and drops out.

"He also that received seed among the thorns is he that heareth the word; and the care of this world, and the deceitfulness of riches, choke the word, and he becometh unfruitful." The emphatic term here is the word "unfruitful." This person is the typical double-minded listener. He seems to "hear the word," but he hears every thing else as well. His life is like a jungle, and the competition of other interests destroys all possibility of fruit.

"But he that received seed into the good ground is he that heareth the word, and understandeth it; which also beareth fruit, and bringeth forth, some a hundredfold, some sixty, some thirty." He hears as the other listeners did, he understands (as they did not), and the symptom of his life and listening is that he bears fruit.

Note carefully that nowhere in the parable is the integrity and quality of the seed questioned. And nowhere is the character of the sower seen as either an advantage or a disadvantage. The sower is merely a role-player in the parable.

Let me attempt to outline the contents in some organized form (view on the next page).

There are three prominent features in the parable. One is the sower, one is the seed, and one is the different kinds of soil. We will examine each of them.

Soil Type No. One	Soil Type No. Two	Soil Type No. Three	Soil Type No. Four
Roadside soil	Rocky soil	Repressive soil	Reproductive soil
Seed On, but not *in*	Seed On & In, but *not Down*	Seed On, In & Down, but *not Up*	Seed On, In, Down, Up, and Out
Seed had no Reception	Seed had no Root	Seed had no Room	Seed had no Resistance
Complete Self-absorption	Confusion of loyalty	Competition for attention	Cooperation with the King
The Satisfied Listener	The Shallow Listener	The Strangled Listener	The Spiritual Listener

I. The SOWER

The first prominent feature of the parable is the *sower*. In verse three, Jesus said, "Behold, a sower went forth to sow." Who does this sower represent?

First, this *sower* represents **Christ.** The Gospel age was launched when the Son of God "went forth to sow." This line comprises a worthy transcript of His entire ministry. He came from Heaven, carrying the "word of the kingdom," and He sowed it wholesale on all types of soil. Here is His simplest autobiography. He Himself explained it this way: "He that soweth the good seed is the Son of man" (verse 37).

The sower in the story also represents *the Christian* in every age. The one consistent assignment, the one continual vocation, of the Christian is to scatter the living seed on all hearts. An Old Testament text states it in this manner: "They that sow in tears shall reap in joy. He that goeth forth and weepeth, bearing precious seed, shall doubtless come again with rejoicing, bringing his sheaves with him" (Psalm 126:5-6). Sometime ago, a former farmer challenged the Scriptures in my presence, stating that some of the analogies the Bible makes of sowing and reaping are inaccurate. He called attention in particular to Mark 4:26-29, where Jesus said that, when seed touches the soil, the harvest is automatic. He said that he had never seen success in indiscriminate sowing while he was farming. I replied that these analogies are not intended to be exact reflections of observable patterns in human farming; in fact, they are intended to set their own standard. I called his attention to Psalm 126:5-6, and asked him if he had ever seen a farmer weeping profusely as he went out into a field to sow. "No I haven't," he replied. "But this is the rule for successful sowing of Gospel seed," I said. You see, Jesus is setting the standard for Gospel sowing, not merely reflecting rules for farming.

Sowing is not a very glamorous or attractive activity. Nobody hurries to a field in the springtime, hoping to win applause by his sowing. However, every farmer knows that unless he sows seed, there will be no harvest. And he also knows that when he sows, he is becoming partner to a miracle. And every Christian should sow for the same reason. When a Christian places the seed of Divine truth on the soil of a human heart, it is something like planting a time bomb under someone's seat. The person who puts it there can depart the scene saying, "I know something he doesn't know." Now the explosions that are caused by Gospel seed are of two kinds: (1) Sometimes the seed "explodes" or germinates inside the sinner with its own life, and he is saved; (2) Sometimes the sinner explodes in reaction against the seed, thus reinforcing his own lostness. One is the germination of the seed; the other predicts the termination of the sinner.

One of the greatest problems in today's church is that the average Sunday auditor in church features himself only as a supporter instead of a sower. Clearly, the assignment for all Christians is to sow, but the harvesting process is destroyed in its inception if Christians do not sow Gospel seeds on human hearts. The entire Gospel enterprise is launched when a sower of Gospel seeds "goes forth to sow." The sower represents both Christ and the Gospel-sharing Christian.

II. The SEED

The second prominent feature of the parable is the *seed*. Luke's Gospel, in particular, is quite graphic in emphasizing the seed. Luke 8:5 literally says, "The seeder went out to seed his seed." Apparently, the seed is very important in the process of farming. And the reality it represents is even more important in the economy of the Gospel. Again, the interpretation is two-fold.

First, the seed represents God's *message*. Verse 19 identifies the seed as "the word of the kingdom," and Luke 8:11 says, "The seed is the Word of God." What an enlightening symbol. God's truth, God's word, "the word of the kingdom," is like a seed.

Here we see the *apparent frailty* of the truth of God. Any word seems frail and helpless, and this seems to be especially true of God's truth. You can take most seeds and hold them between your thumb and your index finger — and they will be hidden from sight. You can rub your finger and thumb together in a grinding motion — and they may disintegrate. James Russell Lowell admitted in his famous poem that truth is easily "crushed to earth."

Sometimes when I stand to preach or teach, I am overwhelmed with the seeming hopelessness of the venture of communicating Divine truth. That truth is as frail as a seed, and may be mistreated like a frail and fragile seed.

But we also see here the *actual force* of God's truth. Christian, don't permit yourself to be deceived by appearances! "It pleased God by the foolishness of preaching (literally, "the thing preached") to save those who believe." "The Word of God is living and powerful, and sharper than a two-edged sword, piercing even to the dividing asunder of the soul and the spirit, and is a discerner (Greek, "critic") of the thoughts and intents of the heart" (Hebrews 4:12). Jeremiah quotes God: "Is not My Word like a fire, says the Lord, and like a hammer that breaks the rock in pieces?" That which is frail to appearance has an unbelievable actual force.

In 1922, English archaeologist Howard Carter was excavating and studying in the famed Valley of the Kings in central Egypt, when he cleared a work area inside a tomb and discovered that it had a false back wall. When he broke through that false wall, he found a new compartment, and that new compartment proved to be King Tut's tomb. Tutankhamen was an Egyptian pharaoh of the eighteenth Egyptian dynasty (reigning from 1348-1339 B.C.)

I have seen the best of the contents of Tut's tomb, which are on display in the Cairo Museum. Among the many items found in the tomb, a metal urn filled with seeds was discovered. Remember that this tomb was approximately 3200 years old when discovered. The urn was opened and some of the seeds within were sent to London for experimentation. A portion of the seeds was planted — and a garden full of plants came up from seeds which had lain dormant for over 3000 years! Friends, the Gospel always has a vital and revitalizing power within it! The Divine life-germ within it merely needs to be planted in good soil, the soil of some Divinely prepared human heart, and a harvest with limitless potential will result.

We also see here the *awesome fruitfulness* of God's truth. Can you imagine the nearly infinite potential there is in just one wheat or corn seed? A seed's power of growth is incredible to consider. Here, Jesus talked about a seed yielding several times more than that which was planted. "Thirty-fold" is 3,000 %; "sixty-fold" is 6,000 %; and "one hundred fold" is 10,000 %. This is a large return. But any farmer knows that for a bushel of corn to produce only a hundredfold would be a meager yield. Corn planted on good ground will produce far more. But, assuming that corn produces only a hundredfold, suppose you had one bushel of corn and were to plant it and its product for so brief a period as fifteen years, how much corn would you have?

At the end of the first year you would have one hundred bushels, at the end of the second, ten thousand bushels, at the end of the third, one million bushels. At the end of the fifteen years you would have enough corn that if it were rolled into corn balls it would make 31,536,188 worlds the size of ours, with a fraction left over! That small fraction left over, we are told, would be enough to feed the present population of the earth for a thousand years. Such is the potential of a few seeds in the vegetable kingdom. Christian, pay no attention to the sad situation around you; just sow the seed! From the seed you might plant, God could bring in to Heaven's granary an infinite eternal harvest.

But the seed not only represents God's message; it also represents God's *man*. So just as the sower had a dual interpreter, so does the seed. In Matthew 13:38, Jesus said, "The good seed are the children of the kingdom."

The growth of the early church in the book of Acts is often reported in terms of the sowing and germinating and reproducing of seeds. Acts 8:1 says, "And at that time there was a great persecution against the church which was at Jerusalem; and they were all scattered abroad throughout the regions of Judea and Samaria, except the apostles." Acts 8:4 adds, "Therefore they that were scattered abroad went everywhere preaching the word." The term translated "scattered abroad" is the Greek term "diesparasan kata." The longer word is a compound word containing the root word "spore," which is the word for a seed. So the picture is that of God sending a persecution and throwing out his people over the world just like a sower throws seeds out over the soil as he sows a field. In verse four, the word translated "scattered abroad" is a similar word, "diasparentes." Again it is the idea of a sower flinging seeds over a wide area in a field. Remember that Jesus had commanded His disciples to be His witnesses "both in Jerusalem, and in Judea, and in Samaria, and unto the uttermost part of the earth." Well, they made it (unaided) as far as Jerusalem! Their comfort zone included Jerusalem, but no more! They were not serious about His command to go to the ends of the earth — but *He was!* So He allowed a severe persecution to arise against them, a persecution that scattered them like seeds over (guess where!) "Judea and Samaria" (!), the second and third places assigned by Jesus in Acts 1:8. Disobedient Christian, determined to enjoy your comfort zone in affluent America and categorically forget the rest of the world, get ready! Tough times are coming! Likely so tough that they will launch large numbers of Christians involuntarily over the world!

  The symbol of a seed representing the Christian has large lessons in it for us. First, what is the *purpose* of a seed? A seed has only one basic purpose — to carry the life-germ of the plant from which it comes and be a vital part of the continuing "line" of that plant. A Christian has only one purpose — to carry the "life-germ" of the Christian movement, the indwelling life of Christ Himself in the Presence and power of the Holy Spirit, and to be a vital link in the continuation of that movement.

Second, what is the *program* of a seed? Jesus declared it when He said, "Unless a grain of wheat falls into the ground and dies, it abides alone; but if it dies, it brings forth much fruit" (John 12:24). There is the program of a seed. In I Corinthians 15:36, the Apostle Paul echoed, "Thou fool, that which thou sowest is not quickened, except it die." Those words of Jesus contain one of the most fundamental and revolutionary life principles He ever uttered. The meaning? The life of Christ will be manifested through us in exact proportion as the Cross of Christ is operative in us. Every Christian must die a certain death before the indwelling life of Christ can be released through him. Do not misunderstand this. Biblically, death is not the mere cessation of existence. It is rather the reduction or resolution of any substance to its primary elements. Once a person is saved, the "primary element," the indestructible and irreducible minimum, is the "eternal life" which he has because of his union with Jesus Christ. His natural life, the life that is concerned solely with the values of this world and of the here and now, must die.

All Christians have an eagerness to succeed for God. Indeed, they may continually try to be productive and cry to Him for spiritual power. But they are usually trying and crying with the flesh protected and intact. The "flesh" is the "me-life" (see Romans 7:18). God cannot use this life for His purposes; it must "die."

Go back to Jesus' analogy. The polished, self-contained seed was, paradoxically, dead because it had not died. What a perplexing paradox this entire verse is! What happened when the "grain of wheat" died? Among other things, it disappeared (!), and deteriorated (!), and disintegrated (!), and was destroyed (!). Think of that seed. Unsown, it is alone. Sown, it appears worthless. If a farmer were to dig up a hundred bushels of seeds two days after they were planted, he could not sell all of them for five cents. But stay with the seed and heed its coming history! That is where its glory lies! Christian, if you wish to be fruitful for God, study this section carefully.

    Third, what is the *power* of a seed? I was somewhere in a western state years ago when I saw a road identification sign which read, "Split Rock Road." I remarked about it to the pastor who was driving the automobile, and he turned around and turned off the main highway and drove down Split Rock Road. "I think you will be interested in this," he said. Some distance down the road, the road divided to go around a huge sandstone boulder, and the boulder was divided into two parts by a huge tree which had grown up through the middle of it! He said, "They say that the wind deposited a little bit of soil and a seed in a tiny crack of that boulder years ago. The seed found enough nourishment to put down a root and put up a shoot, and a tree was born. In time, that tree pushed its roots through the heart of that boulder and split it into two pieces, and that phenomenon supplied the road with its name." The incredible power of a seed! Every homeowner knows that if you allow that tiny maple shoot to continue growing in the crack in the driveway, it will sooner or later heave up the driveway and destroy it. Dear Christian, I am talking about the power God intends to express through *you*!

    But a seed is powerful in quite another way, and so is your life. We are presently in the hottest part of the summer in Memphis, and watermelon season is in full swing! I had a watermelon feast just this morning after I had mowed my lawn. I put aside dozens of watermelon seeds from the slice that I ate. Take just one watermelon seed. It is small, rather flat, and elliptical in shape. I could easily conceal a watermelon seed between my finger and thumb. But place that seed into the ground in the right season and under right conditions and see what happens! With a remarkable intelligence, it will ignore every strawberry, every plum, ever apricot, every squash, etc., etc., and will find only watermelons! And what a miracle it performs with that which it "finds." That relatively small seed will draw up *through itself* out of the soil a fruit that is 200,000 times its own weight! Read that sentence thoughtfully, carefully and prayerfully. Christian, this is what God intends for *you*. He transplanted you into a grace-garden with the intent that you draw out of its nutrients and resources a volume of fruit and resources that are many times larger than yourself! The incredible power of a seed, and dear Christian, that seed represents you! But remember, this power is given only to fulfill God's purposes.

Finally, we see here the *potential* of a single seed when it "falls into the ground and dies." Someone said, "Anyone can count the number of seeds in an apple, but only God can count the number of apples in a seed." The potential for enlarging reproduction in a single seed is almost beyond belief. And again, Christian, you must remember that this seed represents you. "The good seed are the children of the kingdom," Jesus said.

So the seed represents the message of God and the man of God. We have now examined the sower and the seed. The most commanding feature in Jesus' story and its interpretation will now receive our attention — the soils.

III. The SOILS

The last prominent feature in the parable is the one that receives the greatest attention in Jesus' explanation. The last feature is the different kind of *soils* in the story. These soils represent the hearts of men who hear "the word of the kingdom." The soils stand for human understanding and response when the Gospel is proclaimed. The hero or the villain in this story is the Gospel auditor, and the plot is how well He listens to God and His truth.

Two English women were talking at a Christian convention in London. One said, "I'm from Birmingham, and I am privileged to hear the great Dr. John Henry Jowett every Sunday." The other protested, "My dear, that is not a privilege; that is a fearful responsibility!" Hearing Gospel truth is a great enjoyment for a spiritual Christian, but listening to the Gospel is not merely for pleasure; it is for *productivity*. The two main themes of this parable are: (1) Gospel presentation, and (2) How men will respond to it. The soils represent the various responses men make to the presentation of the Gospel. Note from the beginning that God's intent in presenting His truth to men is that the presentation will eventually produce much fruit.

The parable exposes four kinds of *hearts*, each revealed by the kind of soil pictured. It is important to note that apparently all the seed sown in the parable is "sown in the heart" (verse 19). This is said specifically of the first type of soil — the most unresponsive soil. It is when the seed reaches the soil that the condition of it is revealed. The same is true of the unresponsive listener. The seed did reach his heart, though it found that heart impenetrable. The four kinds of hearts exposed in this parable are the solid heart, the shallow heart, the strangled heart, and the submissive heart.

Then the parable exposes four kinds of hearing. Remember that this is a parable about hearing. The four kinds of hearing are surface hearing, which is basically inattentive to the Gospel; superficial hearing, which is very impulsive in making a quick but uncalculated response; *suffocated* hearing, which is very *indulgent* of all ideas; and *spiritual* hearing which *involves* the total person — his mind, heart, conscience, will, and conduct.

Finally, the parable reveals four kinds of happenings which occur when the Gospel is presented. With regard to the first type of soil, the seed is stolen (verse 4), and the enemy is Satan (verse 19). With regard to the second type of soil, the seed is starved (verses 5 &6), and the enemy is the flesh, or the self-life, which gives no accommodation to God's truth ("no depth of earth," "no root in himself"). With regard to the third type of soil, the seed is stifled and smothered (verses 7 & 22), and the enemy is the world or the society which surrounds the listener (verses 7 & 22).

So the three inveterate enemies of all mankind, the world, the flesh, and the devil, are marshaled unanimously and unceasingly against the proper hearing of the truth of God. Remember that "faith comes by hearing, and hearing by the Word of God" (Romans 10:17). Faith starts with the Word of God, stands on the Word of God, steps out on the Word of God, states the Word of God, and stops with the Word of God. We may lose our focus on the importance of the Word of God, but the devil does not. His purpose is served perfectly if he can destroy proper listening of the Word of God, and if he can distract even those who are seeking to hear it. Just as Satan's temptation in the Garden of Eden began with a questioning of the Word of God, he has been seeking to cast doubt on it ever since. He remembers that man was lost by hearing him, and he knows that men are saved by hearing God. Therefore, he has made himself a master of the communicating business, and untaught, undisciplined believers fall right into his hands.

Two men were conversing. One asked casually, "Does your wife ever talk to herself?" The other replied smugly, "Yes, she does, but she doesn't know it — she thinks I'm listening!" When God speaks, He does not intend to merely talk to Himself. He has enlisted man's capacity to hear, and makes man responsibile for his listening. "He who has ears to hear, let him hear."

Basil Matthews, a great English preacher, came annually years ago to the Calvary Baptist Church in New York City for a Bible conference. One year, he shared the program with an Indian preacher from the western United States. The two developed a friendship during their week of service together. One afternoon, they were walking down a busy street toward their hotel. Sounds of subway, elevated trains, cars, and people saturated their ears. Suddenly the Indian preacher stopped on the sidewalk, placed his hand on Matthews' shoulder to arrest his steps, and exclaimed, "I hear a cricket!" After a moment, he walked rapidly to the street corner and crossed to the far side of the street. They were in front of a flower shop. The Indian entered the shop with Matthews hurrying curiously behind. The Indian listened a moment inside the shop, walked over to a series of potted plants on a shelf, thrust in his hand, and pulled out a cricket. The amazed Matthews walked admiringly with him out of the store. Once outside, he remarked, "That's absolutely amazing. How do you do that?" The Indian replied, "My friend, I learned a long time ago that people hear what they *want* to hear. Let me show you." He reach in his pocket, pulled out two half dollars, and threw them down on the sidewalk. Instantly, four people changed their direction and dashed toward the money.

The question is not, "Does God speak?" The question is, "Do men listen?" Do you listen to Him? Do you listen openly, submissively, longingly, deeply, productively?

AT WHAT LEVEL DO YOU LISTEN TO THE LORD?

One Sunday morning, Alexander Whyte, the great Edinburgh pastor, preached a searching sermon about sin and its consequences. He did not know it, but a mother and her college-age son were seated side by side on a seat in church that morning. The boy was home for college for the weekend. The next week, Dr. Whyte received two letters on different days. One was from the mother, and in the letter she angrily blasted the pastor for his forthright exposure and renunciation of sin. A day or so letter, a letter came from the woman's son, who was back at college, and wrote to tell Dr. Whyte that he had been saved through his message on the past Sunday! To some listeners, the Gospel produces a progression of "life unto life," while to others, it leads to "death unto death." Everything depends on the depth and quality of a person's listening. Dear friend, at what level, with what intensity, with what awareness, with what outcome, do you listen to the Lord?

CHRISTIANITY CONDENSED

Philippians 1:21:

"For to me to live is Christ, and to die is gain."

In twelve brief words, the Apostle Paul has summarized the Christian view of life and death. I have used two different titles for this verse. One is "Christianity Condensed," the other is "The Simple Secret of the Christian Life." The verse is a compound sentence constructed by the combining of two smaller sentences. All the words in the sentence are monosyllables, or one-syllable words. You do not need to know the complicated language of theological jargon to live the life that wins. Here it is in twelve brief, one-syllable words. And nine of the twelve words have three letters or less! This means that this verse is the very apex of simplicity. Nothing could be simpler, yet nothing is more profound.

The two shorter sentences are separated by a comma. The sentence before the comma gives the Christian view of *life*, while the sentence after the comma gives the Christian view of *death*. There are three strong words in the verse, the words "me," "live," and "Christ." The middle term, "live," is defined in the union of the two other words, "me" and "Christ." When the two terms, "me" and "Christ" are brought into right relationship, I become "alive unto God." The human finds real life in union with the Divine. This is the only combination that truly deserves to be called "life." The word "life" stands defined in the equation of this verse.

However, in our foolish attempts to find life, we take other extremes and combine them, and we call the result "life." We sometimes say, "To me to live is money." Or, "to me to live is pleasure." Or, "to me to live is fame." But the New Testament answers each of these combinations with this verdict, "Thou hast a *name* that thou livest, and art *dead*." All other combinations fail. The equation is not accurate without the Biblical components. Life is the unique product of a unique union. Jesus said, "This is life eternal, that they may know Thee the only true God, and Jesus Christ Whom Thou hast sent" (John 17:3). This is the theological statement; our text is the practical statement. The word "know" in Jesus' statement is a present tense continuous verb, and may be translated, "go on knowing," or "be knowing." So eternal life is an ongoing relationship or union with God through Jesus Christ. Also, this verb "know" is the same word that is used in the old Septuagint or Greek version of the Old Testament for sexual intimacy. Thus, the Bible says that "Adam *knew* Eve his wife, and she conceived, and brought forth a son." So life is found in intimate, loving interaction between a human being and God. Paul's words echo the Biblical formula for life. "For to me to live is Christ, and to die is gain." Here is the simple secret of the Christian life — and yet, so profound!

I. THE CHRISTIAN LIFE IS DEEPLY PERSONAL

First, the verse indicates that the Christian life is *deeply personal*. "To me to live is Christ." The words, "to me," stand in the emphatic position in the sentence. It is obvious that Paul

CHRISTIANITY CONDENSED

is making a statement of deep personal feelings and preferences here. Jesus Christ is only possessed personally in the life of a human being. If these words do not comprise my personal testimony, then I am not a Christian. Martin Luther said, "Every man must do his own believing, just as every man must do his own dying." And he added, "The most important words in the Bible are the personal possessive pronouns, my and mine."

The Bible says that "God so loved the world" (John 3:16). It says that "Christ loved the church" (Ephesians 5:25). But this would bring me no benefit if I could not say with Paul, "Christ loved *me*, and gave Himself for *me*" (Galatians 2:20). The Bible says that Jesus is the "Good Shepherd who gives His life for His sheep" (John 10:11). It says that He is the "Great Shepherd" (Hebrews 13:20). It says that He is the "Chief Shepherd" (I Peter 5:4). But this would bring me no benefit if I could not say with David, "The Lord is *my* shepherd" (Psalm 23:1).

A cartoon by syndicated cartoonist George Clark showed two women talking over a cup of coffee. One says, "I'm pleased as punch with my weight-watchers club. Last week, we collectively lost 143 pounds among us!" But then she added, "However, I'm sad to admit that none of it was mine personally!" So where was the accomplishment? Where was the victory? She was not a real part of the victory or the accomplishment. You see, dear friend, it is not enough to be closely associated with Christian people, Christian places, or Christian activities. You must know Christ *personally*.

A girl named Edith went to church every Sunday, though nobody else in the family attended. One Sunday, her mother met her at the front door as Edith returned home from church. Edith was smiling broadly. Her mother asked her what she was smiling about. "Mama, the preacher preached from a verse of the Bible that had my name in it!" Edith announced. "Really, what was the verse?" her mother asked. "Luke 15:2, 'This man (Jesus) receiveth sinners, and *Edith* with them!'" she answered triumphantly. Dear friend, unless you have seen the proposition of salvation addressed personally to you, unless you have received Christ personally, unless you have been born of God personally — unless you have heard your name as personally called by God as Edith did, you have never been saved.

Ruth Graham, wife of evangelist Billy Graham, could not believe that she was included in God's life. She struggled and struggled, trying to believe. She finally went to see a pastor with her problem of unbelief. He opened a Bible to Isaiah chapter 53 and directed her attention to verse four, "He was wounded for our transgressions and bruised for our iniquities; the chastisement of our peace was laid upon Him, and by His stripes we are healed." The pastor said to Ruth Graham, "I want you to put your finger on that verse and read it out loud, inserting your own name in place of the word, "our." She did so, and suddenly, God turned the lights on in her inner spirit. "He (Jesus) was wounded for *Ruth's* transgressions." She saw the truth clearly, and entered into her inheritance in Christ. Have you seen yourself as the personal object of God's love and God's search? Do you realize that Jesus died for you as if you were the only sinner who ever lived, or the only sinner who ever needed to be died for? The Christian life is deeply personal.

II. THE CHRISTIAN LIFE IS WONDERFULLY PRACTICAL

Second, the text indicates that the Christian life is *wonderfully practical*. Look at the second pair of words, "to live." "To me to live is Christ." Note that this is a verb, "to live," and not a noun, "life." The verb is the action word of our language. The New Testament is a book about life and living. If I were to ask you, What is the main theme of the New Testament, what would your answer be? Consider this before you lock in an answer. The words "life" and "live" are used over 1,000 times in the New Testament! This alone makes a strong case that the main theme of the New Testament is life and living. Remember that there are three strong words in our text, "me," "live," and "Christ." And remember that the word "live" is the word that is defined by the union of the other two words. Now, living is a very practical thing (!). Someone said, "The problem of living is that it is *so daily*." Exactly! And this is the genius of Christianity. It offers a concept that covers every moment of every day. Jesus said, "I am with you always." "I will never leave you, nor forsake you." If we walk (a practical word) with Him, He will make our lives majestic. However, it must be honestly said that if we don't walk with Him, *He* will make our lives miserable. You see, He is serious in His desire for relationship with the people He made for such a relationship.

A little boy was taking an elementary science exam at school. One question was, "What is salt?" He could not remember the chemical formula, sodium chloride, so finally he wrote, "Salt is the stuff that spoils the potatoes when you leave it out!" Well, Jesus is the One who spoils life — when you leave Him out. There is no maliciousness in the arrangement when you learn that you must breathe to maintain physical life, and there is no maliciousness when you are told that you must have a relationship with God through Christ to have eternal life. No threat, just fact.

The word is "live," not dream, or wish, or hope, or theorize. The Christian life is a continuing experience. Can you imagine anyone announcing, "I'm real tired right at this moment, so I'm going to stop living for two hours and get some rest, then I'll resume the living at the end of that time." No, when a person stops living, it tends to be permanent! I don't live off of moments of inspiration or spasms of faith. I don't just live for one hour and thirty minutes on Sundays, then go dead for the rest of the time. I live every moment of every day and every moment of every night. Even so, Christ is my life every moment of every day and every moment of every night. He doesn't live in me in spells and spurts and spasms.

Many people could be called "hypodermic saints," or "epidemic saints." When they get a "fix," an inoculation, of Christianity in a super-charged atmosphere, they excitedly vow that they will live for Jesus. Their roots are planted in the excitement of the moment rather than in Christ. The "epidemic saint" catches the high-fevered contagion of a meeting or a crusade or an infectious preacher, but he fades away as quickly as he started. He is a chocolate soldier who stays firm in a cool and comfortable place, but melts when the sun gets hot in an exposed place.

A true relationship with Jesus Christ means that every part of my life is affected at all times; every relationship in my life is involved at all times; every moment of my life is to be changed and transformed. Whatever living means to me anywhere and all the time — working or lounging at home, driving a car or a bus, walking along a sidewalk, shopping in a grocery or a mall, reading the Bible or a novel or a newspaper, banging a typewriter or answering a telephone, standing behind a counter or in a line — whether I am tired or in full strength, sick or well, happy or disappointed, whether it is Monday morning or Saturday night, *"to me to live is Christ."* The Christian life is wonderfully practical.

III. THE CHRISTIAN LIFE IS GLORIOUSLY POSSIBLE

Third, the Christian Life is *gloriously possible*. One word in the verse makes it possible. That word is "Christ." Paul did not say, "To me to live is to confess Christ," or, "to me to live is to be like Christ," or, "to me to live is to live for Christ," or, "to me to live is to pray to Christ," or, "to me to live is to serve Christ." These formulas sound wonderful, and are easy replacements for the real thing. No activity, or function, or attribute of the life must be mistaken for the life itself. Jesus Himself is the Source, the Secret, the Substance, and the Solution of the Christian life. Someone said, "Many people are trying to live the Christian life when they don't have The Life to live." No accouterment or accompaniment of the life is the life itself.

Captain Reginald Wallis said, "The greatest day of my Christian life was the day I discovered I could not live it, and God did not intend me to. Then, and then alone, was I willing to invite the Lord Jesus to live His own life in me." Some people say, "The Christian life is out for me. I just can't live it." I've got good news for you. You are dead right; you can't live it! And furthermore, you were never expected to live it as far as God is concerned. Let me say it reverently but firmly. God isn't so stupid as to demand perfection and then expect a thoroughly imperfect person like you to live it!

Billy Graham asked a young man, "Are you a Christian?" "Well, I'm trying to be," was the reply, a quite typical reply to such a question. Graham asked teasingly, "Ever try to be an elephant?" To depend on your own effort is to guarantee failure, but to defer by repentance and faith to Christ's exercise in you is to guarantee fulfillment and fruitfulness.

Pastor Stuart Briscoe was on a preaching mission on the Isle of Man. A lady came to him at the end of one of the services and said glumly, "Mr. Briscoe, I just don't know what is wrong with me...." Briscoe interrupted before she could go further and said, "Ma'am, are you a Christian? Do you know you are saved?" "Why, yes, she replied, but I just don't know what is wrong with me...." Briscoe interrupted again, and politely asked her, "Ma'am, tell me in the simplest terms what happened to you the day you were saved." She thought a moment and replied, "Well, Jesus came into me." He said, "Excuse me, would you repeat that?" "Jesus came into me," she answered. "Please say that again," he insisted. She said, "Jesus came into me." "Again," he said gently. *"Jesus came into me,"* she said. You see, the staggering and stupendous reality of having the eternal Son of God, the Lord of glory, the King of all kings, living in her had never become a vital reality to her, and thus the Christian life was an impossible proposition.

Every Christian has a decisive line of demarcation driven through his life. He has a B.C. (Before Christ) and an A. D. (Anno Domini, "in the year of our Lord") life. He has a Then and a Now. In the B. C., or Then, time, he had to say, "To me to live is (his own name goes here)." "To me to live is Herb." "To me to live is George, or Joe, of Polly, or Sue." Then, by a glorious new birth, he became a Christian. This means that the center of gravity within him shifted from himself to Christ. Do not misunderstand this. The Christian life is not a circle with only one center, Christ. This would violate and destroy your personality. No, the Christ life is an ellipse with two possible centers, you and Christ. Now, "He must increase, but you (the self-centered, fleshly, competitive self) must decrease." As the false usurper, the selfish you, decreases, the true you, the you that you were meant to be, emerges under the administration of Christ's life.

So life is Someone Else! Life is Christ. Shortly after Malcolm Muggeridge, the renowned English journalist, became a Christian, he delivered a sermon in Queen's Cross Church, Aberdeen, Scotland, on Sunday, May 26, 1968. In that sermon, Muggeridge made this confession: "I may, I suppose, regard myself, or pass for being, a relatively successful man. People occasionally stare at me in the streets — that's fame. I can fairly easily earn enough to qualify for admission to the higher slopes of the Inland Revenue — that's success. Furnished with money and a little fame even the elderly, if they care to, may partake of trendy diversions— that's pleasure. It might happen once in a while that something I said or wrote was sufficiently heeded for me to persuade myself that it represented a serious impact on our time — that's fulfillment. Yet I say to you, and I beg you to believe, multiply these tiny triumphs by a million, add them all together, and they are nothing — less than nothing — a positive impediment — measured against one draught of that living water Christ offers to the spiritually thirsty — irrespective of who or what they are. What, I ask myself, does life hold, what is there in the works of time, in the past, now and to come, which could possibly be put in the balance against the refreshment of drinking that water?" *Life is Someone Else!*

In the early 1960s, the heroic Christian leader Martin Niemoller came to America on a speaking tour. Knowing of his experience under the Hitler regime in Germany and of his resistance to the Nazis, two reporters representing large city newspapers hurried to hear him, expecting a sensational discussion of those war years. Instead, Dr. Niemoller preached a warm, Christ-centered Gospel message and yet hardly mentioned his experiences in Nazi Germany. The two reporters left the church greatly disappointed. As they departed, one reporter was heard saying to the other, "Six years in a Nazi prison camp, and all he has to talk about is Jesus Christ!" *Life is Someone Else!*

When John Bunyan was saved, he wrote in his journal, "O, I thought, Christ! Christ! There was nothing but Christ that was now before my eyes! O Christ! O Christ! O Christ! My Lord and my Savior! O Christ! O Christ!" It is *Christ* Who "is made unto us wisdom, and righteousness, and sanctification, and redemption" (I Corinthians 1:30). *Life is Someone Else!*

And life is *someone else*. Note the subtle change, the necessary addition, that is made when a person truly knows Christ. There is not only a shift of the "center of gravity" within him from self to Christ, but there is also a shift from self to other people. "*You* are my joy and my crown," Paul wrote to the Thessalonians (2:19-20). *You* are "my joy and crown," he wrote to the Philippians (4:1). This is the whole point of the Christian life. We become fulfilled and gratified and useful as the focus of our lives turns from ourselves to Christ and others. When the focus of our lives is on Christ, He actually serves us, and, in a reciprocal miracle, we serve Him. When the focus of our lives is on others, we serve them for Christ's sake. If we only relate to Christ without a resulting focus on others, the Christian life becomes self-centered and mystical, an exercise in personal piety alone. This exercise appears wonderful at first, but it is in reality merely another caricature of the real Christian life.

On the other hand, if we sympathetically seek to focus on others without the monitor of a live relationship with Christ, we become mere social contributors — and soon that deteriorates into mere friendship. If I focus on Christ and His Life, then my relationships with others are incredibly sanctified.

We must realize that Jesus does not impart life as something separate from Himself. He Himself is the life which He imparts. "The gift of God is eternal life through Jesus

CHRISTIANITY CONDENSED

Christ our Lord." When we get *Him*, we get *"It."* "He who has the Son has life, but he who has not the Son of God has not life" (I John 5:12). He said, "I am the way, the truth, and the life; no man comes unto the Father but by Me" (John 14:6). We use this verse almost exclusively for evangelistic purposes, but it has a far more profound meaning than merely to say that Jesus is the only way to God and to heaven. After all, He said three things in the verse, not just one.

Explore the phrases, and let me interpret for a moment. He said, "I am the way" — that we might be *saved*. He said, "I am the truth" — that we might be *sure* of it and *sensible* about it. And He said, "I am the life" — that we might be *satisfied* just with Him. One hundred percent of Christians have gotten into the way and been saved. But substantially less than one hundred percent of Christians are *sure* of their salvation and *sensible* about their relationship with Christ. So someone is tampering in our minds and hearts with the authority of Jesus, because the same Christ spoke both sentences. But if there is a large decrease of participation from the first sentence of the verse to the second part, just look at the third part.

"I am the life" — that we might be *satisfied* just with Jesus, that we might find our *sufficiency* only in Christ. How many Christians do you know who have impressed you that they are satisfied just with Jesus? This is a very difficult question to answer. The only way it could be practically tested would be to remove everything but Christ and see if the person is satisfied. When the Apostle Paul came to die, he said, "I have kept the faith." You see, the faith was about all that he had left! But because he had lived a Christ-centered life, he was satisfied and gratified. How many Christians do you know who appear to find their sufficiency in Christ? Do you think you know *even one*?

Now, think carefully of the implications of the fact that Life is Someone Else, that Life is Christ and Christ is Life. Paul's equation is that Life equals Christ, and Christ equals Life. This means that there is no true life from which Christ is absent. Remove Christ, and you have removed life. Insert Christ, and you have inserted life. This means also that for any Christian to know and understand himself, He must get to know Christ — personally, intimately, accurately, and well. Dear Christian, if you are to have an adequate and accurate sense of identity, you must get to know Christ — because He is your Life!

Now, it is just this fact that makes the Christian life gloriously possible. Sadly, most Christians still think they must live the life for Christ instead of allowing Him to live His own life in union with their personalities.

A father came home from work. He saw his son sprawled on the front lawn. "Do you want to play?" the father asked. "Naw, Dad, I'm too tired!" "Why are you so tired, son?" "I've been riding a horse all over the neighborhood," the boy said, pointing to his broomstick horse that was lying beside him on the lawn. "Son," his Dad said, "riding a horse shouldn't make you that tired." "I know, Dad, but when you ride this kind of horse, you have to do your own galloping." A Christian has the winged horse of the universe, Jesus the Son of God, to carry him, but sadly, most Christians still do their own galloping!

In happy contrast, consider the ride which Lucy and Susan enjoyed on Aslan after he had risen from the dead in C. S. Lewis' great story entitled <u>The Lion, the Witch, and the Wardrobe</u>. An incredible story of redemption from sin through death and resurrection, the story climaxes with the two girls commanded to get on Aslan's back and ride. "That ride was perhaps the most wonderful thing that happened to them in

Narnia. And it was a ride on a mount that doesn't need to be guided and never grows tired. He rushes on and on, never missing his footing, never hesitating, threading his way with perfect skill ... " To get the full meaning, do yourself a favor and read the entire book. Go back to your childhood for a little while, and enjoy the ride. The Christian life is gloriously possible because Jesus communicates His Life to you and wants to carry you all the way home.

Every person on earth lives at all times in one of two verses from Paul's letter to the Philippians. The first is our text in Philippians 1:21: "To me to live is Christ." The other is one chapter away in Philippians 2:21: "For all seek their own, not the things which are Jesus Christ's."

> "Only two philosophies occupy life's shelf,
> Either live for Christ, or live for self."

Those two philosophies of life, that of the Savior and that of Satan, confront us in these two verses. Everlasting life is life with Christ at its center, but the other philosophy, that of self-serving, created Satan and agrees with him — and the person who lives that way will have to endure Satan's company forever! Let's finally consider the permanent consequences of the Christ-centered life.

IV. THE CHRISTIAN LIFE IS ETERNALLY PROFITABLE

When a person says, "To me to live is Christ," he will enjoy Christ's company forever. The Christian life is *eternally profitable*. "To me to live is Christ, and to die is gain." A Christian can live or he can die — but he cannot lose! The word translated "gain" in this verse is "*kerdos*," which means gain in the sense of "profit." It was used often in the secular writing of Paul's day to refer to interest gained on invested money. In II Timothy 1:12, Paul spoke of his faith as a deposit (the KJV translates it "commit") of his whole life into Christ's keeping. According to Colossians 3:3 and other Scriptures, this means that Paul's whole destiny went into Heaven's triple-padlocked Safety Deposit Box. We often call this Eternal Security, and it is exactly that. But it is not a mere sterile idea; it is part of a dynamic relationship.

You see, the only person who can give Paul's analysis of *death* is the person who is living out Paul's analysis of *life*. Only the person who can truthfully say, "To me to live is Christ," can fully, accurately and faithfully say, "*And* to die is gain." If a person belongs to Christ in life, he will also belong to Christ in death, and there is victory either way. The Moffatt translation says, "Death means gain." If Christ is my life, then death must be "gain," because it simply means that I get much, much more of what I was living for — Christ! When the time came for Paul to die — he was beheaded near Rome, according to history — you might have said to him, "Do you see the Emperor's executioner approaching?" Paul might have answered, "No, but I see Christ!"

Death meant just one thing to Paul, and that was a complete and unhampered union with Jesus. Paul talked freely, naturally and realistically about death. He called it "the last enemy," because it is just that. Paul never denied its stark reality, nor did he evade its imminence. It is a sure sign of our carnal-mindedness, immaturity, and insecurity that we moderns do not talk of death except in hush-hush voice or in somber tone and tragic mood. Or we swing to the other extreme, the "Polyanna" mood of denial, deliberately acting as if we are invincible or that we will face the dark "king of terrors" only when he gallops across our path. Meanwhile, "eat, drink, and be merry" is our mediocre lifestyle. But Paul not only talked freely and naturally about death; he actually looked forward eagerly to the experience. He knew that death was the limousine that would transport him into the King's Presence, and though the last few miles of the ride might be very rough and bumpy, that "it will be worth it all, when we see Jesus!"

It is the clear teaching of Scripture that *death has two sides to it*, and not just one. For example, Jesus spoke of death as "sleep," and sleep has wakefulness both before and *after* it. Death is an "exodus," and we cannot imagine an exodus from one place without an entrance into another. Death has a before and an after, and one Person holds the key to victory in the life *before* death and in the life *after* death. In the context of verse 21, our text uses a large and expansive word for death. In verse 23, it is referred to as a "departure." Paul said, "I have a desire to *depart* and be with Christ, which is far better." He pictures himself as occupying a "narrow place", like a man walking down a narrow corridor between two solid walls. Paul is between two "pulls," one outward toward his earthly companions, the other upward toward Heaven. He says, "My preference, my desire, is to depart and be with Christ." That is the "gain" of death to a Christian.

The word "depart" (verse 23) is another of those treasure-packed words of Scripture. In Paul's day, it was often used as a *soldier's* term, and it meant to take down a tent — to loosen and remove the pegs, to fold up the fabric, to break camp and to prepare to move to a new location. II Corinthians 5:1 says, "We (Christians) know, that if our earthly house of this tabernacle (portable tent) be dissolved (the work death does), we have a building of God, a house (a permanent residence, unlike a portable tent) not made with hands, eternal in the heavens."

Then the word "depart" is a *sailor's* term, and it meant to loosen the cables and set sail. Think of it. A ship is moored at dockside in a harbor. Then it loosens its moorings and moves out to the threat and the adventure and the prospect of the high seas. Friends and loved ones in the harbor might weep over the departing passengers and say, "Farewell." But a while later, in a distant harbor, other friends and relatives might smile as they hear the cry, "Ship ahoy!" and a few minutes later, the passengers will receive warm and wonderful welcomes from those who greet them in the new land. So is death to a Christian.

The word "depart" is also a *sojourner's* word, and it simply means to move from one location to another. You see, when a Christian dies, he only changes location, he does not change companionship. Who is going to heaven? Those who live in a vital relationship with Christ on earth; those who can validly say, "To me to live is Christ."

If we are to adequately explore the phrase, "and to die is gain," we must at least briefly inventory the Christian's "Death Benefits." In what sense is it true for a Christian to say, "To me ... to die is gain"?

Death is gain for a Christian, first, because it will mean eternal *freedom* from the *problems* of life. As incredible as it may seem, there is coming a time (an eternity!) for a Christian when he will never *sin* again, never *suffer* again, and never *struggle* again! "To die is gain."

Second, death is gain for a Christian because it will mean an eternal *future* in a *place*. Jesus said to His disciples, "I go to prepare a place for you." Note the words "prepare" and "place," and remind yourself that Jesus was a carpenter while here on earth. As of this writing, He has been in Heaven for about 2,000 years — and possibly He has done a considerable amount of *interior decorating* on the place — "for you"! If the language used to describe it in Revelation 21 and 22 is literal language, then it is unbelievably beautiful. If the language is figurative, then the place itself is even more beautiful than figurative language can describe.

Two Christian men died together and entered heaven together. As they were touring the premises, one exclaimed, "Man! This place is spectacular! Why didn't someone tell us in advance how beautiful it was?" The other excitedly replied, "And just think of it! We could have been here ten years sooner if we hadn't eaten all those health foods!" Forgive the facetiousness, but this is something to laugh about and to celebrate. When the prospect has materialized into reality, you may be sure that we will laugh and shout and sing and celebrate — and I am sure there will be enough fuel for our celebration to last forever!

Finally, death is gain for a Christian because it will mark the beginning of unhindered eternal *fellowship* with a *Person*. Jesus said, "I go to prepare a place for you, that where I am, there you may be also." In His great high priestly prayer in John 17, Jesus prayed, "Father, I will that they also, whom You have given to me, be with me where I am."

A dentist had an upstairs office. One day, he was working on a patient in the dental chair. Suddenly, they both heard a loud scratching sound at the door. The dentist laughed as he explained, "That's my dog. I left him downstairs. He has never been in this room; he doesn't even know that it would be a safe place. But he knows that I am here, and he just wants to be with me." It might greatly impress some people to be told that the streets of heaven are made of gold, the walls of jasper, and the gates of pearl. But when a person has lived by this standard, "To me to live is Christ," he would have only one criterion in evaluating heaven: "Forget the furniture of the place, and its location. I want to know one thing: **Is Jesus there?**"

> *"My knowledge of that place is small*
> *The eye of faith is dim;*
> *But it is enough that Christ knows all*
> *And I shall be with Him."*

I want to ask you, dear friend, to finish my sermon for me. The method will be simple. Dare to write out your life philosophy in an honest sentence. If someone were to ask you, "In a word, what are you living for?" what would you say? In a word, what is your dominant aim or motive in life? Perhaps you would have to reply, "To me to live is *money*." Or, "to me to live is *pleasure*." Or, "to me to live is *fame*." Or perhaps your philosophy would be the all-inclusive one, "To me to live is *self*." Now, dare to finish the sentence of Philippians 1:21: "And to die is ..." If you must admit that life to you is summarized in a quest for money, then to die is certainly not gain; it is rather loss, because you can't take it with you. Billy Sunday added, "And if you could, it would melt where you are going!" If life for you is summarized as a quest for pleasure, then to die is loss, because God will not cater to your selfish appetites, sensations, and thrills. Any other motive will end up holding the same loss!

The only person who can say, "To me ... to die is gain," is the person who has happily adopted this lifestyle, "To me to live is Christ." You see, dear friend, "Heaven holds all of that for which you sigh," but it is only yours if you can say, "To me to live is Christ." If Christ is your very life now, He will be your very life forever. "Do you not see that executioner, Paul?" "No, I see no executioner." "*Then what do you see?*" "*Ever and always, I see only Christ.*"

THE PRACTICAL VALUE OF THE WORD OF GOD

II Timothy 3:16a

"All Scripture is given by inspiration of God, and is profitable...."

I am privileged to have a large personal library. Over the years, I have been an addictive reader. I could give up many activities of the moment if I could curl up with a book in a quiet corner. Of the thousands of books in my library, I have had the great privilege of meeting a few of the authors of those books. I will never meet most authors whose books are on the shelves of my library. It is not necessary that I meet the author to benefit from the book. In fact, meeting the author might detract from the blessing received from the book!

With the Bible, however, everything is different. It is vital, *necessary*, **indispensable** to meet the Author if you are to understand the Book. Let me say it as dogmatically as it needs to be said. You will never understand the message and intent of the Bible, nor derive from it the benefit that is there, unless you have a redeeming encounter with its Author. And the good news is that the Author is always available for an encounter with us. He is ready, willing, and eager to meet us (John 4:23-25). In fact, Jesus said that God actually seeks us to initiate that encounter. Every saved person has met God in a transforming encounter. This encounter is so vast and varying in its impact that it is called by numerous descriptive words. As examples, it is called "conversion," or "regeneration," or "reconciliation." In this encounter, Jesus, the Living Word of God, actually comes into the individual at the moment of true faith. When the Living Word comes in, He brings His own affinity (adherence) to the Written Word, the Bible. Suddenly, the new believer is given an insatiable hunger for the truth of the Written Word. The Jesus within Him cleaves to the Bible before Him (just as Jesus did while He was alive in His own body 2,000 years ago). The Delight Jesus had (has) for the Bible is shared with the new believer through their spiritual union.

The Bible has God as its Author, Jesus as its Subject, Man's highest good as its manward Objective, and God's highest glory as its Godward Objective. The Bible is God's Library, containing His own Wisdom about each of these things—and far more. But how is it to be used? What is its practical value? I want to suggest some ten categories of value, some ten uses which the Bible is intended to have in our lives.

I. A REGENERATIVE VALUE

First, the Bible has an inherent *regenenerative* value. The truth of the Book is powerful truth. The Bible communicates the "Gospel of Christ," and the Gospel of Christ is "the power of God unto salvation to every one who believes" (Romans 1:16). This is not merely theoretical, as any truly saved person knows by experience. A saved person bears after his salvation the unmistakable marks of a power-encounter with the Living God through His Word.

Peter, who knew about regeneration through contact with the Living Word *and* the Written Word, wrote, "We are born again, not by corruptible seed, but by incorruptible seed, by the Word of God, which lives and abides forever. For all

THE PRACTICAL VALUE OF THE WORD OF GOD

flesh is as grass, and all the glory of man as the flower of grass. The grass withers, and the flower thereof falls away: But the word of the Lord endures forever. And this is the word which by the Gospel is preached unto you" (I Peter 1:23-25). The experience of any truly born again person echoes these verses. This has happened to me! My life was instantaneously and miraculously transformed when the Seed of Divine Truth had penetrated the "ovum" of faith within me. Following that spiritual "conception," an incredible spiritual birth occurred. I became a "new creature" in Christ (II Corinthians 5:17). Anyone who knew me in that period of my life would have seen a great difference between my "B.C." days and my "A.D." days.

  A member of my own family said (rather reluctantly, because she did not at that time want to receive Christ herself), "I'll have to admit that there is a great difference between what you were and what you are!" The entrance of the Living Word and the power of the Written Word are the only explanation for the miracle! The Bible's regenerative power is Divine, dynamic, distinctive and durable. In James 1:18, the half-brother of Jesus (whose life showed the same Line of Demarcation between sinner and saint—after the Resurrection of Christ), wrote, "Of His own will God begot (sired, Fathered) us through the word of truth." Note the origin of the process within the will of God, and the enactment of the birth through the Word of God. In Luke 8:11, in His interpretation of a powerful parable about the powerful Word of God, Jesus said, "The seed is the Word of God."

  When the movie *Luther*, based on the years in Martin Luther's life which led to the Reformation, came to Memphis, I was one of the first in line to see it. I was not disappointed! I have read several biographies of Luther and hundreds of excerpts about his life, and the movie was historically accurate and Bible-packed, though it could not cover much due to the brief length of the film. I was reminded of the gigantic place the Bible played in awakening Luther from his lostness in sin *and religion*, and in bringing him to the truth of Christ and His salvation. Luther's adviser, John Staupitz, recognized that Luther's agonizing struggle could only be resolved by contact with Scripture, so he engineered circumstances to place Luther in the chair of Bible at a prominent university in Germany. There he came into close and studious contact with the great salvation passages of the Bible. In particular, the Holy Spirit used several of the Psalms (Psalm 22 was especially used by the Spirit) and the great doctrinal sections of the Book of Romans. On the pages of Romans, Luther saw that "the just shall live *by faith*," not by works or religious rituals or religious formalities. There, he met Christ and received His Gift of Eternal Life . . . and the rest is history!

One of the greatest disciple-makers in history was a man named Dawson Trotman, the founder of the international Navigators organization and the leader of the follow-up program for Billy Graham's crusade during the last years of Trotman's life. Let me share the account of Trotman's conversion as it is told in Robert Foster's book, <u>The Navigator.</u> "Dawson's conversion came when he was twenty—through memorizing Scripture. He had had a run-in with the law, the latest of a series, and he made a promise to God: 'Lord, if you will get me out of this trouble with the police, I will go to church this coming Sunday.' As Daws expressed it, 'On the Friday night that I was arrested, Miss Mills was home looking up verses in the Bible, trying to find ten on the subject of salvation which she and Miss Thomas could give to the young people in their church to memorize. Little did she know that the boy for whom they had been praying for six years was going to memorize those verses. When Sunday came along, I decided to go to the young people's meeting. That was a tough decision, for my favorite pool hall was just around the corner—suppose some of the fellows saw me going to church?

"It was the opening night for a contest, and points were to be given for various church activities, among them the memorization of Bible portions. 'Learn ten verses and get fifty points for our side,' said this lovely little blond gal. I went home and dug out my little Testament, and in the course of a week, I had learned all ten verses. Not because it was the Bible, but because of the pretty high school girl! Then they gave me ten more verses . . . on how to grow in the Christian life.

"'How they prayed all that week for me! I went back the following Sunday and got another fifty points for the Red team as well as for the little blond.' Dawson continued with the climax of the story: 'One unforgettable event resulted from that contest. . . I was on my way to work at the local lumber company one day with these twenty verses of Scripture stored away in my memory. I had no plans for using them, except to keep my promise and help win the award for the Reds on the following Sunday.

I was walking along the highway, minding my own business, with my lunch pail in my hand. Miss Mills was still praying, and the Word of God was working through the power of the Holy Spirit, and all of a sudden that morning, as I walked along to work, one of these twenty verses came into my mind: 'Verily, verily, I say unto you, He that heareth my word, and believeth on him that sent me, hath everlasting life . . .' (John 5:24). Those words, 'hath everlasting life,' stuck in my mind. I said, 'O God, that's wonderful—a person can have everlasting life!' I pulled my little Testament out of my pocket and looked it up in John's Gospel, and sure enough, there it was—'hath everlasting life, and shall not come into condemnation; but is passed from death unto life.' There for the first time I remember praying after I had grown to be a man, 'O God, I want this everlasting life!' In that instant, I was born again. That was the beginning. I believed what God had said in His Word, received the gift He offered, and was instantly saved.'"

Just yesterday, I was in the new home of a dear friend. We were discussing one of the features of the new home. He said, "When we prepared to pour the concrete for the sidewalk, though the concrete was going to be four to six inches deep, the builder insisted that we use a plant-killer on the soil because of the power of seeds and plants to break through concrete." Many, many times the Bible speaks of the powerful seed of the Word of God. Just as a seed has an awesome germinal power, the Word of God has an awesome germinal and regenerative power. Just as a seed contains the life germ of the plant-line which it represents, so the Word of God contains the powerful, explosive, germinal "life principle" of the God it represents. That power is mysterious, mighty, magnificent. The Bible's practical value begins in any individual life with its regenerative capability. If you are a person without Christ, and you want to remain that way, you dare not expose yourself to the Word of God. Any seed of Gospel truth planted within you may become like a Divinely-timed bomb, and at any moment you could be blasted off your pedestal of pride and blown into Kingdom Come!

Each point of this study requires a practical implementation if we are to receive the full value of the Word of God into our personal experience. So the question here is, Have you been born again? If not, the Word of God is seeking to penetrate your dead heart at this very moment, bringing its own life (eternal life) with it. As it points you away from yourself and every other point of attention *to Jesus alone*, would you admit your sins directly to Him, realize that your sins are aggressive acts against God and require repentance (a change of mind, will and direction), and then receive the crucified and risen Christ into your heart to save and transform you? Then you will know by personal experience the regenerative power of the Word of God.

II. AN ILLUMINATIVE VALUE

Second, the Bible has a practical value for a person's life because of its inherent *illuminative* value. It brings light to otherwise dark situations, and enables sight for those who have been "issued a new set of eyes" in their new birth. The Psalmist wrote, "Thy Word is a lamp unto my feet and a light unto my path" (Psalm 119:105). Many a pilgrim passing through the wilderness of this world (the opening phrase in Bunyan's Pilgrim's Progress) has found his path aflame with heaven's light through the illuminative power of the Word of God. The Psalmist added in the same chapter, "The entrance of Your Word gives light; it gives understanding to the simple" (Psalm 119:130). Many people, both saved people and lost people, walk in darkness because they refuse the "entrance" of the Word of God into their dark and unbelieving hearts, or because they refuse to be "simple" enough to receive the available light. In Psalm 43:3, the Psalmist made this appeal: "O, send out Your light and Your truth, and let them lead me." Note the combination of light and truth in his appeal. It is wise to appeal to the Holy Spirit for His light before you expose yourself to His truth. It is not enough to have the Word of God. Many people take up the Book and read—and receive no benefit at all. Why? Because they had the truth, but had no light to detect it.

How blind all men are without Divine illumination! How dark their hearts and minds are! "They walk in the vanity of their mind, having the understanding darkened, being alienated from the life of God through the ignorance that is in them, because of the blindness of their hearts" (Ephesians 4:18). How desperately and tragically true! How well do I remember the moment when God "turned on the lights in my inner spirit." My first impulse was to cry, "What is going on? Why have I not *seen this before*? Where in the world have I been?" And I instantly saw the Heaven/Hell, Life/Death, Light/Darkness, Love/*attempt to love* difference between being saved and being lost.

Furthermore, since that time, the Divine Ophthalmologist has been making adjustments on my new eyes. You see, though the Bible does have an *inherent* illuminative capacity, it still must be illumined by the Holy Spirit or that value is totally lost. *Totally* lost! Without the Holy Spirit's illumination and teaching, the Bible itself is just another book! The Holy Spirit has often "opened the eyes of my heart (Greek, *kardia)* and flooded them with light" (Ephesians 1:18; read Ephesians 1:17-19 carefully), and the result is always amazement and enlarged understanding. Some of the Spirit's adjustments are corrective and some are progressive (a part of the growth process), but they are definite illuminative works.

When John Robinson disembarked from the *Mayflower* at Delft Harbor on the eastern shore of this continent, in his opening remarks to his fellow travelers, he declared, "I am convinced that the Lord has yet more light and truth to break forth from His Holy Word." That light will never ceasing breaking forth upon the "simple" (single-minded) believer who is willing to receive and obey it.

In a recent book entitled The Closing of the American Mind, University of Chicago professor Allan Bloom describes how his "uneducated" grandparents lived on a wise and noble level because of the practical influence of the Bible on their daily experience. Bloom says, "*I do not believe that my generation,* my cousins who have been educated in the American way, all of whom are M. D.s or Ph.D.s, *have any comparable learning*. When they talk about heaven and earth, the relations between men and women, parents and children, the human condition, I hear nothing but cliches, superficialities, the material of satire. I am not saying anything so trite as that life is fuller when people have myths to live by. I mean rather that *a* life based on the Book is closer to the truth, that it provides the material for deeper research in and access to the real nature of things." (The italics in this paragraph are mine, not the author's)

How do we reach the practical implementation of this point? We simply read the Bible regularly, all the while dependently asking God to "open the eyes of our hearts and flood them with light" (Ephesians 1:18). We pray with David, "Open Thou mine eyes, that I may behold wondrous things out of Thy law" (Psalm 119:18). What you see in God's Word when this occurs is almost indescribable.

III. A NUTRITIVE VALUE

Third, the Bible has an inherent *nutritive* value for the hungry soul. It contains "the daily minimum requirement of (spiritual) vitamins and minerals" as well as the very "gourmets of grace" for the person who will come to the Lord's table and allow the Host to serve His meal. Jesus said, "Behold, I stand at the door and knock; if any man hear my voice, and open the door, I will come in to him, and will eat with him, *and he with Me*" (Revelation 3:20). I have been studying the Word of God voraciously for over fifty years (!), and I can tell you that no chef on earth can prepare a physical meal that compares with the food of the Word of God! No kitchen table can carry food (no matter who prepares it!) such as the Word of God presents to nourish the soul. Jesus spoke a universal law when He said, "Man (generic man and each individual man) lives not (he *is dead* without this food) by bread alone, but *by every word that proceeds out of the mouth of God"* (Matthew 4:4). Jesus Himself said, "I have meat that you don't know about; my meat is to do the will of Him who sent Me, and to finish His work" (John 4:34). Don't miss the obvious meaning of such statements. To hear and heed the Word of God is to have life, healthy, maturing life, but to fail to hear and heed the Word of God is to starve your true self, the self God intended, to death. What a shock it will be for sense-oriented, self-oriented people to come to the end of the trail and find that they have literally starved the spirit, the eternal dimension of their existence, to death.

Peter addressed the new believer in Christ with this counsel, *"As newborn babes, desire the pure milk of the Word, that you may grow thereby" (I Peter 2:2).* Again, the implication is clear. For a new Christian to regularly take in the milk of the Word is to grow; for him to fail to do so is for him to be stalemated in a pitiful prolonged infancy.

Jeremiah gave personal testimony to the nutritive value of the Word of God when he said to God, *"Your words were found, and I ate them, and your words were to me the joy and rejoicing of my heart" (Jeremiah 15:16).* Jesus suggested the same idea when He said, *"Except a man eat My flesh and drink My blood, he has no life in him" (John 6).* Faith is defined as an assimilation of the very Person of Christ that is like the eating of physical food. When food is ingested, digested and assimilated into the body, it is translated in the inner organism into every necessity that is negotiable. The same is spiritually (actually) true of the believer's intake of the Word of God. When received, the truth is assimilated into the believer's total life and shows up through him as an incarnation of the very life of God. Job 23:12 echoes the same truth: *"I have esteemed the words of Your mouth to be more than my necessary food."* In my values system, Job declares, it is more important to devour the Word of God than to eat a meal. Any spiritual believer will echo and endorse his testimony.

No person reading these words has a normal and deliberate intention to live on earth a single day without the regular eating of meals. In the same way, a Christian should determine that he will not live another day on earth, even a single day, without feeding and nourishing his inner life on the balanced nutrition of the Word of God.

The practical implementation of this point: to receive nutritional value from any food requires appetite, appropriation and assimilation. A person who has no appetite is (at best) unhealthy. His appetite brings him to appropriate (ingest) the food. Then his body assimilates (digests and disperses) the food throughout its parts. A person who has no appetite for the Word of God is either an unsaved sinner or an unhealthy Christian, and both of these are seriously tragic conditions. A Christian who does not ingest substantial amounts of the food of the Word on a regular basis is inviting a spiritually diseased life. The same steps are followed spiritually in receiving the nutritive value of the Word of God that are followed physically in benefiting from daily food.

IV. A REMUNERATIVE VALUE

Fourth, the Bible has an inherent *remunerative* value for the believer who uses it with a devotional spirit on a regular basis. An old hymn says,

> *"Holy Bible, Book Divine,*
> *Precious treasure, Thou art mine."*

Every child of God who walks in the Spirit and lives in the Word will concur that the Bible is indeed a "precious treasure." It contains vast riches of spiritual wealth, and it will make that person fabulously rich who knows how to exploit its riches. The Psalmist who wrote one of the great devotional treasuries of Scripture, the hymnbook of the Bible, wrote, "The Law of Thy mouth is better unto me than thousands of gold and silver" (Psalm 119:72). Ponder that evaluation carefully. It would be better, the verse says, to be impoverished in the things the world counts valuable and to be rich in the things the world disregards, because those riches of God are better than all the wealth the world may offer. David again said, "The judgments of the Lord are true and righteous altogether; more to be desired are they than gold, yea, than much fine gold" (Psalm 19:9). Though it may be made the instrument of either good or evil, gold has no inherent moral value in itself. However, the revelation of God in His Word does have inherent moral value. That immeasurable value is never withheld when a sensitive, seeking soul comes to the Word of God to meet God and receive His treasure trove of truth.

Again, the Psalmist wrote, "I rejoice at Thy Word, as one that finds great spoil." This is far more true today than it was when he wrote those words. The Big Battles of time and eternity have now been fought and won, and now we open the Book to learn what was won for us through the Death and Resurrection of Jesus. Edwin Hodder summarized this dimension when he wrote,

> *"Thy Word is like a deep, deep mine,*
> *And jewels rich and rare*
> *Are hidden in its mighty depths,*
> *For every searcher there."*

Be wise, Christian, and go deep into the "mine" of the Word of God, asking God to help you detect the "jewels rich and rare (that) are hidden in its mighty depths." Determine to be a spiritual "searcher" of the mine, and God will fill your life with a vast inventory of spiritual wealth. The Bible will more than repay the effort of any seeker who wants to meet God on its pages. It has a remunerative value.

Let me give one practical outcome of the remunerative value of the Word of God. Jesus said, "Ye shall know the truth, and the truth shall set you free" (John 8:32). This positive statement has been proven true in the lives of multitudes of spiritual Christians. However, I must add that the flip side of that statement is also true. If you do not know the truth that Christ *is* and the truth that He *tells* and *endorses* in the Bible, you are in bondage to ignorance (and this has nothing whatsoever to do with the number of academic degrees that might be attached to your name). Nothing on earth is more pathetic than to see a "smart" person comfortable in his academic achievement, and pitifully blind to and ignorant of the world of eternal reality.

Now, the practical implementation of this point: you *read* the Word of God in order to *recognize* and *realize* the value it contains and exposes, then you *receive* by faith all the riches it makes known. For example, the book of Ephesians could be viewed as an itemized account of the Christian's inventory. It records the Christian's "spiritual bank account." As you read it, you realize that *all has been given to me because I am in Christ*. But then the question arises, *But how much have I taken of that which has been given?* When I probe these question and their answers, I begin to partake of the remunerative value of the Word of God.

V. A REFLECTIVE VALUE

Fifth, the Bible has an inherent *reflective* value. In a marvelous passage, James the half-brother of Jesus, shows the reflective value of the Word of God. "Be ye doers of the Word, and not hearers only, deceiving your own selves. For if any be a hearer of the Word, and not a doer, he is like unto a man beholding his natural face in a glass (literally, 'mirror'): For he beholds himself, and goes his way, and immediately forgets what manner of man he was. But whoso looks into the perfect law of liberty, and continues therein, he being not a forgetful hearer, but a doer of the work, this man shall be blessed in his deed" (James 1:22-25). What role does the Bible play as a reflector?

First, when we look into the Bible, we see the reflection of *ourselves as God sees us*. The Bible paints our portrait, "warts and all." It points out the devastating truth of our depravity and sinfulness, and it withholds none of the awful truth. Scottish writer R. E. O. White said, "The mirror of the Word is painfully clear." Donald Barnhouse said, "The only safe place to look is in the Word of God, which reflects all things as they are." Every person who has seen the terrible truth about himself on the pages of the Word of God will agree with that assessment of himself. One man said, "The Bible is not such a book as an unaided man *would* have written if he *could*, or *could* have written even if he *would*." Nobody naturally tends to rush to a spot where the horrible darkness of his twisted inner life is exposed. However, when the Spirit breathes upon the Word and the Word shows the sinner his sins, he knows that the picture of him reflected in the Word is accurate.

But the Bible does not merely reflect the accurate picture of the sinner back to himself as he reads, it also reflects the image of Jesus to us as we read it in the Spirit. The Bible not only reflects ourselves as God sees us, it also reflects *Jesus as God sees Him*. In one of the great formula verses of the Bible, II Corinthians 3:18 says, "We all, having had our faces unveiled, and beholding as in a mirror the glory of the Lord (Jesus), are being changed into the same image from glory to glory, even

THE PRACTICAL VALUE OF THE WORD OF GOD

as by the Spirit of the Lord." This is one of the primary purposes of the Bible—to allow us to clearly see Jesus. This verse tells us that we must have all impediments removed from our inner eyes and then we must read the Word of God to gaze upon Jesus. F. B. Meyer, the British Baptist pastor said, "Christian, for every look you take at yourself, take at least ten looks at Jesus." God knows that this rule holds in human life: what you look at longingly, lovingly, and lastingly, you will become like. You will become what you behold; you will be what you see. Since the goal of the Christian life is to be like Christ, He must be regularly seen with the eyes of your inner spirit. This happens as you spiritually read the Word of God. Here is the formula: The child of God looks into the Word of God and sees the Son of God, and the Spirit of God etches the character likeness of the Son of God upon the child of God. This is one of the means by which the Christian is made like Christ. The Bible has a reflective value.

One of the discipleship groups I meet with on a regular basis has begun studying with me John Bunyan's classic allegory, <u>Pilgrim's Progress</u>. As we were discussing the characters of the book, I gave them this suggestion: "Take these personality pictures and carry them like a candle down into your own heart and let God search your inner being with the light they provide—and you likely will come out chastened and changed." You can do the same thing with the reflective Word of God. Take it in hand and look at it as a mirror which will realistically expose you to yourself, then will point you away from yourself to look at Jesus. Hebrews 12:2 says, "Look away from (*aphorao*) everything else and unto Jesus." This is not to be a casual glance; it is rather to be a steady gaze; as you so look, you will experience the reflective value of the Word of God.

How do I practically implement the reflective value of the Word of God in my life? Well, how does one use a mirror? Does he examine the mirror merely to admire and appreciate *it*? No, he uses the mirror to reflect the desired object. Even so, the purpose of the Bible is to reflect a true image of yourself back to you and to reflect a true likeness of Jesus to you. Let the Bible show you yourself as you are, then show Jesus to you as the object of your trust. As you do so, you will experience the reflective value of the Word of God.

VI. A CURATIVE VALUE

Sixth, the Bible has an inherent *curative* value. It is able to heal spiritual diseases and cure the multitudes of spiritual ailments that saints are subject to. Psalm 107:20 says, "God sent His Word, and healed them." Every Christian could borrow these words as part of his own testimony. The Bible has been called "God's Medical Book." The regular taking of this medicine will heal many a diseased part of your life, and will produce great health in your life.

Charles Spurgeon spoke truly when he said, "The medicine that is to reach your case is somewhere between the covers of this book." Some years ago, I recommended to a new Christian a monthly devotional booklet edited by Richard De Haan and published and distributed by Radio Bible Class, entitled "Our Daily Bread." It is sub-titled "The daily meditation book." However, when I sent the note, I read it a final time before dispatching it in the mail. I discovered that I had misspelled one word by just one letter, but what an insight was given by the mistake! I had called it "the daily *medication* book." The Bible is exactly that, and it should be taken as regularly and faithfully as prescribed medication. It will cure many a spreading disease that is operating through the flesh, and it will prevent many a disease which would beset us if we did not have the health-giving medicine of the Word.

How do we implement the curative value of the Word of God? Very simply, we take it in big daily doses. We may never fully know at the time the value of such consumption of the Word, but we will clearly see it one day.

VII. A COMBATIVE VALUE

Seventh, the Bible has an inherent *combative* value. It is inherently valuable for both offense and defense in spiritual warfare. It is a bulwark of defense against the heavy assaults of Satan and his cohorts, and it is one of the two chief weapons for mounting the spiritual offensive that Christians are to engage in. One of my first Bibles had in the flyleaf this written statement: "Either this Book will keep you from sin, or sin will keep you from this Book," and this rule has proven true in over fifty years of being a Christian. The Bible is our best line of defense against the attacks of temptation and sin.

Perhaps the most important and instructive single passage on spiritual warfare in all the Bible is the passage in Paul's letter to the Ephesians where he lists "the whole armor of God" which the Christian is to daily "put on" in order to engage in spiritual warfare. At least six weapons are listed, and one of them is "the sword of the Spirit, which is the Word of God" (Ephesians 6:17). Of the weapons listed, this "sword" is the only one which we can touch with our hands and see with our eyes. The other weapons are either analogies or they are altogether invisible. The Bible is visible and tangible. We have no greater weapon for both defense and warfare in this desperately serious warfare than "the sword of the Spirit, which is the Word of God."

Psalm 91:4 says, "His truth shall be thy shield and buckler." Hebrews 4:12 says, "The Word of God is quick (living) and powerful, and sharper than any two-edged sword, piercing even to the dividing asunder of soul and spirit, and of the joints and the marrow, and is a discerner ('critic') of the thoughts and intents of the heart." You might say that one edge of this mighty "sword of the Spirit" is for offensive battle, and the other is for defensive purposes. When Jesus was tempted in the wilderness by Satan, He defended Himself – and us—by using the sword of the Spirit. When He ministered with His men, He maintained the Gospel offensive by regularly employing this sword in battling the enemies of man and of God.

Years ago, every edition of *Reader's Digest* carried an article designed to help readers enlarge their vocabularies and communicating ability. The title of the article was, "It Pays to Increase Your Word Power." Christian, *it pays gigantic dividends to* increase your WORD power! The Bible will prove to be a fortress against the intrusion of evil and a force for the advance of good to the person who implements and incarnates it in his daily life.

How to implement the Bible's combative value? Make the pledge of David your daily testimony: "Thy Word have I hid in my heart, that I might not sin against Thee." Hide the Word in your heart through daily study, meditation and memorization, and then take the truths gained as your sword for defensive and offensive purposes.

VIII. A PRODUCTIVE VALUE

Eighth, the Bible has an inherent *productive* value. In Deuteronomy 32:2, God said, "My doctrine shall drop as the rain, my speech shall distil as the dew, as the small rain upon the tender herb, and as the showers upon the grass." Throughout the Bible, in every reference to spiritual seed-sowing, harvesting, and bearing fruit, the Bible is the background means of productivity. Any study of the great "sowing" parables of Jesus will reveal that "the seed is the Word of God" (Luke 8:11). We are told that "he who sows sparingly shall reap also sparingly, and he who sows bountifully will also reap bountifully" (II Corinthians 9:6). Jesus said, "Herein is my Father glorified, that you bear much fruit; so shall you be My disciples" (John 15:8). These statements are only brief extracts from an abundance of references to God's design that each of His children plant the seed of His Word in the soil of men's hearts wherever they are and thus become participants in the miracle of His spiritual harvest.

Furthermore, it must be noted that all the references to sowing and reaping in the Bible indicate that God intends each of His children to be involved in the process of *spiritual multiplication*. Every seed carries within itself the life-germ of limitless future productivity and multiplication. As long as the process of sowing is pursued with the product of each harvest, vastly enlarging future crops are guaranteed. To put it simply, every wise farmer will extract seeds from the present harvest for future planting, and each of those seeds will multiply a volume far larger than itself. Here we see the genius of Jesus in commanding each believer to be a disciple-maker. Each believer is thus himself a seed (see Matthew 13:38), and must disciple others who also become seeds. Each believer should sow himself in the lives of others, and lead them to do the same thing. This is the process of hands-on, close-up, disciple building—the investment of your life and the truth you know into the lives of others for the sake of Total World Impact. What an assignment, what a majestic involvement, for each Christian! And the result is guaranteed! In Isaiah 55:10-11, God promised, "As the rain comes down, and the snow from heaven, and returns not thither, but waters the earth, and makes it bring forth and bud, that it may give seed to the sower, and bread to the eater: So shall My Word be that goes forth out of My mouth: it shall not return unto Me void, but it shall accomplish that which I please, and it shall prosper in the thing whereto I sent it." Take the seed of Scripture, Christian, and scatter it over waiting hearts. The fields are white unto the harvest (John 4:35).

How do we implement the productive power of the Word of God in our daily lives? First, be sure that the seeds of the Word are daily sown on the receptive, good soil of your own heart. Someone wisely said, *"Prayer is our sowing seeds on God's heart, but the Bible is God sowing seeds on our hearts."* Allow Him to fulfill His will for you by daily sprinkling His seeds of truth over the fertile soil of your heart. Then, sow the truth received on as many other hearts as are reachable. I think of it this way:

> *O*bjective:
> *T*o
> *H*elp
> *E*very
> *R*eachable
> *S*oul

As you receive the seed in the soil of your own heart, and sow it "bountifully" upon the soil of other hearts, you will join the Holy Spirit in God's great harvest of souls. Thus you will prove the productive power of the Word of God.

IX. A COMPULSIVE VALUE

Ninth, the Word of God has an inherent *compulsive* value. When loosed in the human mind and heart, and when mixed there with faith (see Hebrews 4:2), the truth of Scripture has a most compelling power. A discouraged and disillusioned prophet named Jeremiah discovered this compelling power at the heart of his ministry. Tempted to quit the ministry and defect from his prophetic calling, he discovered that such a response was not as easy as it might seem. In Jeremiah 20:8-9, he wrote, "The Word of the Lord was made a reproach unto me, and a derision, daily. Then I said, I will not make mention of Him, nor speak any more in His Name. But His Word was like a burning fire shut up in my bones, and I was weary with forebearing, and could not stay." I was faced with the ostracisms and persecutions of my society, Jeremiah said, on a daily basis. I tried to quit preaching and teaching in the Name of the God who had called me to speak for Him. But when I vowed to be silent, I discovered that I had a raging fire dammed up in my breast which had to be released. I discovered that my silence was far more wearying than the problems I faced, and I could not stop speaking in His Name. This, dear friend, is an example of the compelling power of the Word of God. Every true believer and minister of God has experienced the same compulsion that Jeremiah spoke about.

Samuel Chadwick, a preacher of a past generation of our history, illustrated this power in this picturesque account. "On the river yesterday, I saw a little steamer, fighting against a strong headwind. Unaided, the boat would have been at the mercy of the wind, but it was actually making stubborn and persistent headway—because a burning fire was shut up in its heart. So it is with the true man of God."

Hear an echo of the same truth from another prophet: "The lion has roared, who will not fear? The Lord God has spoken, who can but prophesy?" (Amos 4:8). Here again is a testimony to the compelling power of the Word of God.

Now, let me direct you to the New Testament and to one of Paul's letters for a final testimony of the compelling power of the Word of God. Paul wrote, "Though I preach the Gospel, I have nothing to glory (boast) of: for necessity is laid upon me; yea, woe is me, if I preach not the Gospel. For if I do this thing willingly (that is, my motive is love), I have a reward; but if against my will, a dispensation ('stewardship,' in which every item of the service is scrutinized legally) of the Gospel is committed unto me" (I Corinthians 9:16).

To implement this point in your life, just live with a tender heart before the Word of God, maintain regular contact with it by daily reading and study, and the Word will exert its own compulsive force.

X. A SUPERLATIVE VALUE

Finally, I will mention a *superlative* value of the Word of God. This note is struck with regularity in the devotional parts of the Bible. David spoke for millions of transformed people when he said, "My heart stands in awe of Thy Word." May God pity the arrogant self-sufficiency of the natural man's sinful heart that forces him to totally miss the superlative glory of the Word of God. To that pitiable and pitiful man (however able or academic or affluent), the vast "parallel world of reality" is replaced by the temporary baubles and bubbles of sensory life. Jesus said that he may "gain the whole world" and yet "lose his own soul" (his true identity as a God-related human being, his true destiny with God forever). His *capax Dei* ("capacity for God") is left empty, while he tries to fill it with trifles and trinkets, or with ideas and empty philosophies. Far too soon, he will see what he has missed—and despair over the loss.

In Psalm 138:2, David acknowledged the superlative nature of the Word of God when he said to God, "Thou has magnified Thy Word above all Thy Name." That is, there is simply nothing higher in life as we experience it than the Word of God and the truth He brings to us through it. I declare this to be absolutely true—in my experience, in my relationship with God, in my daily life. When I "walk with the Lord in the light of His Word, what a glory He sheds on my way!" When I don't do so, how dry-as-dust is everything I think and do, and how unfulfilling is the "best" activity.

Thomas Carlyle spoke for those who have touched the live current of the Spirit's power in the Bible and have been transformed by the truth of the Word of God attended by the great power of the living Holy Spirit. Carlyle simply said, "There never was a Book like the Bible, and there never will be another." Dear Spirit of God, thank You for the superlative power of the Book You wrote for us, and thank You for Your willingness to attend our minds and hearts today as we open it to hear from You.

About 1600 years ago, Aurelius Augustine, a renegade sinner, heard a young child behind a hedge cry out the words, "Take up and read! Take up and read!" The Spirit of God empowered the child's challenge in the sinner's mind, and he went into the nearby house, picked up a Bible as an "accident of grace," "just happened" to open it to the thirteenth chapter of Paul's letter to the Romans, where he read, "Put ye on the Lord Jesus Christ, and make no provision for the flesh (the drives of the self-life), to fulfill the lusts thereof." Directed by the Holy Spirit and attended by His power and grace, Augustine repented of his terrible sins, clothed himself by faith in the Lord Jesus Christ, and received His Covering of Righteousness, and was instantly saved. Again, the rest is history . . .

Long ago, Thomas a Kempis said, "I am never happier than when I am in a nook with The Book." Dear friend, why don't you seek a quiet "nook" and spend some time in The Book, and prove the truth of what you have been reading?

PRAYER THAT PREVAILS

John 15:7:

"If ye abide in Me, and my words abide in you, ye shall ask what ye will, and it shall be done unto you."

Can there be any question that Jesus Christ expected — and received — answers to His prayers? None whatsoever. And in all of His recorded teachings, He leads us to believe that we (also) shall be able to obtain, through prayer, what otherwise would not be ours.

However, we have only to compare the promises of Jesus and the experience of Christians as seen consistently in their biographies or personal confessions, to discover a wide difference between *His assurances* with regard to prayer and *their actual experiences* in prayer. These variations are often so wide that Christians lower their expectations concerning answers to prayer, and finally pray only in a mediocre manner, governed more by unbelief than by faith.

In a recent "Peanuts" cartoon, Lucy said to Linus, "If you hold your hands upside down, you get the opposite of what you pray for." Many Christians must feel that they pray with their hands in the upside-down position! They have become so accustomed to disappointment in prayer that an unmistakable answer to prayer would shock them. All of us must confess a large measure of shame at this point. We have asked so many things which we have never received; we have sought so much without finding; we have knocked repeatedly, but the door has remained tightly closed. We have excused our failure by rationalizing that our prayer was probably not according to God's will, or that God withheld the answer to give something else, even something better. We forget that *if we prayed as we should, we would necessarily and inevitably ask what is according to His will*. If we "delight ourselves in the Lord, He will give us the desires of our hearts," because our desires are conditioned and determined by our delight in Him. He can trust that kind of prayer — and will favorably answer it. But we tend to evade the plain words of Christ, "Whatsoever ye shall ask in my name, that will I do."

We have only to selectively read the life stories of the great devotional saints (actually, *just Christians*) of history to see that they had discovered a great secret with regard to prayer and its answer, a secret which apparently has eluded many of us. A great library of prayers, intercessions, and supplications stands recorded in heaven, but some are answered, and some are not. What determines the difference? Why are some answered, and the prayers of some Christians answered *with regularity*, while the opposite is true of others?

We will turn for the answers to these questions to Christ's "legacy of love," the instructions He gave in His last lengthy interview, or "teaching session," with His disciples before the great redeeming events of His Death and Resurrection. These instructions are recorded in John thirteen through sixteen. In this crucial passage, Jesus gave the fullest instructions about prevailing prayer which He ever expressed. We will focus on John fifteen, though we will range around that chapter in a wider circle, gathering *the prerequisites of prevailing prayer* which are stated by Jesus Himself. In this passage, Jesus teaches that any prayer which is to prevail with

God and receive His favor and His answer, must pass five crucial (this word is based on the Latin word for "cross," and means "as serious as the cross") tests. It will be seen that these five tests could be regarded as only different shades of the same attitude. However, each is important for the testing of our prayers. Before we examine them, let me also add that these are not mere tests (a word which suggests only discipline and severity to some people); these are touchstones of delight to the surrendered and devoted heart.

I. SEEK THE GLORY OF GOD ALONE

First, if my prayers are to be favorably heard, and answered, I must be a person who *seeks the glory of God alone*. Jesus stated it as His own sole motive, "That the Father may be glorified in the Son" (John 14:13). The one and only purpose of Christ on earth was to glorify the Father, and at the close of His life here He was conscious that He had perfectly fulfilled this purpose. "Now is the Son of Man glorified, and God is glorified in Him." And this earthly satisfaction was perfectly consistent with, and an extension of, His eternal being. Each of the three Persons in the Holy Trinity has always been (and remains) devoted to upholding and displaying the moral beauty of the Other Two. The Father glorifies the Son and exalts the Spirit. The Son glorifies the Father and exalts the Spirit. And the Holy Spirit glories the Son and exalts the Father. This devotion for The Others is total and equal in Each Member of the Godhead at all times. Having completed His work of redemption and having sat down at the right hand of the Majesty on high, Christ still pursues His cherished purpose of making His Father known, loved, adored, and glorified. Thus, no prayer can hope to succeed with Him, with His Father, or with the Holy Spirit, which is out of harmony with this sublime and selfless intent.

Any prayer you offer to God should be consciously submitted to this standard — can I be confident in the Presence of Christ that my request will promote the glory of the Father? Marshall the evidence, present the reasons, and establish the grounds for your prayer. If your claim can be satisfactorily made "to the glory of God the Father," your prayer is already granted. But you may be sure that it is impossible to seek the glory of God consistently if selfish desires and aims dominate your life. Prayer is submitting to God and His glory, *not subverting God to yourself and your glory*. The glory of God and the glory of self can no more co-exist in the same person than light and darkness in the same space. The glory of God can only triumph in a man at the expense of self, and the glory of self can only triumph there at God's expense. Surely no one can truly *pray* for God's glory unless he is *living* for God's glory. The Christian who can state his motive in Paul's words, "That Christ may be glorified in my body, whether by life or by death," will touch the tenderest spot in Christ's glorified nature, and will awaken all of His mighty power in answer to his prayers. Christian, should we not (you and I) make a repentance-and-faith adjustment of our lives to the glory of God at this moment, so that God can show His promised answers to our prayers?

II. SUBMIT YOUR PRAYERS TO THE STANDARD OF CHRIST'S CHARACTER

Second, if my prayers are to be favorably heard, and answered, then I must *submit my prayers to the standard of Christ's character*. Jesus said, "Whatsoever ye shall ask *in My name*, that will I do." Throughout the Bible, a person's *name* stands for that person's *nature*. So Jesus said, You must ask *in My nature*. That is, when we pray, it must not be the self-nature that dictates the prayer, but the Christ-nature within the believer. But what are the distinguishing marks of the Christ-nature? The Christ-nature excludes boasting and practices humility. The Christ-nature is pure, peaceable, and loving. The Christ-nature is not swayed by the glare of the world. In short, the Christ-nature is full of Gethsemane, Calvary, Pentecost and Olivet. It is full of self-surrender, of the death-stance of the cross, of the breath of the Holy Spirit, and of the heavenly life of the Ascension.

Believer, get alone with God just now. Pour out your deepest heart to Him in prayer. Let the Christ-nature, which is in you by the Holy Spirit, speak to Christ Himself on the Throne of the universe. Thus, your heart becomes the prayer chapel for a dialogue between God the Father, God the Son, and God the Holy Spirit. This kind of prayer starts at the Throne of God as He governs your life, descends to you through a particular need (or *sense* of need), cycles through your heart as its prayer chapel, receives an answer, and then returns to God in the form of praise. Thus, the river of the water of life has descended from the Throne of God in the Eternal City, flowed right through your heart, and returned right back to its source. Its "outbound" course has sought the low point of your human need, and its "inbound" course has sought the high point of God's glory. It began with God's glory and ends with God's glory, and when it can find a matching point on earth, it will seek that point. It began with Christ's nature and it will end with Christ's nature, and when it can find a person who seeks consistency with His nature, it will hear and answer the prayer that is prayed according to the standard of that nature. This is what is meant by praying "in Christ's name."

If our prayers are to prevail with God and in behalf of men, we must get quiet enough before God to let the Christ-nature speak. We must be quiet and submissive enough that

He can create our petitions at His throne and countersign them in our hearts, thus endorsing His own purposes by means of our answered prayers. If this litmus test were properly applied to our prayers, surely many of the petitions we now offer so idly would never leave our lips. We would rise far above our usual petty praying, and would occupy the heavenlies with Him, both in person and in purpose. Many a prayer of mine has been like a frail little boat, leaving the shore of my unschooled heart, only to be dashed to pieces on the steadfast rock of God's purpose. If I would only learn to pray according to the nature of Christ within me, that nature would *become* the rock to which my prayers would anchor. The name of Christ must be predominant in my conversation, and the nature of Christ must be predominant in my character, if I am to be effective in prayer. I must know the meaning of, and practice the discipline of, praying in submission to the standard of Christ's character.

III. STAY IN UNHINDERED UNION WITH HIM

Third, if my prayers are to be favorably heard, and answered, then I must *stay in unhindered union with Christ.* He said, "If ye abide in Me, ... ye shall ask what ye will, and it shall be done unto you" (John 15:7). The day you were saved, you were transplanted out of Adam as your representative man, and into Christ. You are now "in Christ," having been placed there by a miracle of the Holy Spirit at the moment of your trust in Jesus Christ. You entered into union with Christ at that moment, and that union is forever. However, its conscious enjoyment and practical usefulness will be real only as you "keep all channels open" between you and Christ. This is called "abiding in Christ."

You see, your arm may be in your body, and yet be dislocated and useless. If I were to board a train in Memphis, Tennessee, today, intending to go all the way to St. Louis, Missouri, all that would be necessary for me to arrive at my destination would be to resist the temptation to get off the train at any of the stations along the way. It would be necessary for me to remain on the train until I arrive at my chosen destination. That's the word — *remain.* Stay put. This is the meaning of the word, "abide." To abide in Christ is to *keep the contact intact* between me and Jesus. Like the rider on the train, the faithful Christian must be careful to resist every temptation or suggestion to depart from full communion with Him by any act (even the tiniest act) of disobedience or unbelief.

While you are abiding in Christ in daily fellowship and moment-by-moment communion, it will not be hard for you to pray accurately and confidently, because Jesus has promised to abide in you as you abide in Him. The very Life of Christ in the moving Presence of the Holy Spirit will work in you, producing in you desires and petitions similar to those which He ceaselessly presents to His Father. Throughout this age, Jesus has been asking of God the Father. This perpetual communion is the constant attitude of the Son toward the Father. He cannot ask what the Father will not give. So we may be sure of success when we get into the current of His prayer. Abide in Him so that He may freely abide in you, not only in the activities and routines of your daily life, but in the intercessions and supplications of the specific time of prayer as well. Your delight in Him will increase with communion, and your communion will increase with that delight. As the relationship remains unhindered, you may "ask what ye will, and it will be done unto you."

IV. SIFT YOUR PRAYERS THROUGH HIS WORDS

Fourth, if my prayers are to be favorably heard, and answered, I must *sift my prayers through the sieve of His words.* My life and prayers must be monitored by the Word of God. Jesus said, "If my words abide in you, ... ye shall ask what ye will, and it shall be done unto you" (John 15:7). Christ's words may be compared to a jury of wise and serious persons, sitting in the court of eternal reality to try my prayers before they pass on into the Father's presence. If His Word pronounces an unfavorable verdict on my prayers, they will not be answered. But if His Word gives approval to my prayers, they will be answered. Hearing His Word quickens me to ask on the basis of revelation. It was when Jesus *mentioned* the Living Water that the Samaritan woman said, "*Give* me *this* water." Her request was prompted and conditioned by His revelation.

Suppose that I pray a prayer that is earth-born and earth-bound, "of the earth, and earthy," and stained with selfishness. As the prayer approaches the throne of God, this verse stands like a sentinel at the throne: "Seek ye first the kingdom of God and His righteousness," and the prayer is turned away. I am surprised and ashamed by my own spiritual vagrancy, and I discard that prayer as unworthy of Christ's blessing.

Suppose I pray a prayer that is marred by criticism and unkindness towards another human being, even toward another Christian. That prayer is stopped in its tracks by this solemn word of Jesus: "Love your neighbor as yourself," or a broader word, "Love your enemies, and pray for them that despitefully use you," and the unworthy prayer hastens away from the holy Throne.

Or suppose I pray a prayer that is tainted by a heart of murmuring and complaint because of the weight of Christ's cross and the restraint of Christ's yoke. The sentinel of the Word touches me with the sword-point of this notable declaration of Jesus: "In the world ye shall have tribulation; but be of good cheer, for I have overcome the world," and I pull back, aware that the mixture of complaint with communion cannot be allowed in the Throne-chamber of heaven. Like the accusers of the woman taken in the act of adultery (John 8:1-11), prayers like these are inwardly convicted of unfitness, and go forth from the Master's Presence, ashamed and unanswered.

I attended a meeting some time ago in which the moderator opened the meeting by saying, "As we begin, I want to ask the preacher to say a little prayer." Friends, *there is no such thing as a "little prayer"! If it reaches God, it has a magnitude beyond description; if it doesn't reach God, it isn't a prayer at all.*

The words of Christ forbid unsuitable prayer, but that ministry is negative and will only produce a sterile blank if it does not lead to a correction. *The words of Christ should also stir the heart with enlarging desires* for the possession of those good things which Christ has promised to them that love Him. Then prayer becomes a dialogue between the Master who says, "Seek ye my face," and the sensitive spiritual disciple who responds, "Thy face, Lord, will I seek" (Psalm 27:8). As you sift your prayers through the sieve of His words, His words will slowly condition your life so that your prayers will agree with Him — and He will agree with your prayers.

V. SERVE OTHERS IN LOVE, EXPECTING DIVINE FRUIT TO RESULT

Finally, if my prayers are to be favorably heard, and answered, then I must *serve others in love, expecting Divine fruit to result from the service.* Jesus said, "I appointed you that you should go and bring forth fruit, and that your fruit should remain: that whatsoever ye shall ask of the Father in my name, He may give it you" (John 15:16). In other words, answers to prayer will depend very largely (much more than we think) on our ministry to others. You see, it is the sign of a maturing Christian that the focus of his attention and action is increasingly on others, and not merely on himself. I saw a desk motto which read, "No turtle ever moves forward as long as he is enclosed within his shell." No Christian should expect to have his prayers answered as long as he remains imprisoned in the shell of self.

A Christian came upon a fellow believer from behind and startled him. The startled one exclaimed, "You almost made me jump out of my skin!" The other replied, "That just might be a good thing!" Lillian Smith, in her book, <u>The Killers of a Dream</u>, says that there are two journeys every believer must make. One, into himself, should lead him to accept, confess, and surrender what he finds there. The other, into the world, should lead him to regard it as the workshop of his service for Christ. Paul Tournier said essentially the same thing when he wrote, "Every Christian needs two conversions: one out of the world and one back into it." The Christian simply must move beyond personal piety to a consuming concern for other people all over the world. We live in a consumer society, and tragically, the church has often been turned into a consumer community, but where is the Christian who is willing to be consumed — for the glory of God and the good of others?

"Only two philosophies occupy life's shelf;
Either live *for God and others*, or you will live *for self.*"

Recently, I read the challenging life-story of William Wilberforce, the little hunchbacked Englishman who led the fight to free the slaves throughout the British Empire. The drama of the story is greatly heightened when we realize that slavery was at the very foundation of the economy of England at the time. When the struggle was most intense, and Wilberforce was showing physical signs of his part in the battle, a friend asked him, "William, how is it with your soul?" Wilberforce, who was spurred on by his marvelous Christian faith, replied, "I forgot that I had a soul." He meant that he had become so absorbed in ministering to others that he had forgotten himself. What a picture of Jesus' statement, "He who would save his life shall lose it, but whoever would lose his life for my sake and the Gospel's, shall save it." To be a healthy human being, according to Jesus, is to exist "between give and take" (or perhaps the proper order is "take and give"). However, we must be sure that the taking is a reception of God's resources, and the giving is a transmission of those resources to others, producing Biblical "fruit."

A wise Christian will hold himself accountable with this question: Do I live in a house of mirrors (always seeing and pampering myself), or in a house of windows (seeing others and ministering to them)? Many of us need to immediately replace our mirrors with windows. We need to balance the "outside-in" living of constant intake, with a suitable "inside-out" ministry of equally constant output. We need to focus on giving until giving matches getting in our lives. We need to change to the mentality of service instead of selfishness, to contribution and not mere acquisition.

> *"Self is the only prison that can ever bind the soul,*
> *Love is the only angel who can bid the gates unroll;*
> *And when he comes to call thee, arise and follow fast;*
> *His way may lie through darkness, but it leads to life at last."*

Many years ago, when Albert Schweitzer visited America, his journey took him to the city of Chicago. He was greeted there by a committee of prominent Chicago citizens, as well as by a great crowd of reporters at the railroad station. Schweitzer suddenly dismissed himself, pressed through the crowd, and helped a struggling little old lady with her baggage. When he returned to his welcoming crowd, he said wryly, "Sorry to keep you waiting, gentlemen, but I was just having my daily fun." A reporter later wrote, "That was the first time I ever saw a sermon walking." Whether that would qualify as "fruit unto God" is surely debatable, but the action and the attitude were unquestionably right. We must serve — for Christ's sake and for the sake of others — and we must get far enough in that service that it becomes the greatest fun of our lives.

Let me repeat this last test: According to Jesus, answers to prayer depend very largely on our ministry to others. If we are prompted by desire for our own comfort, peace, enjoyment, or advantage, we will have a poor chance of receiving answers from Him in prayer. If, on the other hand, our prayers are connected with our fruit-bearing (that is, prayer is for the purpose of bearing "fruit unto God," and the "fruit unto God" is thus merely the extension of our prayers), the golden scepter will be extended to us, as King Ahasuerus extended it to Queen Esther, saying, "What is your request? Even to the half of the kingdom it shall be granted."

When pastor Wallace Bassett was in the central American nation of Panama, he visited the Panama Canal. "Imagine my surprise," he later said, "when I was told that I could lift one of the great ships that pass through the canal." "How am I to do that?" I asked. "Just press this button," was the reply. When Dr. Bassett pressed the specified button, the great canal lock closed and filled with water, lifting the ship in it to the next level. Dr. Bassett remarked, "What a picture of prayer! Prayer is the Divinely-given means for weak believers like myself to elevate Heaven's great causes among men, and to lift life's great and crushing loads." In light of the vast needs, opportunities and responsibilities of today, could any believer make a more strategic contribution than to join with other believers in concentrated prayer?

What is the conclusion of the matter? Simply this: the temple of prayer is guarded from the intrusion of the unprepared footstep by several crucial tests. At the very door, we are challenged by the watchword: Seek the glory of God alone. If our lives do not harmonize with God's glory, we are allowed to go no further. Then, the key that unlocks the door is engraved with the name of Jesus. Submit your prayers to the standard of Christ's character. The locked door to the Audience-chamber will only open to the hand in which His nature is pulsating. Then, we must stay in obedient union with Him. We must abide in Him and He in us if His to plead in and through us. Then, His words must monitor and monopolize our lives if our prayers are to be answered. And finally, we must serve others in love, expecting Divine fruit to result from the service. It is as we serve our Master according to His orders that we can count absolutely on His answer to our prayers.

As we accept and apply and act upon the mandates given by these "tests," we can expect that prayer will become ever more engrossing and rewarding. We will discover the door of the prayer closet to be the little door that opens to The Largest Life. May God help us to keep the hinges of that door well-oiled and the Throne-room well-visited! Go into the Holy of Holies, spread His Book open before the Mercy Seat and between you and Him, wait until the Shekinah ("Presence") Light shines upon its sacred page, and when you have had an audience with the King and caught His pulse beat, rise to go out and serve in His name. Surprising fruit will be the result.

WANTED: MEN WHO WILL MODEL CHRIST — AND MEN WHO WILL FOLLOW THE MODEL

Philippians 3:17:

"Brethren, be followers together of me, and mark them which walk so as ye have us for an ensample" (King James Version)

"Brethren, together follow my example and observe those who live after the pattern we have set you" (Amplified Bible translation)

This text might immediately throw a shallow Christian into protest. He might say, "Who but an egotist would say, 'Brethren, join in imitating me'?" However, this assessment overlooks several very important facts from the life of the Apostle Paul, as well as several important facts revealed in the context of this verse.

Fact Number One: the moral confusion of the world of Paul's day is known to have been very great. *People needed moral and spiritual examples that could be trusted.* Paul did not back down from this duty, and he encouraged other believers to also assume the responsibility of Christian example.

Fact Number Two: the *context* of this verse corrects the possibility of a charge of egotism against the one who wrote these words. Paul has just stated in no uncertain terms that he was not perfect. "I have not already reached the goal of the Christian life, nor have I become perfect, but I press on in order that I may lay hold of that for which also I was laid hold of by Christ Jesus" (verse 12). In fact, Paul clearly indicates that the only worthy example of a Christian is the person who admits he is *not* perfect but is nonetheless pressing on. He has just said that he personally has no righteousness of his own, that any righteousness he has is provided by Another (verse 9). Thus, the only righteousness others are to respect in Paul is the very righteousness of Christ Himself.

Then, look just beyond our text (verse 17), and read verses 18 and 19: "For many walk, of whom I have told you often, and tell you now in tears, that they are the enemies of the cross of Christ, whose end is destruction, whose god is their belly, whose glory is in their shame, who mind earthly things." After reading those words, it becomes quite obvious why Paul wrote what he did in verse 17. There were plenty of *bad* examples to observe, but all men (including Christians) need *good* examples.

Fact Number Three: in this verse, Paul called on the Philippian Christians to imitate not only him, but also other exemplary Christians. Hear the words again: "Brethren, be followers together of me, and mark them which walk so as ye have us for an example." The New American Standard Version says, "And observe those who walk according to the pattern you have in us." So Paul guards both himself and his disciples in this statement. He guards himself against the pride of thinking that he is the only exemplary Christian on the premises, and he guards them against following him exclusively, which might tend to create a cult. Nevertheless, Paul lovingly and boldly asks them to imitate and follow him.

I. THE PRACTICAL METHOD OF MAKING DISCIPLES

Here we see *the practical method of making disciples.* Just as it did with Jesus, disciple-making begins with a model, a mandate, and a method. The model provides the incarnational example of the process. The mandate clearly shows that disciple-making is the responsibility of each Christian. The method combines the model and the mandate in a practical procedure, and shows how disciple-making is to be accomplished.

A. The model is in personal example

The New Testament *model for disciple-making is in personal example,* and each Christian is expected to supply such an example. Christian, the truth is that people will either take you as an **example of** Christ, or as an **exemption from** Christ. You cannot escape the exerting of influence, the setting of example. D. L. Moody was probably correct when he said, "Of one hundred men, one will read the Bible, and the other ninety-nine will read the Christian." You see, everything we say is a profession of faith, and everything we do is a promotion of faith—or these things are preventions of faith in the lives of others. Our words and works are either an encouragement in favor of good, or of less good, or of evil. We daily influence our intimates and the immediate circle of associates just beyond them, whether we are conscious of our influence or not. A stone thrown into a pond does not merely disturb the water in the spot where it hits it. Around that point of impact, great concentric circles form. We simply cannot control our influence, though we certainly can largely control the kind of influence we exert.

> *"I have a little shadow, That goes in and out with me;*
> *And what can be the use of him, Is often more than I can see."*

Behind these ideas rests a gigantic law of spiritual life, and it is this: Christianity is propositional, to be sure, but its first attraction to human beings is generally personal. It is instructional, but it is first incarnational. Historian Robert Wilken said it wisely when he said, "Before people are doers, they are first spectators." Christianity is not merely audible, it is also visual and tangible (see I John 1:1-3). So it must have models as well as mouthpieces; it must have pacesetters as well as proclaimers; it must have examples as well as exhorters. This is one of the roles Jesus plays for mankind — "leaving us an example, to follow in His steps" (I Peter 2:21).

This is a key role, also, for every disciple-maker. He cannot expect his disciples to be what he is not, or to do what he does not do, or to go where he does not go. It is true that the disciple-maker's life must not be the end of the disciple's quest, but merely the example of one seeking to be a follower of Christ. But it is example that gives credibility to leadership. Jesus exemplified the standard of disciple-making before He exhorted it.

Reconsider for a moment the characteristics of a disciple. A disciple is one who: (l) has a regular relationship with his disciple-maker, his teacher (compare Mark 3:14a); (2) receives revelation (systematic truth) from his disciple-maker, his teacher (see Matthew 10:5); (3) repeats the truth received to other potential disciples (II Timothy 2:2); (4) shows increasing resemblance to his disciple-maker, his teacher (see Luke 6:40); and (4) becomes a reflection of his teacher in both concept and conduct. So a disciple-maker must be a model and a pace-setter, and he must expect his disciples to follow him and his example. Indeed, he must humbly invite them to do so, as Paul does in our text.

B. The mandate is in personal exhortation

Clearly, the New Testament *mandate* to disciple-making *is presented in the form of personal exhortation.* Let's examine our verse more closely, in order to be sure that we understand the dimensions of responsibility that are presented here. Indeed, we must recognize that the responsibility is two-fold. Paul had to show it and say it, and the Philippian readers had to see it and submit to it. The two key verbs, "join in following my example," and "observe those who so walk," are both in the present tense. Again, we must note that Paul boldly urged Christians to follow the example of the testimony and technique of other Christians. This means that the following of right examples should be the consistent and continuous activity of every Christian. It also suggests that most Christians need to be encouraged by another Christian to do this, or the concept will lapse in their minds.

Pastor Rick Yohn, in his book, <u>Living Securely In an Unstable World</u>, wrote, "In my later teen years, I had the privilege of being supported by a number of mature Christian men. They spent time praying with me, counseling me, and encouraging me in my Christian walk. I developed a boldness for witnessing by following the example of one man. I established a consistent prayer life by following the example of another. I developed a deep desire for studying the Scriptures by following the example of a third. The more I associated myself with such men, the more I experienced a personal spiritual growth and the sanctifying work of God's Holy Spirit." Christian, you are following somebody's example at this very moment. You spend your minutes, days, weeks, months, and years living out the influence that people have exerted on your life.

Note that you are to give positive and selective attention to those who set the right example for you and others.

"Mark them which so walk," Paul says. The Greek word translated "mark" is the word "skopos," from which we derive our English word, "scope." Perhaps you have heard someone say, "We scoped it out," referring to a careful and critical examination of a certain object. The word means to "keep an eye on." In Romans 16:17, this word is used for an examination that leads you to avoid something, but here, the examination is made in order to appreciate and imitate something.

Look also at the word, "example" in our text. It is a big, big word. The Greek word is "tupon," from which we get our word "type." The word "type" is a special word, and it has a specialized meaning in the New Testament. It comes from a root that means "to strike," and it describes the creating of an impression by striking the image into a receptive surface. Technically, it was the impress or figure made by a seal or a die, such as the die that is used in minting new coins.

This was the same word Thomas used when he said about Jesus, "Except I shall see in His hands the print (the 'tupon'— the "impression") of the nails, and put my finger into the print ('impression') of the nails . . . I will not believe" (John 20:25). Thomas was saying that the marks of crucifixion in the body of Jesus were all he had to go by, and all other impressions were not to be trusted. This is the word translated "example" in our text. The example of a Spirit-walking Christian is the only trustworthy impression most people will ever have. However, it is evident that Christians do not automatically set a Christian example for others to follow. Unless we are "imitators" of Christ in the fullest New Testament sense, we will leave false impressions with others as to Who Jesus is and what Christianity is all about. And note this: the impressions we make are the result of a die already cast, a Life already lived — and we have been stamped with the Image of it!

So a Christian must constantly ask himself, "Is my life worth copying?" Would I want to live in heaven among a society of Christians who have lived their lives by the impression I have made on them? The word translated "example" suggests a "copy-pattern" or a "mold." Close examination of Paul's letters in the New Testament will disclose that this idea is quite common in his writings. In I Thessalonians 1:7, Paul says, "You were examples to all that believed in Macedonia and Achaia." He made the same appeal to the Corinthians that he presents in our text when he said, "I beseech you, be ye followers of me" (I Corinthians 4:16). And again in I Corinthians 11:1, which proves the point we made earlier about Paul's humility: "Be ye followers of me, even as I also am of Christ." There is Paul's guard, there is his proviso, there is his protection, there is his qualification — follow me, but only as I follow Christ. In II Thessalonians 3:7-9, Paul put the appeal even more powerfully: "You know how (why) you ought to follow us: for we did not behave ourselves in a disorderly fashion among you: neither did we eat any man's bread without return; but we worked with labor and pain night and day, that we might not be chargeable to any of you: Nor because we have no rights, but to makes ourselves an example unto you to follow us." So the Christian disciple-maker and teacher should make self-conscious effort to provide the right example, and to appeal to his disciples to follow that example. Like the teacher who writes the "copy-pattern" on the chalkboard and assigns the pupils to copy it, Paul places the pattern of his own life in Christ before the Philippian Christians, and asks them to "copy" it.

Johann Gutenberg is credited with building the first printing press. Living and working in the Rhineland of Germany in the 1440s, he gave to the world one of the most important tools ever invented. Before that time, all copies of information — records, facts, etc. — were made by hand. You see, Mr. Modern, there was a time when fax machines did not exist! I heard about a man in a Memphis business who was trying to fax a message to the west coast, but he accidentally got his tie caught in the fax machine—and ended up in Los Angeles himself! Before moveable type, before typewriters, before Xerox, before computers, before fax, there were people who had to copy documents by hand if the documents were to be preserved. This is the way the earliest transmissions of the Bible were made. The copyist had to be very careful to copy everything correctly. In Jesus' time, the scribes mentioned in the Bible were very important people. They were the copyists who were responsible to preserve and transmit the text of the Bible.

The scribe was himself carefully trained for this task. Jesus referred in Matthew 13:52 to "the scribe who is instructed," and the word translated "instructed" is the verb form of the word "disciple." "Every scribe who is *discipled."* Intensive training was required for the copyist's technical job to be done well. In his training, the master scribe or teacher would give the disciple, the apprentice, the aspiring young scribe, a piece of paper with the letters of certain words written picturesquely across the top. These letters contained every "stroke" (remember the word, "tupon") that the copyist would be expected to make. The young copyist would practice copying the words again and again, until he had mastered the printing of those letters. He literally followed the "example" (copied the"tupon") that was set before him. After he had followed the example enough times, the stroke of the pen came naturally to him.

Dear Christians, all of us are copies, and copyists, and then we are responsible to be copy-patterns for someone else to copy! We are to follow the examples of worthy Christians until the "tracing of the strokes" of the Christian life become natural and automatic in our own lives. We are responsible to carefully choose the examples we will follow. These examples will play an incredibly large part in making us who we will finally become.

So we see that our text combines the proper model (Paul and others) and the proper mandate (the urgent encouragement to follow their example) for making disciples. Both the model and the mandate are essential. If I only see a model of the Christian life, I will not be able to follow it with full intelligence. If I only hear the mandate, I will think it is too visionary and impossible to receive my serious consideration and commitment. Both are essential.

II. THE PERSONAL MODEL FOR DISCIPLE-MAKERS

This text also suggests that *disciple-makers also need (and have) personal models*. The original model of disciple-making was Jesus Himself. From all eternity, He had been His Father's disciple. When He came to the earth, Jesus taught a small group of men and made them responsible to teach others. He made disciples, each of whom was then responsible to make other disciples. We could say that He not only made disciples, He made disciple-makers, and they then trained other disciples, who in turn would also become disciple-makers. So an ever-enlarging network of trained disciple-makers emerged from the training process which Jesus initiated with His Twelve.

A generation later, a disciple-making leader emerged in the Christian movement who functioned in the Spirit and Vision of his Master. Though Paul had apparently never seen Jesus in the flesh, he was so influenced by His disciples that he learned about being a disciple of Christ (remember Stephen,

Acts 7) and building disciples (remember Barnabas, Paul's disciple-maker) from them. In turn, he said to a young disciple-maker, "The things which you have heard from me, the same things commit to faithful men, who will be able to teach others also" (II Timothy 2:2). We must see this as simply an extension of Jesus' own life. Jesus said, in effect, "The things that I, Jesus, have heard from My Father, I have committed to (invested in) twelve faithful men, who shall be able to teach others also." Our text for this study was written by that second-generation man who was a crucial "link" in the chain of disciple-making. Just what kind of example did he set? What kind of model was he? What copy-pattern can we detect in him? Well, it is very interesting that you asked that question! The third chapter of Philippians gives us a profound portrait of Paul. In order to see the dimensions of his example, let's see what kind of man he was. We will use the verses preceding our text as our foundation.

In verses 12-15, Paul said, "I am not as one who has already 'arrived,' nor am I anywhere near perfection: but I am following hard after God, so that I may fully 'grasp' that for which Christ Jesus has grasped me. My brothers, I have not fully grasped it yet: but this one thing I do, forgetting the things which are past, and reaching ahead toward those things that are still before me, I strain toward the mark for the prize of the upward calling of God in Christ Jesus. As many as are maturing in Christ, I ask them to join me with the same mentality."

Here is a veritable world in words! Each sentence is an ocean of content, enticing the swimmer-in-training to dive in and exhaust himself. However, because of the nature of our study, we will focus our attention on the kind of man Paul was — in order to see the model he gave, the example he set, before disciples and disciple-makers.

A. Healthy Dissatisfaction

First, Paul was a man of *healthy dissatisfaction*. Anybody who has studied the life of Paul extensively has become aware that Paul was very dissatisfied before he became a Christian. And his dissatisfaction had been extremely intense! Someone said, "A psychotic is a person who says that two plus two is five; that is, a psychotic is really out of touch with reality. However, a neurotic is a person who says, 'Two plus two may be four, but I don't like it!'" In other words, the neurotic is in touch with reality, but it does not suit him. Before he became a Christian, Paul was something of a religious neurotic.

Winston Churchill often told the story of a family who was picnicking by a lake one day when their five-year-old son accidentally fell into the water. A stranger passing by saw the situation and, at great risk to his own safety, dived in, fully clothed, and rescued the child from drowning. The rescuer presented the boy back to his mother, but instead of thanking the stranger for his heroic deed, the mother snapped feverishly, "Where's Johnny's cap?" Out of all the possible facets of this traumatic event, this was the detail the mother emphasized. There are some people, no matter what is done for them, who choose not to be satisfied. They are perennially unhappy with themselves, with others, and with reality itself. I strongly suspect that Saul of Tarsus fell into this group before he was saved. But this is the same man who in Philippians chapter four declared himself to be "content in any circumstance where I find myself."

But Paul was not only dissatisfied before he became a Christian. He was also marked by a healthy dissatisfaction after he became a Christian. Indeed, any true Christian is a profound mixture of happy satisfaction and healthy dissatisfaction. It is crucial that a Christian keep a wholesome balance of these two things in his life. Someone wisely said,

"A Christian cannot recommend the Bread of Life or the Water of Life to others if he himself looks as if those foods disagreed with him!" But we still must recognize that healthy dissatisfaction is a vital part of the Christian life. The Christian has had a deeply satisfying drink of the Water of Life, but he is always thirsty for more! He became an instant winner in Christ, but he then realized that there are a lot of other races to be won and fights to be fought since he got his first gold medal. The Christian life involves a sanctified dissatisfaction as well as a settled contentment. Why? Because, though I am positionally perfect in Christ, I am still very imperfect in my daily practice as a Christian.

Paul expressed this creative tension between positional perfection and practical progress in these words: "I am not as one who has already arrived, nor am I anywhere near perfection . . . but I seek to know the Person of Christ better and better, and to 'grasp' His purpose for me with a more complete grip each day." It is this healthy dissatisfaction that keeps the Christian moving ever deeper into the Treasure and the treasury of the Christian life. Paul modeled this healthy dissatisfaction, and every Christian should reveal it as well. Christian, just remember that wherever you are at present, it's not where you could be. Then let the margin of difference between what you are and what you could be provide the dissatisfaction that moves you toward the desirable goal.

B. Heart-felt Devotion

Second, Paul was characterized by a *heart-felt devotion.* "This one thing I do," he said. We would call this concentration or focus, and that is what Christian devotion is. Vision, focus, and concentration are indispensable ingredients of every Christian's daily life. Paul was a specialist, and so should every Christian be. His focus was not on a dozen things, or even two, but only on one. His vocation was Christ and His

Purpose; his avocation was anything else that called for his attention and effort. Vance Havner once said, "Most Christians could be called 'hypodermic saints,' because they run as if they are energized by 'shots' of the Gospel. They live the Christian life by spurts, spasms, or turns, but not consistently and continually." Then he divided Christians into three categories — workers, shirkers, and jerkers — and he said that most Christians are jerkers whose devotion is unsteady and unreliable.

When a lion-tamer at the circus allows himself to be locked in with all those vicious lions, why does he carry a three- or four-legged stool in his hand? This is not an arbitrary act. The person who holds the chair knows something very important about the constitution of a lion. He knows that when you put several points of focus before him, the constitution of the lion requires him to try to focus on all of them. Thus, his attention and energies become fragmented and divided, and the lion is largely neutralized. In the Bible, Satan is described as "a roaring lion" (I Peter 5:8). Christians could easily neutralize Satan by simply striking on all assigned 'fronts,' on all commanded points of focus. Jesus was a wise strategist when He commanded us to witness "both in Jerusalem, and in Judea, and in Samaria, and unto the uttermost part of the earth" — striking with equal force and efficiency at all times on all of these assigned fronts. Instead, however, our attention has been introverted into our own lives and our local church situations, and even there, our attention is divided to a thousand petty things — and thus Satan has divided us and neutralized us. Our "one thing" is the pursuit of Jesus Christ and His purpose of total world impact. This goal is worthy of the heart-felt devotion of every Christian.

There is great power in concentration. Let the sun disperse its rays over the earth, and it has a substantial power.

But let a few rays of the sun's light be focused through a powerful magnifying lens, thus concentrating it, and that concentrated light and heat can burn its way through a sheet of solid metal! If each Christian would practice heart-felt devotion to Jesus Christ and His purpose to make disciples and impact the whole world, and join with a few others of similar devotion, the impact would be enormous! Paul was the walking model of such whole-hearted (concentrated) devotion.

C. Heavenly Direction

Third, Paul lived a life of *heavenly direction.* "Brethren, . . . I forget those things which are behind, and reach forth unto those things which are before" (verse 13). Throughout this passage, Paul employs another sports illustration. He sees in his mind's eye a sports stadium, a running track, and a corps of runners sprinting for the finish line. Each runner is exerting maximum effort to reach the finish as the winner of the race in order to receive the victor's reward.

Every runner on a track team is mindful of two foundational rules in running a race: (1) Don't look back; and (2) Focus on the finish line. Don't look back! "Forgetting the things which are behind." When hurdlers in a track meet hit a hurdle while running a competitive race, they don't turn around to look at the hurdle, nor do they stop and go back and pick it up. Any sports fan knows how ridiculous it is to suggest such action, but Christians are usually not as wise as hurdlers on a track team. They often stop to look back, and break their momentum toward the finish line.

Paul says that Christians should forget the things that are past. Someone outlined this responsibility toward the past in these points: (1) Past *sins* must be *forgiven*; (2) Past *sorrows* must be *forgotten*; and (3) Past *successes* must be *forsaken*. An 80 year old man facetiously said of his feeble mind, "My memory is what I forget with!" The Christian must deliberately use his memory to forget the past.

Clara Barton, the founder of the American Red Cross, received much criticism, but she bore the burden of it cheerfully. One day a friend reminded her of a particularly mean thing that had been done to her. When Clara's face showed a blank expression, the friend exclaimed, "Surely you remember that, Clara!" "No," Clara Barton replied, "I distinctly remember forgetting it!" Every Christian should be marked by such distinct and discriminating forgetfulness.

"We thank Thee, Lord, for memory To live again the past;
That in remembering bygone days The fruits of joy shall last.
But for the power to forget We thank Thee even more:
The stings, the slights, the hurts, the wounds Can never
hurt us more."

Most of all, the Christian must forget all failures of the past, whether they be sins of omission or commission. David committed several crimson sins as king of Israel, but when he had "come clean" with God and sought His forgiveness, he prayed, "Restore unto me the joy of thy salvation, and uphold me with Thy free Spirit. Then will I teach transgressors thy ways; and sinners shall be converted unto thee" (Psalm 51:12-13). David rested in the mercy and grace of God, and refused to allow a sad history of failure to determine his future life.

In the 1986 major league baseball season, Bob Brenley, catcher for the San Francisco Giants, set a major league record when he made four errors in one game. However, in the same game, in the last of the ninth inning, the same Bob Brenley came to bat with the score tied. Brenley hit a home run for the Giants, and they beat the Atlanta Braves by a score of seven to six! Dear Christian, no matter what errors are behind you in earlier innings of the game, you still may deliver a winning hit for God's side if you will forget the failures of the past and focus on the responsibilities and possibilities of the present and the future. A disciple-maker who stops to pick up the hurdles he has knocked down will never win the race. A batter who is dejectedly focusing on earlier errors will not likely deliver a winning hit. Don't look back!

Then, the disciple-maker must be sure that he keeps his attention on the clearly defined goals of Total World Impact, the Building of an Army of Disciples, and the Training Process by which the soldiers in that army train others. Paul followed his athletic metaphor still further when he said, "Strain forward toward those things that are before you." One can see the runner with every muscle straining toward the tape, his total focus on the finish line, and his full effort given to the race. He knows that he cannot allow distractions to divert his attention from the running of the race.

A Christian should look at the past in just about the same proportion as a driver glances in the rear view mirror while driving an automobile. The rear view mirror is a handy instrument to have in the car for the sake of safety, but there is no safety in the driver keeping his attention focused through that mirror on objects behind the vehicle! Christian, through which do you look the most — the rear view mirror, or the windshield?

There is an old parable which I have read and studied many times. It is called "Atalanta and the Golden Apples." It is the story of a king's daughter named Atalanta, who was blessed with the gifts of beauty and fleetness of foot. When she had matured into a young woman and her gifts were well known far and wide, her father the king offered her hand in marriage to any man who could beat her in a prescribed race on a racecourse. Many tried and failed, and, as a consequence, forfeited their lives. At last a young Greek named Hippomenes applied to run the race against her. When he arrived on the day of the race, he was wearing a small sash around his waist, and a small sack hung from the sash.

When the race started, she teasingly slowed her pace to let him get ahead. Then suddenly, she put on a burst of speed and started to pass him. However, as she did, he reached into the small bag and pulled out a golden apple. As she went by him, he rolled the apple diagonally across her pathway. The gleam of its beauty attracted her eye. When she saw the flash of gold, she knew it also had a great value. So she stopped and turned aside just long enough to retrieve it, quickly returning to the course to resume the race. She easily caught Hippomenes again and threatened to pass. Again, he rolled an apple across her path, and again she turned and quickly retrieved it. She returned to the race and caught him again. As she began to pass, he threw the final apple across her course. Again, she turned to retrieve the apple, thinking she still had enough time to make up the distance and win the race. But he had calculated correctly, because he breasted the tape at the finish line as she trailed by a step. Hippomenes won the race and the beautiful maiden — and the kingdom — not by his superior speed, but by the cunning of distraction. She lost because of her own folly in leaving the course for a mere trinket. Even so, it has often been the ruin of many a saint in the most glorious race of all that, for the three golden apples of the enticements of the world, the seduction of the flesh, and the allurements of Satan, he has failed to "strain toward the prize of the high calling of God in Christ Jesus." The disciple and disciple-maker must maintain his heavenly direction with consistency throughout his Christian life.

D. Holy Determination

Finally, Paul was a man of *holy determination.* Isolate the words, "I press toward the mark for the prize of the high calling of God in Christ Jesus." Paul is not picturing a quiet stroll in the park, but a vigorous and draining run. Objects held in the hand might not be noticed in a stroll in the park, but such objects become a hindrance when one is running. One of the great tragedies of the Christian life is that many Christians never win any significant victories for the cause of Christ, never capture any enemy territory or troops, never destroy any strongholds of the enemy in their homeland—in short, they never win any real victories in spite of the extreme and aggressive language that is used again and again in the New Testament. The words used in our text and in countless other similar passages in the New Testament are far too vigorous to describe the casual, relaxed, easygoing type of Christian life that is so often exemplified among us. We must not sit back on padded seats in an air conditioned building and listen and look. We must strain every nerve of our moral and spiritual being to run this race and win this prize.

Paul said elsewhere, "The pioneers who have blazed the faith-trail, the veterans that have run the race before us, are like spectators in a heavenly grandstand, loudly and lustily cheering us on as we run the same race today. We must strip down, start running—and never quit! No extra spiritual weight is permissible, and no parasitic sins. We must deliberately take our eyes *off* of everything else, and keep them fastened *on* Jesus, Who not only started the race but knows how to triumphantly finish it as well. Study how He did it! He never lost sight of where He was headed. Because of the anticipation of an exhilarating finish, He could put up with anything along the way—the cross, the shame, whatever. And now He's there, in the place of honor, beside the King's throne.

When you find yourselves flagging in your faith, go over that story again, item by item. That will shoot adrenalin into your souls! And keep running! It will be worth it all when you, too, are invited up to sit with Jesus beside the King's throne."

In conclusion, pause just a moment and remind yourself of our theme—disciple-modeling, disciple-making, and disciple-multiplying. And remember that God has placed *you* in Square One to begin the process. Remember, too, that the product of your ministry with your disciples is to create impact that extends to the ends of the earth until the end of time. Place yourself in our text—and move out for Jesus.

A middle-aged man and his wife had walked out on a long dock that extended into the Mississippi River at Vicksburg, Mississippi. They had seated themselves at the end of the dock, and were dangling their legs over the end as they held hands and "whispered sweet nothings" in each other's ears. Suddenly, their romantic absorption was broken when they heard running footsteps on the dock behind them. They both looked back and saw a man dressed in a business suit, running as fast as he could toward the end of the dock. They thought he was running to them, but as he reached them, he maintained his fast speed. They parted just in time for him to leap from the end of the dock. With a "wahoo" yell, he sailed through the air and splashed into the water several feet from the end of the dock. Alarmed, the couple raced out to the end and helped him out of the water. The woman asked, "What in the world are you doing?" Panting and spitting water, the man answered, "Do you see that man back up there on the hill? Well, he just bet me a million to one that I couldn't jump across the Mississippi River. Now, I knew within reason that I couldn't do it—but at those odds, I couldn't just stand there and not try it!"

This disciple-making task may seem exceedingly difficult to us, if not altogether impossible. The task of total world impact is indeed a formidable assignment. A world full of lost people is a forbidding concept. **But in light of what is at stake, can we simply stand still and do nothing**???

HIS LAST WORDS, HIS LAST WILL

Acts 1:8:

"But ye shall receive power, after that the Holy Ghost is come upon you: and ye shall be witnesses unto me both in Jerusalem, and in all Judea, and in Samaria, and unto the uttermost part of the earth."

George Orwell, the renowned author of <u>1984</u> and <u>Animal Farm</u>, once wrote, "we have now sunk to a depth at which the restatement of the obvious is the first duty of intelligent men." In today's church, the obvious is revolutionary. Nothing is so poorly obeyed as the "obvious" commission of Jesus. When the obvious is restated and applied, the church is shaken at its foundations.

The commission of Jesus was stated in each of the four Gospels and in the Book of Acts. The Book of Acts is a continuation of the gospel narratives. It is written in chronological sequence and follows an easily discernible geographic pattern, a pattern specified in Acts 1:8: "Jerusalem...Judea...Samaria...the end of the earth." The Book of Acts may be divided into three segments (1-7, 8-12, 13-28), with the first segment showing how the early church continued in Jerusalem the work that Jesus had begun (Acts

1:1). The second part concerns Gospel progress in Judea and Samaria, and the last part "to the ends of the earth."

Verse eight of Acts one contains the last words that Jesus Christ spoke to His disciples just moments before His ascension to Heaven. The Gospels of Luke and John reveal that the first time Jesus met with His disciples following the resurrection He charged them to be witnesses to all nations. He repeated the charge at least once the same evening. He repeated it again later on the mountain in Galilee as recorded in Matthew 28. And now He is outside the city of Jerusalem, 40 days later, just before His ascension. Thus, the commission should be quite obvious to us. However, one practical question will reveal that we have actually paid it very little attention. How much of what you do, think, say, or make impacts the whole world? You see, Jesus was intense about world involvement, but relaxed about methods. We reverse this! We go to one conference after another on methods, but side-step the necessary involvement.

Jesus' command called for action. The Great Commission was never given just to be studied. It is a plan for action. In this study, we will merely examine it again, using Acts 1:8 as our foundation. But, the critical question is: Will you make yourself available at each step for the fulfillment of the Great Commission?

I. STRATEGY FOR GOSPEL ADVANCE

First, we see in this statement the *strategy* for Gospel advance. The strategy is contained in the word "witness." This is a cosmopolitan word with an overload of content. The original word is "marturia," which should inform us immediately that this is not a tame word. It is the word from which we get a transliterated English word, the word "martyrs."

So, the lifestyle pictured in this word is a risk-taking lifestyle. To be a "martyr-witness" is a life-and-death proposition.

Virginia Owens wrote, "Being a Christian is an extreme position, not a safe one. One doesn't follow Christ down the middle of the road toward respectability." One theologian who had begun to appreciate the "extreme position" of Christianity wrote, "Let us collect all the New Testaments there are in existence, let us carry them out to an open place or up on a mountain, and then, while we all kneel down, let someone address God in this fashion: 'Take this Book back again; we men, such as we are now, are no good at dealing with a thing like this, it only makes us unhappy.' My proposal is that like the inhabitants of Gadara, we beseech Christ to 'depart out of our coasts.'" These writers have begun to grasp the radical "martyr-witness" demand of Jesus.

Martyr, this word "martus," occurs over 30 times in the Book of Acts, and is one of the keynotes of the book. It informs us that we are to forget any thought of a "safety-first" lifestyle. A farmer took his dog hunting in the woods several miles from his house, only to discover that he had forgotten his lunch pail. He put his gun down and told the dog to stay by the gun until he returned. While the farmer was gone, a forest fire swept through the woods and the dog was killed. Later, the farmer found the dog's charred body beside his rifle. He sadly said, "I always had to be careful what I told that dog to do, because he would always do it." Christian friends, Jesus Christ wants us to be so concerned with doing what He says that we forget about the forest fire.

A biology professor expressed a matter-of-fact rule of science in class one day when he said, "Self-preservation is the first law of nature." A Christian student smilingly observed to him after class, "It's most interesting to see the contrast between nature and grace. Self-preservation may be the first law of nature, but self-sacrifice is the first law of grace." He was right!

See the Calvary-sacrifice that is at the very heart of God's grace, and then be reminded that the first principle of Christian discipleship is in these words of Jesus: "If any man will come after Me, let him *DENY HIMSELF*, and *TAKE UP HIS CROSS*, and follow Me." To deny myself means that I say to myself what Peter said about Jesus when he denied Him: "I never heard of the man; I do not know the man." To "take up his cross" means that the Christian walks in daily death to his own will and wishes in order to follow Christ.

Bruce Morgan wrote, "The trouble with Christians is that nobody wants to kill them anymore." Eugenia Price echoed that thought when she said, "The greatest sin of the church is that it has TAMED Jesus Christ." The kind of witness which is called for in Acts 1:8 is quite apparently of such a nature that it gets us into constant trouble (but also produces in us constant joy, and is attended by constant miracles).

A meeting of hundreds of religious leaders from across America was held in which the agenda was, "How can we be used to turn this nation back to God?" Each attendant was given opportunity one evening to make a brief response to the question. One black leader arose and said, "Brethren, Christians in America will never again have the desired impact on this society until they lose their fear of dying," and he sat down. Many in the meeting concluded that his may have been the best answer given by anyone present.

Years ago, a great missionary spokesman named Robert Wilder visited tiny Hope College in Michigan to bring a chapel message on world missions. He placed a large map of India in the front of a chapel and installed a metronome before the map. In the message, he declared that every time the

HIS LAST WORDS, HIS LAST WILL

metronome clicked, a soul died in India without ever having heard of Christ. That day, Christ and His world vision captured the heart of a young college senior named Samuel Zwemer. As the vision flamed in his heart, he asked God to place him in the hardest spot on earth.

In the course of time, he established residence on the Island of Bahrain in the Persian Gulf, at the very heart of the Islamic world community. This island was often identified in newscasts and newspaper reports of the recent "Gulf War." Zwemer began to print and circulate Gospel tracts in the Arabic language, though he hardly had the approval of the Islamic government of the island. In one week, Zwemer's two small daughters, ages four and seven, both died from illness and the oppressive heat. Samuel Zwemer asked the Bahrain officials for permission to bury the bodies of his two precious daughters on the island, but permission was refused on the ground that they were Christians and their bodies would contaminate the soil. Zwemer appealed and permission was granted —if he would dig the graves himself. He did so, and after the burial, he erected a marker which said, "Worthy is the Lamb who was slain to receive riches." This is the heroic, give-all-unto-death lifestyle Jesus called for.

One early missionary society sent 70 missionaries to the nation of Cameroon, the vital "hinge" between west Africa and south and south central Africa. (Incidentally, the Muslims are engaged in a concerted effort today to "capture" Cameroon.) Of the 70, 68 of them died on the field. The average life span of these 70 after arrival on the field was 1-1/2 years! Many of them actually shipped their coffins with them to the field, knowing that it was unlikely they would return! This is the heroic, give-all-unto-death lifestyle Jesus called for.

A family of missionaries went to China with a "faith missions organization" to proclaim the Gospel there. They went as public school teachers. They were there when the Tiananmen Square Crisis occurred. When they returned, they came back as typical furloughing missionaries—with a box of slides and a visual presentation of their work. "Have slides, will show" seems to be the universal motto of furloughing missionaries. When their presentation and explanation was concluded, a question-and-answer period was allowed. One church member stood and said, "Weren't you afraid you would die over there?" The calculated answer of the husband was, "No, because we died before we went." This echoes the word "martus," or "martyr-witness."

    Charles Crowe, Methodist pastor, was driving around the Chicago Loop to his church one morning, as he had done many times before. The church building was renowned as having on its top the tallest steeple of any church building in North America, and on top of it was a large cross. On this particular morning, as Pastor Crowe passed in front of the building he saw a considerable group of people gathered on the sidewalk in front of the building, and they all were looking up. He leaned forward in his car and glanced upward to see what they were gazing at. He turned into the parking lot, parked his car in the "Reserved for Pastor" place, then hurried back around to the front of the building and joined those staring upward.

    On top of the cross was a painter with a bucket of paint attached to his suit. He was buckled in place to the cross, and he was slowly painting his way down that metal cross. The cross perceptibly swayed against the sky with every movement he made. The people were watching his delicate and dangerous work. After a few minutes, Charles Crowe left the gathered crowd and started toward his office in the church. Suddenly the Holy Spirit seemed to say, "My child, you have driven that same route hundreds of times and never before was anybody on that sidewalk looking up at the cross. What made the difference today? Simply this: TODAY THE CROSS HAD A MAN ON IT! The world will always stop to see when a true man is really on the cross."

Today the world is saying to the church what Thomas in his doubt and ignorance said about Jesus, "Unless I shall see in His hands the print of the nails, and put my finger into the print of the nails ... I will not believe." They are looking for the unassuming sacrifice of a Christ-centered Christian, or they will not believe.

It would be well for us to pause a moment and remind ourselves of the only alternative to this Christian lifestyle. Jesus said, "Whosoever will save (protect, defend, preserve) his life shall lose it: and whosoever will lose his life for my sake shall find it." The first clause defines the safety-first, me-centered, save-myself-at-all-costs lifestyle. The second clause defines the investing, self-disinterested, other-centered, other-building, Christ-consumed lifestyle — the lifestyle of a Christian.

Two travelers were caught in a heavy blizzard in the far north. As they struggled against the storm, they came upon a man frozen in the snow and thought to be dead. One said, "I have enough to do to keep myself alive; I'm going on." The other said, "I cannot pass a fellow human being while there is the slightest breath left in him." He stooped down and began to warm the frozen man by rubbing him with great vigor. At last the poor man opened his eyes, gradually came back to life and animation, and walked along beside the man who had restored him to life. And what do you think they saw as they struggled along together? They saw the man who took care of his own safety— frozen to death in the snow. The "good Samaritan" had preserved his own life by the vigorous effort required to save the other man. The friction he had produced had aroused the action of his own blood and kept him alive. The rule never fails. "Whosoever (Christian or church) will save his life shall lose it: and whosoever will lose his life for my sake shall find it."

C. S. Lewis captured the adventure of the Christian life when he had this to say in a child's fantasy story entitled <u>The Last Battle</u>: "I'd rather be killed fighting for Narnia than grow old and stupid at home and perhaps go about in a bath chair and then die in the end just the same." Friends, we are going to die one way or another. The Christian commitment is "that Christ may be magnified in my body, whether by life or by death."

To paraphrase Jesus, "Believer, you are my evidence, my credentials, my arguments, my recommendations, my publicity, my advertisements, my commercials." And, the Cross is at the center of any true representation of Christ. George Bernard Shaw asked, "Must a Christ be re-crucified in every generation because the world lacks imagination?" The answer to your question, Mr. Shaw, is "Yes," and we are to be the unselfconscious lambs. "You are my martyr-witnesses." This is the strategy of Gospel advance.

II. SOURCE OF THE GOSPEL WITNESS

Second, we note the *source* of the Gospel witness. The source of the Gospel witness is seen in the threefold occurrence of the word "you." "*Ye* shall receive power after the Holy Ghost has come upon *you*, and *ye* shall be witnesses unto me." The "you" and "upon you" are plural. The commission is given to the whole Body of Christ and is fulfilled by each member of that Body. You, dear Christian, are involved big-time in the strategy of Jesus. You are the source of the Gospel witness.

Note that the word "you" outnumbers the mention of the Holy Spirit by three to one in this verse. This certainly

HIS LAST WORDS, HIS LAST WILL

does not minimize His role; it maximizes your responsibility. Who is the "you"? Not angels, nor supermen, nor special people. The text identifies the "you" in the preceding verses. Verse 2 specifies them as "the apostles whom Jesus had chosen."

Friends, all the apostles were men. This does not minimize the role of women; it maximizes the responsibility of men. The Holy Spirit apparently anticipated the problem of Christian history, that men would tend to easily abdicate their responsibility and turn it over to women. So, today we have mission groups in our churches called "Women's Missionary Society." Thank God for concerned, Godly women; but this is primarily a man's responsibility! You see, if you capture a man, the God-appointed leader in society's basic unit, you stand an excellent chance of capturing everybody in his constituency; but if you capture one of his constituency first (wife, children), you may never capture the leader or any others in his constituency.

Early one cold Good Friday morning some years ago, the People's Church building of downtown St. Paul, Minnesota, caught fire. It was shortly after midnight and the fire department was hindered by the cold in its attempts to put out the fire. By the time they had adjusted, the building had burned to the ground. Early the next morning, church members and townspeople began to gather on the corner where the building was still smoking and the ruins smoldering. The building had been a kind of art museum for religious art, as well as a church building; and, thus, it was a popular spot for tourists.

Right behind the pulpit had stood a replica of "The Appealing Christ," an eight-foot-tall, gleaming white marble statue created by the Danish sculptor, Thorsvalden. As an aside, Stanley Jones, missionary to India, was on a tour of Copenhagen, Denmark, years ago, when the guide brought them to The Church of Our Lady in Copenhagen, where the original of the statue was kept. The statue pictures Jesus standing with face bowed to the ground, hands extended to the world. It is based on Matthew 11:28, "Come unto Me, all ye that labor and are heavy laden, and I will give you rest." As the group was leaving the church, the guide asked, "Did anyone see the Master's face?" Jones answered, "How could we? It is bowed down to the ground." The guide quietly answered, "That's the point, sir. If you would see the Master's face, you must first kneel at His feet!"

When The People's Church building burned, the statue fell with the floor and caved into the basement below. In the late morning of the following day, several men of the church secured permission to go down into the ruins and see if there were any valuables that survived the fire. They found the statue, streaked and charred, but unharmed except for a large chip out of the square base. They carefully cooled it down, and late that afternoon they picked it up and carried it out of the ruins and onto the street corner. They assigned six men to cordon it off so the passersby and observers would not damage it, then they went back down into the ruins to look again. When they returned to the corner a short time later, the crowd was no longer merely staring down into the ruins of the destroyed building. Instead, they were jockeying for position around the circle, all trying to get a look at the great sculpture.

May I spiritualize the illustration to make a crucial point? You see, Jesus had been *in* that church all the time, but He had been "chained to the pulpit," and the people on the street had never seen Him. It was only when the church caught fire (!) and the men of the church (!) picked Him up and carried Him out onto the street corner (!) that the "outsiders" saw Him for the very first time! You, Christian believer, are the source of the Gospel witness.

III. SUBJECT OF THE GOSPEL WITNESS

Then our verse points out the *subject* of the Gospel witness. Jesus said, "Ye shall be witnesses UNTO ME." Our witness is not to focus on a church, or a denomination, or a creed, or a doctrine, or a system. It is to focus on Christ. It is our happy privilege to present Him as He presented Himself in His Word, as Redeeming Savior (Acts 1:3), as Risen Lord (1:3), and as Returning King (1:11). What a fathomless Subject! What a captivating theme.

A painting on the wall of a German art gallery illustrates this part of our assignment. The picture shows Martin Luther, the great German reformer, preaching in the high pulpit of a German church. He has a Bible in one hand, is pointing a protruding finger with the other hand, and his mouth is open as if caught in the act of proclamation. He is preaching the Gospel. You see both preacher and audience. But, if you look closely, you observe a peculiarity. No one in the audience is looking at Martin Luther, the preacher! As you follow their gaze, you make a happy discovery. In the corner of the building, there is the dim but unmistakable form of Jesus, the Son of God—and every eye in the place is on Him. They are listening to Luther, but they are looking at Jesus! This is the desirable outcome of our witness for Christ. We proclaim Him, and He introduces Himself through our witness, so that the attention of the "listener" rests finally on Him.

IV. THE SCOPE OF THE GOSPEL WITNESS

The text also reveals the *scope* of the Gospel witness. Note carefully its closing words, "Ye shall be witnesses unto Me BOTH in Jerusalem, AND in all Judea, AND in Samaria, AND unto the uttermost parts of the earth." So, the near people are our assignment—"Jerusalem"; the neighboring people are our assignment—"Judea"; the neglected people are our assignment—"Samaria" (Samaria represents the people of your worst prejudice); and the next people are our assignment—"unto the uttermost part of the earth." And note carefully that it is not "either/or" with regard to these people, it is "both/and." Jesus Christ seriously expects us to take on the whole wide world! How? By learning and following the disciple-making strategy by which we see the masses through the man, and build the man to impact the masses—the strategy Jesus followed with His Twelve.

The Book of Acts is one of the few books in the Bible that conveniently outlines itself. Chapters one through seven reveal the witness of the early disciples in Jerusalem; chapters 8 through 12, in Judea and Samaria; and chapters 13 through 28, "unto the uttermost parts of the earth."

The real measure of the power and effectiveness of a local body of Christ is: How far does its influence reach? **God seriously expects the local church to take on the whole world!** After all, Jesus did it with twelve men, and He did it before telephones, televisions, telethons, and tel-electronics. He only had *tell-a-person*! Yet, He impacted the civilized world of that day through His small, rag-tag group of men.

Today, we tend to think that we must win our communities at home before we give the attention He commanded to the world. But that order is reversed. "The light that shines farther necessarily shines brightest near home." Every church should be plotting constantly how it can get the Gospel to as many places in the world as quickly as possible; and its goal should be to build world-visionary disciples who will impact the entire world to the ends of the earth 'til the end of time. God said, "Ask of me, and I will give thee the heathen for thine inheritance, and the uttermost parts of the earth for thy possession" (Psalm 2:8). Then why do we *not* have the heathen for our inheritance and the uttermost parts of the earth for our possession? The only possible reason is, we are not asking! Quite apparently, the church-at-large does not have on its heart what God has on His heart. What about your church? What about you?

Note, too, that the verse says, "both in Jerusalem and in all Judea, and in Samaria, and unto the uttermost part of the earth." It is not "either/or," it is "both/and." We are to be witnessing in all these places at once, and we are to have them all on our hearts. How? By building a vision for the whole world, and then by building individuals to implement that vision. The scope of our assignment is the whole world.

V. THE SECRET OF THE GOSPEL WITNESS

Jesus' words reveal, finally, the *secret* of the Gospel witness. "Ye shall receive power," He said, "after that the Holy Ghost is come upon you." Note the title, "Holy Ghost." Most Christians prefer the better translation, "Holy Spirit," and for obvious reasons. I like the term, "Holy Ghost," for one reason. We think of a ghost as the part of the person who remains when the body has departed—and that's Who the Holy Spirit is. The best simple way to think of the Holy Spirit is as Jesus without a body. The Holy Spirit is essentially Christ's Replacement in the earth, doing what He did, and carrying on His work.

A little boy said to his mother, "Mama, how does God make it rain?" Then, as an afterthought, he answered his own question: "Oh, never mind, I already know. He gets the Holy Spirit to do it. After all, He does all the work!" The Holy Spirit is the Executive Person in the Godhead. Today, He does all the work!

Then think of the word "power." The Greek word for power is the word "dunamis," and we all know that we derive our English word "dynamite" from that Greek word. However, that association creates a significant problem for us. We associate the word "dynamite" with something highly explosive; and, thus, we tend to expect a highly explosive experience of God's power as representative of Jesus' promise. The problem is two-fold: one, there is no highly explosive experience in the Gospel; and two, the Greeks didn't have dynamite! Dynamite was invented by Alfred Nobel (of Nobel Prize fame) in 1866! To translate the word "dunamis" by our English word "dynamite" is likely to be misleading, causing Christians to seek a "boom" experience instead of allowing the Holy Spirit to produce the efficiency of character and vocation which marked the life and ministry of Jesus.

The power of Acts 1:8 is the power of character transformation, the power of illumination, the power for communication, the power for steady action. It is power *to* witness, as well as power *in* witnessing. Someone defined character power as "the forceful expression of personality," and this is a good definition of God's power. It is the forceful expression of God's personality. It may take the form of a cataclysmic display, but it is far more often expressed as *persuasion* deep within a person's character, and *conviction* that impacts him and others around him. The works of the Holy Spirit promised by Jesus—conviction (John 16:7-11), illumination (John 16:13-16), communication (John 15:26), and world impact (Acts 1:8)—fall far more into the area of dynamic persuasion than the area of demonstrative "boom" experiences.

Note that this power is "received." "Ye shall *receive* power." It is not achieved; it is received. It is not attained; it is obtained. No great talent is required to receive a thing. Both rich men and paupers may receive something that is offered. Presumably, one simply takes it. God is eager to give you the power of the Holy Spirit—but only on His terms and only for His purposes. He has commanded you to be filled with the Holy Spirit, the Person who is God's power.

I John 5:14 says: "This is the confidence that we have in Him, that if we ask anything according to His will, He heareth us." Since He has commanded us to be filled with the Spirit, we may be confident that this is His will. Thus, we may expectantly ask Him to fill us with His Spirit and simply receive His Fullness. Then we may confidently know that the Person of the Holy Spirit is always "traveling with us" as we live to fulfill the Great Commission of our Lord.

DOES OBEDIENCE PRODUCE SLAVERY OR FREEDOM?

Philippians 2:12-18:

"Wherefore, my beloved, as ye have always obeyed, not as in my presence only, but now much more in my absence, work out your own salvation with fear and trembling. For it is God which worketh in you both to will and to do of his good pleasure. Do all things without murmurings and disputings: That ye may be blameless and harmless, the sons of God, without rebuke, in the midst of a crooked and perverse nation, among whom ye shine as lights in the world; Holding forth the word of life; that I may rejoice in the day of Christ, that I have not run in vain, neither laboured in vain. Yea, and if I be offered upon the sacrifice and service of your faith, I joy, and rejoice with you all. For the same cause also do ye joy, and rejoice with me."

The second chapter of Philippians has two themes — a large, major theme and a small, "minor" theme. The major theme of the chapter is *humility*. Indeed, this is without question the greatest chapter in the Bible on the subject of humility. The master-key of this chapter, and the master-key of Christianity, is humility. The "minor" theme of the chapter is *obedience.* Our text is an example of the importance of obedience.

Modern man, captured by secular humanism, has raised his voice in loud protest against the virtues of humility and obedience. He cries, "Humility is an unnecessary cowering and groveling before a supposed God — because of a superstitious fear of the unknown. And obedience is nothing short of slavery." He taunts the Christian with the words, "Where is this 'freedom in Christ' we hear so much about, if we must *obey* Him?"

The brilliant poet Shelley spoke for such men in one of his poems:

> "Power, like a desolating pestilence,
> Pollutes whatever it touches; and *obedience,*
> The bane of all genius, virtue, freedom, truth,
> *Makes slaves of men*, and of the human frame
> A mechanized automaton."

The italics in Shelley's poem are mine. "Obedience makes slaves of men," said Shelley, and his complaint may be valid in some cases. As examples: (1) There is extreme peril in full obedience to any mere mortal man. Such unquestioning obedience may easily become slavery. (2) There is grave peril also in full obedience to any church or religious system (indeed, to *any* system of any kind). I was astounded to read Ignatius Loyola's statement in the Constitution of the Catholic Jesuit order: "We must, if anything appears to our eyes, white, which the Church declares to be black, also declare it to be black." This is dangerous, debilitating, and likely damning, obedience to a church and a religious system. This makes religious slaves of men, and the most binding, demanding, and destructive kind of slavery is religious slavery.

DOES OBEDIENCE PRODUCE SLAVERY OR FREEDOM?

The Christian's obedience is to be only to the Lord! And yet, we must make the practical acknowledgment that we will likely render obedience to Him only if we first hear His truth through His church. When Christ's minister speaks to us the Word of the Lord, and we obey it, we are obeying Christ. So the Christian's powers of discrimination and discernment must be developed (Hebrews 5:14) so he can detect the difference between the Word of God and the mere words of men. Again, disciple-making is a paramount necessity for this development. Jesus said, "If any man will *do* His will, he shall *know* of the doctrine, whether it comes from God or some other source." If any Christian sincerely wants to hear the Word of God that he may earnestly obey it, he will hear it — with understanding.

No Christian dares to obey any man purely passively and unthinkingly, lest Shelley's charge becomes true and that Christian becomes "a mechanized automaton." But the obedience to Jesus Christ rendered by a Spirit-filled Christian is not liable to this error. We can trust Jesus Christ as we can trust no mere mortal man. For one thing, His guidance is perfect, and for another, He only seeks our highest good.

Having said all of that, it must also be stated that it is a badge of honor and freedom in the New Testament for a Christian to call himself "a bondslave of Jesus Christ." The early Christians applied this designation eagerly to themselves. The word is the opposite of "free" in I Corinthians 7:21. Now the paradox: The Christian is decidedly, decisively, deliberately, definitely not free. But conversely, the Christian is definitely and decisively free! No true and free Christian ever serves Christ against his own will. You will recall that a slave happy in his master's service could voluntarily be bound to that master for life (see Exodus 21:1-6). The Christian has freely yielded himself to the possession and control of Jesus as his Savior and Master. And when Paul (and other writers in the New Testament) uses this word for himself, it does not set him apart from the rest of the believers, but identifies him as one of them. All of them happily thought of themselves as slaves of Jesus Christ.

The truth is that obedience to Christ is the fulfillment of man. This is the revelation of Jesus and the Bible, and this was Paul's Gospel — and anyone who proves it in practice finds it to be wonderfully true. Paul gloried in being a slave of Jesus Christ because it gave him a freedom undreamed of before: the freedom to fulfill his own true self.

Take a violin in your hand. That violin is a poor instrument when it is used as a sledge-hammer or a broom, because he who thus uses it obviously does not know what it is for and how to use it. Design and intention indicate purpose. In the hands of a master violinist, the violin "comes into its own," by its own "obedience" to its owner's loving and skillful employment. Man, too, is a poor instrument when owned and used by another man, or by a tyrannical system, or by himself (can you imagine a violin trying to play itself?). He "comes into his own" when He who designed him with intent and purpose and value takes him in His own hand. Man is "taken in hand" by the Master the day he is saved, and he plays out his role for the rest of his days in the manner prescribed in our text.

Our text also unwittingly confronts us with the age-old argument between those who hold two quite opposite views of salvation. One view could be called the haughty man's view of salvation (the vanity of salvation by works), and the other could be called the humble man's view of salvation (the victory of salvation by God's grace through faith in Jesus Christ). Some have tried to argue that this text supports the Pelagian

DOES OBEDIENCE PRODUCE SLAVERY OR FREEDOM?

view of salvation by self-effort, but a little careful examination of the text will show clearly that this is not the case.

Some people say, "I never accept anything that I haven't earned and deserved." This is sheer, utter, perfect (!) nonsense! Such a person certainly didn't earn the very gift of life itself. Furthermore, he does nothing to earn and deserve the air he breathes. And he is incapable of survival outside of the provision of God and the support of society. And he didn't cause, invent, earn or deserve any of these things! He is "a beggar at Heaven's gate" with regard to all worthwhile things, and "beggars cannot be choosers." Beggars have never been renowned for their earning power!

Note that the text does not say, "Work *for* your own salvation," but rather, "work *out* your own salvation."

Two other phrases deserve our attention before we actually explore the matter of Christian obedience. Paul reminds the Philippian believers that they had obeyed him while he was with them, and now he counsels them to obey (note that there is no object; he does not tell them whom or what to obey) "now much more in my absence." They had rendered "eye-service" when Paul was there with them, but he encourages them to obey all the more since he has gone away from them. So Christians are to live "dependently *in*dependent lives." They are to become so dependent on the Lord that, if necessary, they can live independently of Christian leaders. And this raises the whole issue of "following the leader."

Many Christians were brought to Christ and have grown in Him under the leadership of a charismatic and dynamic Christian leader. In large measure, Paul was this type of leader. This type of leadership has both advantages and disadvantages, both delights and dangers. All Christians, both leaders and led, must be alert to the dangers and determine to live balanced lives here as in all matters of the Christian life.

Some of the dangers of charismatic, dynamic leadership in the community of believers are:

(1) The temptation of clerical tyranny (absolute and unquestioned control by pastoral leaders) or clerical autocracy (this is the leader's temptation; here the pastoral leadership assumes self-rule over the Body), or the temptation of clerical worship (this is the temptation which confronts those who are led by such a leader). Both temptations are subtle and potentially deadly, and must be answered by the humble obedience (of both leader and led) featured in our text.

(2) The temptation of the leader to be the Lord's proxy or substitute. To have a pastor whom one can simply obey without argument solves a lot of problems for simple souls. Such a leader usually presents only a sterling side of his character. He never manages to confess a real sin, and thus he is always admired as if he were a perfect leader. This stance misleads both the leader and the people who are led.

(3) The temptation of unquestioning submission among the followers. This kind of submission reached its extreme in Jonestown, the cult led by Jim Jones, and the Branch Davidian compound led by David Koresh in Waco, Texas. But these are only extreme examples of those who have allowed themselves to be Satan-duped into blind following of such leaders. Most unquestioning submission to dynamic leaders is much less drastic and detectable than in those cases, but it is still very dangerous.

Paul's counsel in verse 12 of our text will provide a sure guide for us with regard to "following the leader." We will see in this study what Paul's real object was. It was to make them obedient to the Lord rather than to himself. They had been leaning on him at Philippi, *perhaps (probably?) too much,* when he was with them. The right business of the Christian pastor is to lead his people into a complete dependence upon the Lord. Ideally, he should do this to such a degree that he works his way out of a job. I say "ideally," because sheep will never be fully independent of their shepherds! The right way of securing this is to be the kind of man Paul was — one who himself practiced total self-commitment and obedience to Christ. He often gave such counsel as this: "Follow me — but only as I follow Christ." Nevertheless, the temptations mentioned above are always subtly present to leaders and followers.

One further item will introduce the actual study of the text. The clear and consistent Biblical view of salvation is that it operates in three grammatical tenses — the past tense, the present tense, and the future tense. Past-tense salvation ("I *have been saved*") is salvation *in possession* — once I have it, I have it forever. Present-tense salvation (*"I am being saved"*) is salvation *in process*. While past-tense salvation is perfect and invariable (there are no degrees of regeneration and justification), present-tense salvation has much fluctuation and variation in it. Future-tense salvation (*"I will yet be saved"*) is salvation *in prospect* — there is coming a day when I will be perfectly saved in a full, final, forever way. This will occur in the day of completed redemption that is referred to many times in the New Testament. The theological name of past-tense salvation is *justification*; the theological name of present-tense salvation is *sanctification*; and the theological name of future-tense salvation is *glorification*. *Justification* of the sinner (past-tense salvation) is gained in a *crisis* moment when the sinner is broken over his sins, repents of them, and trusts and receives Christ as his personal Lord and Savior. Justification is point action (it occurs at one moment of time). *Sanctification*, on the other hand, is gained through a continuing process. It is linear (ongoing) action, and the process must continue through every "now," every present moment of the believer's life. *Glorification* is also point action, beginning at a moment of time. It begins with the crisis of the believer's death, and its results continue in the Presence of God perfectly and forever.

It is important to remember as we study our text that this passage concerns *only* our *present- tense salvation*. It concerns only our sanctification. No part of this text concerns our salvation from the eternal penalty or eternal punishment of our sins (past-tense salvation). It concerns our responsibility for our own sanctification — while endowed by the Presence and power of God. Remembered that we have chosen to explore the matter of obedience from this text, we will now turn to the study itself.

I. THE DEMAND FOR OBEDIENCE

First, we note the *demand for obedience* that is made in the text. Verse twelve says, "Wherefore, my beloved, as ye have always *obeyed*, not as in my presence only, but now much more in my absence, . . ." The Greek word translated "obeyed" is based on a root word which means "to obey as a result of listening." We have already examined some matters about Christian leaders, and we will later be told in this text the importance of "the word of life." These two — Christian leaders and the Word of life — are to function together. The Christian leader's primary ministry is to "hold forth the Word of life." If God has called him to do this (pity him and his followers if He has not!), He has also called people to hear what he says. And they are to hear with a certain predisposition. They are to "hear underneath the truth" (the exact meaning of the Greek word translated "obedience"), not merely listening, and not merely appraising, but listening in full submission to Jesus as Lord as He reveals His truth. This is the word for "obedience" in the New Testament. And this is the obedience that is commanded in our text.

We see here the *responsibility* for this obedience. It is stated in these crucial words, "Work out your own salvation." This is the commanded responsibility of every Christian. There are no exemptions, exceptions, or exclusions — every Christian. Every Christian is responsible to work out his own salvation. But what does it mean to "work out your own salvation"?

The words presuppose the possession of salvation (that past-tense salvation has already occurred). The verb, "work out," is a present middle imperative verb. The present tense means that this is a present responsibility — each believer is to be doing this at every moment. The middle voice means that, as the believer fulfills his responsibility, the results (the *benefits*) come back to him (!). And the imperative mood means that this a command of God, a command that has equal force to any one of the Ten Commandments, or of any other command of God.

The term translated "work out" is based on the Greek word that gives us our English word "energy." This tells us that the command here insists on highly energetic action on the part of the Christian. Do we see such action generally among Christians today? No? Then we can only conclude that most dull, sluggish, inactive Christians are *radically disobedient*.

Now, let's explore the meaning of the words, "Work out your own salvation." I am from the state of Arkansas. Arkansas has a small town in it that bears the name, "Bauxite." That's right, Bauxite, Arkansas. You can guess its background. Years ago, it was discovered that the terrain there was rich in bauxite ore. By whatever process or crisis, God had previously worked that bauxite into the earth there. When man discovered it, he moved in and began a process of development to exploit the riches God had earlier worked into the earth. Man began to "work out" what God had already "worked in." We will look further at God's in-working later, but at the moment, we are looking at our responsibility to work out something God has already worked into us. British commentator Guy King said it beautifully: "I am to *mine* what is *already mine*." Salvation comes only by a crisis miracle of God's in-working, but once we have it, we are mutually responsible with Him to work out that which He has worked in. So present-tense salvation (sanctification) is a "co-op" between God and His child.

This can be seen Biblically in the great salvation/sanctification text of Ephesians 2:8-10. "By grace are ye saved through faith." Salvation is all of grace, but it implicates man's response of faith. "And that not of yourselves." Nothing that arises out of you can contribute to your salvation. "It is the gift of God." It has been fully provided by God Himself, free of your effort and merit. "Not of works." Your performance cannot contribute to your salvation. "Lest any man should boast." If one sinner could contribute one one-hundredth of one percent of the necessary work to gain personal salvation, heaven would never hear the last of it! He would boast all over heaven forever! But your salvation is so arranged as to totally exclude human boasting.

Paul summarizes verses eight and nine at the beginning of verse ten in the words, "For ye are God's workmanship." Then he adds the Christian's responsibility when he states, "We are God's workmanship, created in Christ Jesus unto good works, which He has previously ordained that we should walk in them."

Remember the past, present, and future tenses of our salvation. God *has* worked, God *will* work, and God *is* working *now* — and it is on the basis of His present work in us that we are to "work out our own salvation." Here is a garden. God has already worked in all the vital elements of earth and sun and rain, but a gardener must now "work it out" by breaking up the soil and planting and cultivating the flowers. There was a time when every garden was a mere opportunity or a mere possibility. The fertility of the field and the availability of the elements were gifts of God, but those gifts were improved, or "worked out," by a gardener's labor.

Here is an illustration much closer to my own heart. A noble book is a gift. It is the distilling of much wisdom gained from varying experiences of life. But before we can make it ours we must expend time, mental intensity, and persistent effort in order to "work it out." Indeed, we must "sell" all other books, for, as John Ruskin said, "If I read this book I cannot read that book." Christian, apply these illustrations to our text and you will see Paul's meaning.

There are several actions prescribed in our text which help to explain what it means to work out our salvation. The verbs are "obey" (verse 12), "shine" (verse 15), "holding forth" (verse 15), "run" (verse 16) and "labor" (verse 16). This is not intended to be an exhaustive list for "working out your own salvation" but we may take the liberty to regard it as a suggestive list. So the Christian vocation of "working out our own salvation" could involve such practical activities as obeying Christ, shining the Gospel light into a dark world, holding forth the Word of life, running the Christian race, and laboring in Christ's service. Most of these terms call for urgent, consistent, energetic action. If there is no such urgent involvement in your life, and you know that you are a Christian, you are radically disobedient. The responsibilities are to "work it out," verse 12 (this refers to your salvation); "shine it out," verse 15 (this refers to your influence), and "hold it out," verse 16 (this refers to your witness). "Work it out" is primarily a matter of *character*; "shine it out" involves both character *and conduct*, and "hold it out" (the Word of truth) involves character, conduct *and communication*.

To summarize: Our salvation comes solely from God; it is God's gift to us and God's accomplishment in us. However, our working it out is our acceptance of the gift and our relentless and unremitting effort to co-operate with God's grace by giving over our wills and our actions to God as He works in us. And the word that is used here, *katergazesthe* (try to pronounce that!), means to "work on to the very finish." So this is the one life's vocation that should command the attention and effort of every Christian all day long every day. This is the believer's *responsibility*.

Then note the *requirement* that is specified for the fulfillment of this responsibility. "Work out your own salvation *in fear and trembling*." At first glance, it would seem that these words enforce the secular humanist's charge of "slavery" and "slavish fear" when he evaluates the Christian duty of obedience. But first impressions are often wrong, and this is no exception. One translation renders this phrase, "with reverence and healthy respect." J. B. Philips translates it, "with a proper sense of awe and responsibility." Alan Richardson translates it, "seriously and reverently." Marvin Vincent says, "Not with slavish terror, but wholesome, serious caution." All of these are reasonable translations of the basic words.

Why does Paul put this qualifying clause with the responsibility to work out our salvation? He is fully aware of the tendency of the Christian to become casual, glib, and irreverent about the great salvation God has produced in him. The words, "How shall we escape, if we neglect so great salvation?" were not written to lost people, but to Christians! In fact, we are commanded in our text to "work out our own salvation" precisely because it is so easy to have it and *neglect it*. Salvation may be free, but it is not cheap! A wise Christian will not permit himself to slide into careless and disobedient living, serving and obeying his own preferences, tastes and desires more than he serves and obeys Christ. History has shown again and again that it is disastrous to be part of a Christian experience that lacks solemnity in the Presence of God and commitment in the service of Christ.

The "fear and trembling" of verse twelve are not anxiety and doubt about God, but *about our own selves*. When we realize how easily we can block and frustrate God's work in us by stubbornly resisting the working of His grace we must fear and tremble for the possible consequences. Our "fear and trembling" concern our awesome responsibility.

Basil, the great bishop of Cappadocia in the fourth century, wrote candidly to a friend, "I hesitate to write what I myself do in this solitude, night and day, seeing that, although I have left the distractions of the city, which are to me the occasion of innumerable evils, *I have not yet succeeded in forsaking myself.*" The grim fight was still on for him (as for you and me), the titanic struggle to transfer his trust from self to God. Thus, the "fear and trembling" of our text — the acknowledgment of a wholesome distrust of self which will free us to trust God.

Then note the *reasons* for this obedience. Look at the word "wherefore" at the beginning of verse twelve. Actually, there are two "wherefores" in the context, one in verse nine and the one in verse twelve. The first one is found in the greatest passage on the Person of Christ in the entire Bible (verses 5-11). Humble obedience was infinitely rewarding in our Great Example, Jesus (study the "wherefore" of verse nine), and the "wherefore" of verse twelve indicates that humble obedience to Him in our lives today would have similar results. Jesus, the Son of God, was obedient while living in a world filled only with disobedient people. As a result, heaven will be full of disobedient sinners (you and I included) who became convicted and broken enough to bow at His feet, confess Him as Lord, and receive His salvation.

The introductory word "wherefore" in verse twelve dares to link our little lives with the glorious life of our exalted Lord. Paul fixes his wondering and worshiping gaze upon the humble obedience of the Lord Jesus — "He humbled Himself, and became unto death, even the death of the cross" (verse eight), and then he asks us to act in a similar way. So the first reason for *our* humble obedience is *His* humble obedience. His conduct becomes our command; His model becomes our mandate; His example becomes our exhortation.

The second reason for our obedience is found in a phrase in verse thirteen: "His good pleasure." This phrase may refer to: (1) The will of God, or (2) The pleasure, satisfaction and gratification of God. In either case, the motive of our obedience is to please and glorify Him. God Himself is pleased and gratified when we obey Him and when His purposes are accomplished (remember, His purposes are always perfect and always good). We are forever asking God to make *us* happy; would it not be wise if we occasionally stopped to ask *Him* how *we* can make *Him* happy?

One writer said, "Divine sovereignty and human responsibility meet at the crossroads of some mighty decisions. And remember, the sign marked 'His good pleasure' is the only one worth following."

The final reason for our obedience is mentioned in verse sixteen: "That I may rejoice in the day of Christ, that I have not run in vain, neither labored in vain." A Day of Evaluation is coming for every Christian, and the terms of the test are stated throughout the New Testament. The Bible reveals that each Christian will either "receive a reward" or "suffer loss," and that he will live with the result forever. Paul seems to live with his eye fixed on "that day." Even in this passage, his appeal to the Christians at Philippi is motivated by "that day." He tells them that he has made an investment (ponder that word carefully; investment is made to get a dividend, to draw interest) in them which is now at stake. Having preached to them, taught them, and discipled them, he is looking for returns "in the day of Christ" -- the day when we will receive suitable rewards for service rendered (see II Cor. 5:10). Paul's expectation of reward included not merely those to whom he has personally ministered the word of life and personally discipled in the Christian life, but also includes the number of people who will be won in turn through *their* soul-winning and disciple-making multiplication. So he urges them to "work out their own salvation," to "hold forth the Word of life," and to "shine as lights in a dark world." As he writes, he is gazing ahead to the "day of Christ," and he asks them to follow his gaze.

Here, then, is a lengthy look at the demand for obedience in these verses. We have looked at the Christian's responsibility of obedience, the requirement of obedience, and the reasons for obedience. Now we will go a step further.

II. THE DYNAMIC OF OBEDIENCE

Second, we will look at the *dynamic of obedience* that is revealed in the text. After the command to "work out your own salvation," the text then says, "For it is God which worketh in you both to will and to do of His good pleasure." So the text balances *our outworking* with *God's in-working*. God's *demand* to "work out your own salvation," is attended by God's *dynamic*, "for it is God who is working within you."

Note the *Person* Who provides this dynamic. "It is God Who works in you." You see, dear Christian, before your conversion, God worked *on* you by His Holy Spirit. Now, since you are saved, He works *in* you — by His Holy Spirit. When a sinner is saved, Jesus Christ comes into that sinner in the Presence and power of the Holy Spirit. "If any man have not the Spirit of Christ, He does not belong to him." If He is not in us, we are not Christians at all. But He is in every born-again person, and His Presence is the dynamic for this obedience and the accomplishment which comes through it. His "working in us" is the dynamic for our "working out of our salvation."

The verb of the phrase, "It is God who works in you," is a present tense, active voice verb. The present tense means that God is at work in you at this very second. Think of it! The Eternal God has stooped to work within the narrow limits of your inner life. Your heart may be as filthy as a stable, as dark as a cellar, as stifling as an over-crowded room. But He, Whom the heavens cannot contain, and in Whose sight they are not clean, is steadily at work in the unpromising, uncongenial confines of your heart. Should we not be very careful to make Him welcome, and to remove every hindrance to His work? On one occasion in the ministry of Jesus, He went into the Temple, looked around, and immediately began to overthrow all the hindrances to His free work in His House. What might He do in you, in me, today?

"God works in you." The word translated "works" is the root word from which we get our word, "energy," or "energize." It means that an energetic God lives inside of every Christian, and He is going to work every moment to fulfill His purposes there. Let this make a deep impression on your mind, Christian. The Christian life involves Divine dynamic, Divine energy, Divine work, Divine accomplishment. It is not (I repeat, not) a passive, indolent life. It was said of Jesus that "virtue went out of Him," and the same is true of Christ in you — and frankly, it will also be true of you in Him.

DOES OBEDIENCE PRODUCE SLAVERY OR FREEDOM?

A close examination of the text will reveal that the word "energy" is used three times in two verses — once in verse twelve ("work out"), and twice in verse thirteen ("God is the One energizing in you to will and to energize according to His good pleasure"). The Holy Spirit made the entire passage to pulsate with energy, and that energy is the dynamic by which a Christian is to "work out his own salvation." Because there is an Energetic Worker within, there is the possibility of an energetic outworking as well. This energy is first experienced, then it is expressed. The stream flows out only because the spring rises up. Jesus implanted His life in us the day He entered our lives. And now He imparts His Presence and power to us moment by moment. He entered us then; He empowers us now. He saved us then; He sanctifies us now.

Note the *provinces* of this dynamic. Paul is even more specific about the work that Christ does in us each day. "God (emphatic) it is Who works in us, both to *will* and to *do* His good pleasure." So He works on our *desires* and He works on our *deeds*. He seeks to sanctify our desiring and our doing. And what else *is* there in the Christian life? So God does not do His work in us mechanically or by iron force. He works by inner promptings, inner movings, inner checkings, inner suggestions, inner inspirations, inner whispers that are delicate and sensitive. No wonder we are counseled to "Grieve not the Holy Spirit of God" (Ephesians 4:30). If we treat these inner workings with neglect or rebellion, they subside. Remember, this present-tense salvation involves a cooperation between us and the Holy Spirit.

God works in us "to will." God does not treat His children like lifeless machines. He deals with us as moral agents who can say Yes and No. He will not compel us to be saints, or force us to be holy (though He does have strong means of persuasion!). There are certain signs that God is willing His good pleasure within you -- if you have a holy discontent with yourself; if you have a hunger for a better Christian life; if you have a determination to live for "God's good pleasure." And there is a necessary conclusion that must be drawn from this truth. It means that every holy impulse that has ever been expressed within His child comes from Him, and from Him alone.

> *"Every virtue I possess, And every victory won,*
> *Every thought of holiness, Are His and His alone."*

But God not only inspires the will, God also energizes the work. "God works in you both to will and to do His good pleasure." He not only puts the desire into our hearts, He also provides the drive to carry out His will. He inspires the earliest impulse and He empowers and directs the final accomplishment. God leads us to purpose His will, and then He lends us the power to perform it.

Can you imagine what would happen if all Christians became aware of this truth and began to implement it in their daily lives? But we must sadly admit that this is hardly true. We are more like the truth revealed in a Dennis the Menace cartoon. Dennis is standing in his front yard with his little female "friend," Margaret. A lawn mower is standing idle in a yard that is half-cut. Dennis says indignantly to Margaret: "It is *so* a power mower — and here comes the power!" And he points to his father, Mr. Mitchell, who is wiping his sweating face with a towel as he comes around the corner of the house. Honesty would force many defeated Christians to say, "The Christian life may be a power-life, but I have to supply the power!" This text takes us worlds away from such a sad confession.

A father came home from work one evening to find his small son sprawled in the grass of the front yard. "Are you ready to play, son?" the father asked. The boy feebly replied, "Naw, Dad, I'm too tired." "Son, what did you do that made you so tired?" "I've been galloping on my 'horse' all over the neighborhood," the boy answering, referring to the stick-horse he sometimes played with. "Son, I've ridden a horse many times, but it has never made me that tired," the father teased. "Yeah, but Dad, your horse carries you, but when I ride, I've got to do my own galloping." Every Christian has the Lord of the universe — and all of His resources — within him, and yet most Christians are still "doing their own galloping." Who is doing the "galloping" in your life, you or God?

Let me share with you at this point a practical paragraph from the pen of the great British preacher, F. B. Meyer: "God may be working in you to confess to that fellow Christian that you were unkind in your speech or act. Work it out. He may be working in you to give up that line of business about which you have been doubtful lately. Work it out — and give it up. He may be working in you to be sweeter in your home, and gentler in your speech. Work it out — and begin. He may be working in you to alter your relations with some with whom you have dealings that are not as they should be. Work it out — and alter them. This very day let God begin to speak, and work and will; and then work out what He works in. God will not work apart from you, but He wants to work in and through you. Let Him. Yield to Him, and let this be the day when you shall begin to live in the power of the mighty Indwelling One." Amen — and may God help us!

Note one final thing about the dynamic of the Christian life. We can also see in these verses the ultimate *purpose* of this dynamic. Read verses twelve through eighteen again, and note that there is an order, a progression, to these verses. We have not mentioned much about verses fourteen through seventeen, but this in no way diminishes their importance. Here is the order:

God works in you.

You co-operate with Him, "working out His in-worked salvation."

Christian character is developed.

This Christian character enables you to minister to **others** (verses 15, 16a).

God's focus is on *others*, and the focus of the God-shaped Christian will also be on *others*. So we can see again the clear purpose for our Christian development. Our character is to be developed to serve others, and wonderful things develop in our character while we live to serve others. Thus, the best and happiest Christians are those who have forgotten themselves by burying their lives in the spiritual welfare of others. You see, all strength and effort that are consecrated to the service of others react upon our own character with eternal benefits.

Here, then, is the dynamic of the Christian life. We have seen the Person who provides this dynamic, the provinces in which it operates in our lives, and the ultimate purpose of it. Now, let's quickly examine one final happy thing in the text.

III. THE DELIGHT OF OBEDIENCE

Finally, we will look at the delight of obedience as it is vividly stated in our text. Let me remind you that the main theme of the book of Philippians is "joy." In fact, Greek scholar A. T. Robertson labeled this book, <u>Paul's Joy in Christ</u>. Guy King quaintly said that it shows us "the joy way." In verse 16, Paul used the word "rejoice." But look especially at the climax of our passage. "But even if I am being poured out as a drink offering upon the sacrifice and service of your faith, I rejoice and share my joy with you all. And you too, I urge you, rejoice in the same way and share your joy with me."

We must realize that joy is a *command* of God, and we must continually obey the command. In verse seventeen, "Rejoice," and the verb is a present imperative verb. So the Christian is commanded to rejoice — now.

We must realize, too, that to rejoice is a *choice*. Some years ago, two Christian psychologists wrote a book entitled, Happiness is a Choice. Earlier, Paul had commanded the Philippians to "do all things without murmurings and disputings" (verse 14). So Christians may choose to grumble, or they may choose not to grumble. They may choose to be argumentative, or they may choose to not be argumentative. Here, they are commanded to make the choice to rejoice. What a happy place the fellowship of believers would be if all Christians would make this choice — and say so!

We must realize, too, that rejoicing is contagious. The pattern of verses seventeen and eighteen never fails. "I rejoice, and share my joy with you all. And I urge you, too, to rejoice in the same way, and share your joy with me." If one person got such a good case of the contagion of joy that he couldn't hide it, many others would come down (rise up!) with it, too!

For Paul, it was joy all the way home, whatever the circumstance! The Philippian Christians are serving Christ (Paul speaks of "the sacrifice and service of their faith"), and Paul is serving Christ (he speaks of his life being freely "poured out like a drink-offering"). Note this principle: the joy is mutual when the service is mutual. The more Christians that are in the network of service, the more will be in the network of joy.

Though we didn't stop at every point along the way, our journey through this great passage is complete. We have been reminded of our salvation, of our responsibility, of our relationship to Christian leaders and their relationship to us, and of the importance of obedience in the Christian life. We have seen the demand for Christian obedience — the responsibility for it, the requirement of it, and the reasons for it. We have seen the dynamic that is necessary for us to be obedient — the Person Who gives it, the provinces in which it is exercised in our lives, and the purpose of it. And finally, we have seen the delight of Christian obedience — we have viewed that delight as a command, a choice, and a contagion. Let's close with a tiny reminder from the annals of history, an adage that stands forever: "To obey is better than sacrifice." Then let's listen to God's commands — and rise up to obey them.

THE DANGER OF LOSING SIGHT OF JESUS

Luke 2:40-52:

"And the child grew, and waxed strong in spirit, filled with wisdom; and the grace of God was upon him. Now his parents went to Jerusalem every year at the feast of the Passover. And when he was twelve years old, they went up to Jerusalem after the custom of the feast. And when they had fulfilled the days, as they returned, the child Jesus tarried behind in Jerusalem; and Joseph and his mother knew not of it. But they, supposing him to have been in the company, went a day's journey; and they sought him among their kinsfolk and acquaintance. And when they found him not, they turned back again to Jerusalem, seeking him. And it came to pass, that after three days they found him in the temple, sitting in the midst of the doctors, both hearing them, and asking them questions. And all that heard him were astonished at his understanding and answers. And when they saw him, they were amazed: and his mother said unto him, Son, why hast thou thus dealt with us? Behold, thy father and I have sought thee sorrowing. And he said unto them, How is it that ye sought me? Wist ye not that I must be about my Father's business? And they understood not the saying which he spake unto them. And he went down with them, and came to Nazareth, and was subject unto them: but his mother kept all these sayings in her heart. And Jesus increased in wisdom and stature and in favor with God and man."

Note some important features from the text. In verse 40, the term "child" means "little child," but in verse 43, a different word is used which means "the boy." In verse 40, the word "grew" is in the passive voice, which means that no force of will was necessary on Jesus' part; the growth was inevitable. The word apparently refers to physical growth. The statement that he "waxed strong in spirit, filled with wisdom," indicates that His inner growth kept pace with His physical growth.

There is a volume of meaning in verse 41. Note that "His parents (plural) went to Jerusalem every year at the feast of the Passover." The plural word "parents" unfolds the entire story to us. You see, only the male head of the family was mandated by the Law to attend the required Jewish feasts in Jerusalem each year. The attendance of the wife and mother was optional. What a testimonial to the spiritual character and hunger of Mary that she went every year!

"When Jesus was twelve years old, they went up to Jerusalem after the custom of the feast" (vs. 42). A very important time had come for the young boy, the time of His "Bar Mitzvah," or His becoming "a son of the Law." This marked His official induction into manhood and into the full privileges of the Jewish Law. This also provides the probable answer to the charge of parental delinquency that is sometimes made against Mary and Joseph because of this story. Normally the travel caravans from areas of the country divided into male and female groups. The women usually traveled a short distance ahead of the men, and the men "cleaned up camp" before departing. Up to this time, Jesus had always traveled with the women when the Galilee caravan had gone to Jerusalem for the Passover Feast. So Joseph undoubtedly thought Jesus was doing what He usually did. But since He had reached His Bar Mitzvah, the time of His majority as a Jewish male, Mary naturally would assume that He has begun

THE DANGER OF LOSING SIGHT OF JESUS

traveling with the men. So neither Mary nor Joseph was delinquent, just careless.

Verse 43 says, "When they had fulfilled the days." Can you imagine what the days of the Passover meant to Jesus? They were days of absolutely holy delight, in which His pure heart would swell with growing awareness of some connection between Him and all the features and functions of the Passover.

Please read every phrase of this text with great care. The story closes with this monumental verse, "And Jesus increased in wisdom and stature, and in favor with God and man." The word "increased" is an engineering term which literally means "to chop forward," the word for a corps of engineers clearing a pathway. Previously (vs. 40), His growth was automatic, but now, strenuous energy and activity are required on His part. And note that when His will is involved in the growth process, "wisdom" (His inner growth) moves ahead of "stature" (His physical growth). He also "increased . . . in favor with God (His spiritual growth) and man" (the development of His personality, His social growth). So here is the picture of a perfectly balanced and symmetrical human life. He lived the only absolutely normal human life ever lived. There was perfect balance between the physical, the mental, the spiritual, the social, and the domestic. At each stage of His life, He was perfect for that stage. As a child, His perfection was that of innocence; as an adult, it was that of holiness.

Now, let's use this familiar story in an unfamiliar way. Let's think of what it reveals about "The Danger of Losing Sight of Jesus." Years ago, I wrote this sentence in the margin of my Bible - "Every sin a Christian commits results from a loss of perspective." Indeed, a Christian never sins except when he misplaces his attention from its Proper Object. The saint's secret is in the phrase, "Looking away from all else and unto

Jesus" (Hebrews 12:2). But what happens (what doesn't happen!) when he loses sight of Jesus?

THE REASONS FOR LOSING SIGHT OF JESUS

First, we will consider *the reasons for losing sight of Jesus* that are suggested in the story.

The first reason suggested in the story is *sheer carelessness*. Many have wondered how in the world Mary and Joseph could have made the mistake they made in leaving Jesus in Jerusalem, thinking He was with them on the return journey. However, careful thought will reveal that there was absolutely no delinquency on their part. Remember that this was the season of Jesus' "Bar Mitzvah." When families and communities traveled to the feasts, the women traveled in one group and the men in another, with the women going ahead. Because Jesus had always previously traveled with the women as a small child, Joseph assumed He was in His usual place. But, because it was the official time of His entrance into manhood, Mary assumed that He was with the men. So there was no delinquency on the part of His parents, only carelessness. But carelessness had the same effect delinquency would have had! Note verse 44, "But they, supposing Him to have been in the company." "Supposing" is extremely dangerous in the Christian life. Mary and Joseph did not deliberately plan to displace Jesus; they just drifted into the loss!

On December 31, 1989, the daily newspaper of Memphis, Tennessee, my home city, contained this article, datelined in Nashville, Tennessee:

Five-year-old Tyler Payne was on his way home to Texas with his family after a Christmas visit with grandparents in Knoxville when he took advantage of a service station stop in Nashville to use the restroom. The restroom door stuck.

THE DANGER OF LOSING SIGHT OF JESUS

The family car pulled out. Young Tyler was left behind. Glenn Payne and his wife, Kris, noticed a small absence among the five boys and one girl snoozing in the back of their station wagon about two hours later in Jackson, Tennessee. Back in Nashville, Tyler had been rescued by a woman who had heard him screaming for his mommy. "This is embarrassing, but I'm glad he's safe," said Payne, the boy's dad, an electrical engineer. Payne said the family usually does a head count before embarking, but he had turned the driving over to Mrs. Payne. Nobody counted. Sobs turned to smiles when Tyler saw his family. *Tyler Payne says he'll never go to the bathroom again.*

Undoubtedly, this understandable oversight is quite similar to that of Mary and Joseph in our Gospel story.

In John Bunyan's classic Christian allegory entitled Pilgrim's Progress, when Christian lost his great burden of sin in God's forgiveness at the Cross, he was immediately met by "three Shining Ones" (representing God the Father, the Son, and the Holy Spirit). Each confers upon him a great spiritual benefit. The third one (the Holy Spirit) "set a Mark on his forehead" (representing the sealing of the Spirit - Ephesians 1:13, 4:30), "and gave him a Roll . . . which he bid him look on as he ran, and that he should give it in at the Celestial Gate." This "roll," or scroll, represents the Bible, the believer's manual for guidance and his assurance of admission into Heaven. However, a short time later, Christian had to climb a long, steep hill called "the hill Difficulty." He found the hill very difficult, indeed, and so, when halfway up, he saw "a pleasant Arbor" (the arbor of ease), he decided on his own to turn aside and rest. "Thus pleasing himself a while, he at last fell into a slumber, and then into a fast sleep . . . and in his Sleep his Roll fell out of his hand." He was abruptly awakened, realized the error of prolonged ease, and hurried back to the narrow path over the hill. Soon he ran into a major crisis, whereupon "he felt in his bosom for his Roll, that he might read therein, and be comforted; but he found it not." When he faced a major crisis, and desperately needed his appointed resource, he discovered that he had lost it — through sheer carelessness!

In Jesus' parable of the ten young women, five wise and five foolish, the five foolish ones surely did not deliberately plan to take no oil with them; they simply "supposed" they could acquire oil conveniently along the way, or borrow it from those who had it in an emergency. But the point of the story is that the crucial spiritual values of life are non-negotiable and non-transferable in a crisis. The supposition that you can borrow from another's stock is sadly erroneous. They, like Mary and Joseph, supposed, and their supposition was fatal!

When I was a teenager, I traveled with my family on a vacation trip to the northeastern United States. We traveled for some distance on the Pennsylvania Turnpike, which at that time had just been completed. At one point, our trip was stalled because of a major wreck in one of the turnpike's mountain tunnels. While we were waiting with the stalled traffic, a state trooper was visiting with us. He stated that the turnpike had been built to relieve the traffic congestion and number of accidents on the smaller state highways, but actually the opposite effect had occurred. The number of accidents and fatalities had increased during the first year it was open. Puzzled, my father asked why. The trooper explained that the consistency and ease of travel on the new highway had induced what he called "Highway Hypnosis," which meant that the drivers were sedated into carelessness by the steady conditions that allowed them to "suppose" security. The problem was corrected, he explained, by sharply varying the highway terrain and by installing occasional bumps on the highway surface to alert the drifting driver.

THE DANGER OF LOSING SIGHT OF JESUS

What a picture of one of the subtle but major dangers of the Christian life. It's possible to lose sight of Jesus by sheer carelessness.

Then, a Christian may lose sight of Jesus through a *substitute concentration*. Once the first false suppositions had been made, Mary and Joseph became too busy to notice any problem. They were so absorbed with family, friends, and the festive pleasures of the trip that they went a long distance before they were shocked into awareness of Jesus' absence. Mary and Joseph didn't even know they had lost Him. And a similar tragedy occurs far too often in every believer's life. At one time or another, we give primary attention to secondary things — and tragically lose sight of Jesus. A popular slogan has appeared in many places in recent times: "The Main Thing is to keep the Main Thing the Main Thing." This needs to be emblazoned on the heart of every child of God.

When Gypsy Smith, the renowned evangelist, was an old man, a lady took her small boy to one of his crusades just so the little boy could meet the great evangelist before he passed off the scene. After the crusade service, the moment of introduction finally arrived. When she introduced evangelist and boy, Gypsy Smith heartily extended his hand, but the little boy stood completely still, holding his mother's hand in his left hand. The mother said, "Son, give Brother Smith your hand." The little boy just stood there, unmoving. The mother said sharply, "Give the preacher your hand!" The little boy broke his left hand loose and extended it. "No, no, son, you know better than that! Give him your right hand!" The little boy soberly said, "Mom, I can't." She said, "Why can't you?" He replied, "Because I've got my marbles in my right hand." This is precisely why many Christians never give God the right hand of their best dedication: they've got their "marbles" in their right hand. It's possible to lose sight of Jesus through a substitute concentration.

Again, it's possible to lose sight of Jesus because of the *social crowd*. Notice the phrases in verse 44, "in the company" and "among their relatives, neighbors, and friends." How many are like Zacchaeus at this point! "He wanted to see Jesus who he was, but could not for the crowd, because he was little of stature" (Luke 19:3). How many combine Zacchaeus' two handicaps - pygmy stature and a pressuring society — into a deadly loss of the sight of Jesus.

Others lose sight of Jesus because of *selfish conceit*. When Mary and Joseph found Jesus, He was "in the temple, sitting in the midst of the doctors, both hearing them, and asking them questions. And all that heard Him were astonished at his understanding and answers" (verses 46-47). At this point, these scholars and religious leaders of the people gave respect to Jesus because of His incredible sensitivity and insight with regard to spiritual realities. But later, it was this same camp that became violently incensed over the threatening teachings of this apparently innocent, erudite child. Later, they would say, "We are the religious authorities, and He is only a carpenter's son. It isn't sensible that we should listen to Him, and that He should assume authority over us!" Here we see the insane imbalance of selfish conceit. How subtly and powerfully pride distorts our inner lives at any moment!

A little girl went with her mother to visit her grandmother in a distant city. The first morning of their visit in the grandmother's home, the little girl awakened beside her mother in a strange bed. Looking around to get her bearings, she noticed a large mirror at the foot of the bed. As she looked, she observed a reflection of a picture of Jesus at the head of the bed. She sat up to get a better look, but when she did, she projected her own body into the line of the reflection, and thus blotted out the reflection of Jesus. After a few "trial runs" of this exercise, she awakened her mother. "Look, Mommy," she said, "when I can see myself, I can't see Jesus; but when I can see Jesus, I can't see myself!" Exactly! But how many of us daily lose sight of Jesus through an inordinate over-attention upon ourselves. We lose sight of Jesus through selfish conceit.

The final reason suggested in the story for losing sight of Jesus is a *sterile church*. You won't mind me stretching the story a bit to make a valid point. The people who loved Him most lost sight of Him, and they did it in the very place least likely to induce such a loss — at church. The church is the most likely place to get a life-transforming vision of Jesus, but it may also sadly be the very place where many lose sight of Him. How many conventional churchgoers have not had a soul-shaking, sin-conquering, service-motivating fresh look at Jesus in years!

We must sadly admit that sometimes the church itself is responsible for this failure. To paraphrase Vance Havner, the church is often a firecracker institution while professing to believe a dynamite Gospel. It can easily substitute activity for vitality, the idolatry of size and success for the influence of spiritual power, coldness in place of Holy Spirit warmth, and formality for faith. "It is time for judgment to begin at the House of God" (I Peter 4:17). Much of the responsibility for society's misdirected gaze lies squarely at the door of the church. And often the church is sterile because it has permitted a lapse of its own look at Jesus.

But we must fairly say that one reason many lose sight of Jesus in church is solely because of the churchgoer himself. Many people attend church actually looking for distractions or focusing on inferior objects. And attitude is all-important. Any bad spirit in a churchgoer — anger, pride, hostility, protest, envy, jealousy, prejudice, lust (you complete the list), will cause the tragic loss of a clear look at Jesus.

Just as in the Old Testament, the written Word was lost in church and the people suffered fearful consequences; here the living word was lost in church and the ones suffering the loss were thrown into deep distress. This scene could be reproduced many times over in churches every Sunday.

So Christians may lose sight of Jesus at any time because of sheer carelessness, a substitute concentration, the social crowd, selfish conceit, or a sterile church. What may be done about such a loss?

THE REMEDY FOR LOSING SIGHT OF JESUS

There is a powerful, perfect *remedy for losing sight of Jesus* suggested in the text. Mary and Joseph reveal the proper pattern.

First, they *stopped*. Verse 44 says, "they went a day's journey" without Him. Friends, even one day's journey without Christ is too far! And one day's journey without Him can (and often does) lead to another day's journey without Him. The loss may seem innocent enough at the moment, but direction and momentum tend to become more irreversible with each reinforcement. Beware of even "a day's journey" without Him! When they became aware of His absence, they immediately went into an emergency alert. They stopped all progress toward home, refusing to take another step without Him. Oh, that we were as wise as they! We often become aware of emptiness, sterility, powerlessness and all the other deficiencies that attend a lost vision of Jesus, but instead of calling a halt to everything until the vision is restored, we rush on through the traditional and expected activities — without Him! The approval of countless others is worthless if Jesus is absent! But we need to take the same absolutely radical measure Mary and Joseph took; we need to stop everything until we vitally see Him again. Many of us need to take a spiritual inventory, echoing the words of William Cowper:

"Where is that blessedness I knew, when first I saw the Lord, Where is that soul-refreshing view, Of Jesus and His Word?"

Then, they *switched directions.* Verse 45 says, "They turned back again." This phrase, when viewed spiritually, combines the gigantic words, "repentance" and "conversion." To "repent" means to rethink your present and past life and spiritual status with a view to redirecting your life away from all distractions and toward Jesus Christ.

Let me give you a crazy riddle that has a crazy answer — but it illustrates an eternal truth.

Question: Do you know why the ram went over the cliff?

Answer: *Because he didn't see the ewe turn.*

Do you know why people go to hell? It is because they ignore the *"you-turn,"* the absolute necessity for repentance. The primary Greek word for repentance is "metanoia," which means "a change of mind." Everything begins with a spiritual re-evaluation of life and destiny, now thinking from God's point of view. This change of mind leads to a change of character, which in turn leads to a change of direction. Then comes a change of conduct. All of this means a change of eternal destiny.

Conversion (which is not merely an initial experience, but an ongoing lifestyle) is the actual turning from all lesser objects unto Christ. Just like the needle of a magnet, when released from all distracting pulls, will invariably turn to focus on polar north, so the heart of every born-again believer, when released from the multitude of sinful distractions, will turn invariably to its True Focus, Jesus.

Finally, Mary and Joseph *sought Him*. Verse 44 says, "They sought Him (a very strong word which means to 'search up and down')." And verse 45 says, "And when they found Him not, they turned back again to Jerusalem, seeking Him." When they found Him, Mary said, "Thy father and I have sought thee sorrowing" (vs. 48). We would each be wise to conduct a sorrowful search for Him when the Spirit convicts us of the sin of distracted vision. And where will we find Him? Precisely where we lost Him! And you really *know* where you lost sight of Him. Was it when you began to omit Bible study from your daily habits? Was it when you began to drift away from the prayer closet? Was it when you began to accumulate unconfessed sins in your heart? Was it when you began to be careless about church attendance? Was it when you became silent in your personal witness? How many Christians lose sight of Jesus and then try to go on without correcting the loss. But God is not a God of unfinished business. To try to make progress without a full, fresh view of Him is inviting disillusionment, despair, and disaster.

Do you remember the account of the lost ax-head in II Kings 6? When the ax-head flew off the ax-handle, the man who suffered the loss went quickly to Elisha (a picture of Christ) and reported the loss. Elisha's first response was, "Where did it fall? Where did you lose it?" Dear friend, if you are at this moment conscious that your faith-view of Jesus has blurred or gone, stop what you are doing, switch directions, and, sorrowful over the loss, engage your heart in The Search that never goes unrewarded. Then, you can join the multitude about whom it has been said, "Then were the disciples glad, when they saw the Lord."

An Addendum

Eight important questions will enable us to explore this story:

(1) *Who* "lost" Jesus? Mary and Joseph! His own family (today, His Family is the Church made up of His own children)! The ones who loved Him most!

(2) *In what sense* did they "lose" Him? They only lost *fellowship with Him;* they only lost sight of Him. They *did not* (in fact, *could not*) lose *relationship* with Him. They had not lost their *love* for Him; they had not lost their *faith*. They had lost *Him!* We must be very careful to understand this point. Though they "misplaced" Him and got out of *fellowship* with Him, they were still His parents, and He was still their son. Even so, a Christian may get out of *fellowship* with God, but once he has become God's child, this *relationship* cannot be broken.

(3) *Where* did they "lose" (or, lose sight of) Him? In the most unlikely place! They lost Him in church! There is nothing about merely being in church that guarantees encounter and relationship with Jesus there. In fact, it is very easy to lose sight of Him in church—for various reasons. How many times have each of us gone to church, only to stay in our cocoons of coldness, or criticism, or cynicism, or carnality while we were there!

(4) When did they "lose" Him? During the Passover season! When every article and particle of Passover observance pointed to Him! At a time when Messianic expectation was alive at a fever pitch, Mary and Joseph, of all people, should have had a very high level of such expectation, and should have strongly suspicioned that Jesus was central to the Passover observance. Today, Christians should never "lose"

(lose sight of) Jesus in church. Sunday worship should remind every Christian of the Death and Resurrection of Jesus, and of the Presence and Power of the Holy Spirit. These things should dynamically focus our attention upon Jesus.

(5) *How* did they "lose" Him? They lost Him for the most unlikely reason! They were guilty in Jerusalem at the very end of the Passover Feast of the most unlikely of sins, and that sin caused them to lose Jesus. Indifference! Carelessness! The text says, "They, *supposing* Him to be in the group." Here we see the deadly danger of drifting, the sin of supposing. When we go to church taking everything for granted, without proper preparation, without advance thought, we will lose sight of Jesus there.

(6) *How long* did they suffer the loss? The text says that "after *three days* they found Him in the temple." *Three days!* Sometimes we go long distances without seeing His face, don't we? Even *one day* without Jesus is too long. A one day's journey without Jesus (verse 44) is too far. Furthermore, until they turned around, they were only increasing the distance between Him and themselves.

(7) *How did they find Him again?* They went back to the very spot where they had lost Him. "They turned back to Jerusalem, seeking Him" (verse 45). A train that runs from Kansas City to St. Louis and back again must enter the train's turntable in St. Louis (and in Kansas City) to make the return trip. It must be turned around. When a believer "loses" Jesus, he must turn around as God acts upon His mind and heart. Thus, he is *turned around* by the agency of Another, and he *turns around* by his own choice. Urged by their embarrassment, by their desperation, and by their desire to correct the loss, Mary and Joseph turned back to the place where they had "lost" Him.

(8) *What did they do when they found Him?* They resumed the old relationship! "And He went down with them, and came to Nazareth" (verse 51). They went back to daily life together. They went on together, and so shall we — when all problems in our relationship with Him are made right.

FROM THRONE TO THRONE BY WAY OF THE EARTH

Philippians 2:5-11:

"Let this mind be in you, which was also in Christ Jesus; Who, being in the form of God, thought it not robbery to be equal with God: But made himself of no reputation, and took upon him the form of a servant, and was made in the likeness of men; And being found in fashion as a man, he humbled himself, and became obedient unto death, even the death of the cross. Wherefore God also hath highly exalted him, and given him a name which is above every name: That at the name of Jesus every knee should bow, of things in heaven, and things in earth, and things under the earth; And that every tongue should confess that Jesus Christ is Lord, to the glory of God the Father" (King James translation).

"Keep on fostering the same disposition that Christ Jesus had. Though He was existing in the nature of God, He did not think His being on an equality with God a thing to be selfishly grasped, but He laid it aside, as He took on the nature of a slave and became like other men. Because He was recognized as a man, in reality as well as in outward form, He finally humiliated Himself in obedience so as to die, even to die on a cross. This is why God has highly exalted

Him, and given Him the name that is above every other name, so that in the name of Jesus everyone should kneel, in heaven, on earth, and in the underworld, and everyone should confess that Jesus Christ is Lord, to the praise of God the Father" (Williams translation).

Let Christ Jesus be your example as to what your attitude should be. For he, who had always been God by nature, did not cling to his prerogatives as God's equal, but stripped himself of all privilege by consenting to be a slave by nature and being born as mortal man. And, having become man, he humbled himself by living a life of utter obedience, even to the extent of dying, and the death he died was the death of a common criminal. That is why God has now lifted him so high, and has given him the name beyond all names, so that at the name of Jesus every knee shall bow, whether in Heaven or earth or under the earth. And that is why, in the end, every tongue shall confess that Jesus Christ is the Lord, to the glory of God the Father." (J. B. Phillips paraphrase).

"Let your bearing towards one another arise out of your life in Christ Jesus. For the divine nature was his from the first; yet he did not think to snatch at equality with God, but made himself nothing, assuming the nature of a slave. Bearing the human likeness, revealed in human shape, he humbled himself, and in obedience accepted even death — death on a cross. Therefore God raised him to the heights and bestowed on him the name above all names, that at the name of Jesus every knee should bow — in heaven, on earth, and in the depths — and every tongue confess, 'Jesus Christ is Lord', to the glory of God the Father" (New English Bible).

"Let this same attitude and purpose and (humble) mind be in you which was in Christ Jesus. Let Him be your example in humility -- Who, although being essentially one with God and in the form of God (possessing the fullness of the attributes which make God God), did not think this equality).with God was a thing to be eagerly grasped or retained; But stripped Himself (of all privileges and

rightful dignity) so as to assume the guise of a servant (slave), in that He became like men and was born a human being. And after He had appeared in human form He abased and humbled Himself (still further) and carried His obedience to the extreme death, even the death of the cross! Therefore (because He stooped so low), God has highly exalted Him and has freely bestowed on Him the name that is above every name, That in (at) the name of Jesus every knee should (must) bow, in heaven and on earth and under the earth, And every tongue (frankly and openly) confess and acknowledge that Jesus Christ is Lord, to the glory of God the Father" (The Amplified Bible).

The study of the doctrine of the Person of Christ is technically called "Christology." This great doctrinal passage from Paul's letter to the Philippians is nothing less than a systematic Christology. In fact, it is so full of great truths about Jesus Christ that it is easy to turn it into a mere study, and the heart fails to rise in praise to Jesus as it should before such a parade of truths. Every serious Christian should use this passage as a vehicle for adoration, pausing regularly in the passage to worship and adore the Person who is presented here. In this passage, we read of such breathtaking truths as the Preexistence of Jesus, the Incarnation of Jesus, the Humiliation of Jesus, the Crucifixion of Jesus, the Ascension of Jesus, and the Exaltation of Jesus. So it is indeed a systematic Christology! And the way these great truths are presented is even more remarkable. The passage contains a chain of mysterious and marvelous statements about Jesus, any one of which might make the subject for an entire volume of study. As a matter of fact, I have one volume of Christology in my personal library (A. B. Bruce's <u>The Humiliation of Christ</u>) which is essentially about one word (Jesus "stripped," or "emptied," Himself) in the text — and Bruce's large volume contains 447 pages! So the substance of eternity is contained in this paragraph of Scripture.

However, we must note the innocent setting in which such great truth is found. The church in Philippi had a small-scale problem of division in it. The tiny signs of a church split could be seen by a concerned observer. And Paul writes to nip this problem in the bud. In doing so, he incorporates into his statement the greatest paragraph on the Person of Christ ever written in human language. What is an *incidental* in the Philippian letter is the most *fundamental* of revelations about the Person of Christ. This is just like the Holy Spirit! How many times He hides fundamental realities in incidental occurrences, or sublime realities in simple settings. This passage spans the eternities; in fact, it could be called, "Jesus From Eternity to Eternity." It begins with Jesus in eternity past, follows the dizzying drop of His incarnation and humiliation, then attends Him in His Heavenly exaltation, which will continue forever. This passage will only be understood by the personal combination of an *anointed mind* and an *adoring heart*. Christ's redeeming activity has two great movements in it. First is His human emptying and second is His heavenly exaltation. Each of these two movements must be examined carefully.

HIS HUMAN EMPTYING

The first large movement in the text concerns *the human emptying* of Christ. We might study this humiliation of Jesus under four divisions which are revealed in verses six through eight. Each division contains a staggering truth about the condescension of Jesus.

Movement Number One: *He who was totally God also became truly man.* "Christ Jesus … being in the form of God, thought it not robbery to be equal with God: But made himself of no reputation, and took upon him the form of a servant, and was made in the likeness of men." "Being in the form of God, ... He was made in the likeness of men." Study carefully the various translations at the beginning of this study (and any more you may have). Compare the separate phrases in the different translations. We will need every possible shade of meaning in every word and phrase to see into these great truths. The Phillips paraphrase says that "Jesus had always been God by nature." The New English Bible says that "the divine nature was His from the first." The Williams paraphrase says, "He was existing in the nature of God." The Amplified Bible translates it: He was "essentially one with God, and in the form of God (possessing the fullness of the attributes which make God God)."

At the very doorway of this great passage, we are confronted with the great *fact* of the preexistence of Jesus Christ. Jesus is a uniquely eternal Person! His life did not begin when He was conceived in the womb of the virgin Mary, or when He was born in Bethlehem. Oh, no! The word "being," or literally, "existing," clearly indicates that our Lord had a previous existence before Bethlehem. He Himself preceded and predated all the events of His own earthly life! The word used here for "being" occurs fifty-nine times in the New Testament and every time it has reference to prior existence. Prior to His birth at Bethlehem, Jesus the Son of God had existed for all eternity with God the Father and God the Holy Spirit. Jesus, with the Father and the Spirit, is everlastingly the living one.

Jesus Himself claimed preexistence. He often proclaimed His eternal existence to those around Him. In a classic passage in John six, He said that He "came down from heaven," and He indicates that He will return to where He was before. In another classic passage, He said, "Before Abraham was, I am" (John 8:58). The Jews understood His claim, because the text tells us that they immediately picked up stones with the intention of killing Jesus, for they recognized that He was implicitly identifying Himself as God, and they thought He was guilty of the "blasphemy" of making Himself equal with God. In John 17, the chapter which records the great High Priestly prayer of Jesus, verses five and seventeen refer directly to the eternal preexistence of Jesus. He asks the Father for the very glory which He had possessed with the Father "before the world was."

Jesus' claim of preexistence agrees perfectly with all of the writers of the New Testament.

Consider briefly the testimony of the Apostle John. In John 1:1-2, he used a verb ("was") which indicates that Jesus *always was*, and that there was never a time when He was not. Consider, too, the testimony of the Apostle Paul. In II Corinthians 8:9, he wrote, "For ye know the grace of our Lord Jesus Christ, that, though he was rich, yet for your sakes he became poor, that ye through his poverty might be rich." Jesus could only have been "rich" in Heaven before coming to the earth and becoming a man. Therefore, He existed prior to coming to this world.

Furthermore, we can see the *nature* of Christ's incarnation in this verse. When a rich man becomes poor, his mode of existence has changed, but not his nature as a human being. When Jesus became "poor" in His incarnation, His mode of existence changed, but not His nature as God. Then, in Colossians 1:17, Paul said, "He (Jesus) is before all things, and by Him all things consist." The preposition that is used denotes that which is prior in time to all other things. All created things had a point of origin, but Christ did not. In fact, the Bible tells us that "all things were created by Him (Jesus)." The One through whom everything was called into existence necessarily existed before all else was created. Just as the artist existed before the portrait that he painted, and the architect existed before the building that he designed, so God the Son existed before the universe that He brought into being. The writers of the New Testament unanimously agree about the preincarnate existence and glory of Jesus Christ.

But this passage tells us much more. It not only reveals the *fact* of His preexistence; it also points out the *form* of it. "Christ Jesus, existing in the *form of God.*" "Existing in the nature of God," the Williams translation says. "Being essentially one with God (possessing the fullness of the attributes which make God God)," the Amplified Bible puts it. "He had always been God by nature," the Phillips paraphrase translates it. The word translated "form" in the King James translation does not refer to a physical or outward form or shape.

God is Spirit (John 4:24), and does not innately possess outward form or shape. The word "form" in our text means "essence" or "reality." Jesus was throughout eternity past in the "essence" or "reality" or "nature" of God. To say that Jesus was "existing in the nature of God" is the highest possible claim that He is *totally God*, or as the old creed says, "He is very God of very God." Jesus is Himself absolute Deity, a co-participant with God the Father and God the Holy Spirit in that Divine essence which constitutes God, God. So Jesus Christ is perfectly identified here with the being, nature, and personality of God — *Himself being God!*

While the great astronomer, Johan Kepler, was observing the stars one night, he explained his activity with these words: "I am thinking God's first thoughts after Him." But the thoughts expressed in our text predate the stars! Here, we are thinking over again the first thoughts of God. Here the vastness of eternity unfolds before us.

Now we come to the "dizzying drop" which I referred to earlier. He who was totally God *became truly man.* Again, Phillips translates it, "He who had always been God by nature, did not cling to His rights as God's equal." "He did not snatch at his rights," another translation says. We are great "snatchers" of rights and advantages — just look at the daily newspapers! "He did not regard His equality with God a thing to be seized upon." The word means to "clutch," or "cling," or "hoard." Jesus was so absolutely sure of His Godhood — of His total equality with God *as* God -- that He did not have to hoard it. He could freely give up His rights, advantages, and powers, knowing that no loss could permanently threaten Him.

Here was the contest of redemption. The first Adam made a frantic attempt to seize equality with God (Genesis 3:5); but Jesus, the last Adam, being sure of Godhood, voluntarily gave up His Divine rights and advantages.

"And He was made in the likeness of men." Let these words reach the deep of your person: *God became man!* The word "likeness" means similarity but with a difference. Jesus became a man, similar to each of us — but with a difference! Though He was genuinely human, He was unique among humans in that He was without sin. The New Testament writers use an impressive array of words and phrases to present the incarnation ("in-fleshment") of God in Christ. John 1:14 says that He "became flesh." Galatians 4:4 says that he was "born of a woman." Romans 1:3 says that "He was born of the seed of David according to the flesh." I Timothy 3:16 declares that "God was manifested in the flesh." Hebrews 2:14 indicates that "He became a partaker of flesh and blood." And His time on earth is referred to as "the days of His flesh" (Hebrews 5:7).

We must never allow the incarnation of Christ to fade in our minds or hearts. "Jesus" is the human name of God!

And we must not confuse this truth. The incarnation is not the *deifying of man*; it is the *humanizing of God*. It is not man rising into Godhood; it is God condescending into manhood. In His incarnation, He was as perfectly united with man as He had always been -- and remained -- perfectly united with God. This incredible fact brings many previously impossible things into the human situation. For example, when God became man in the incarnation of Christ, for the first time in His eternal existence, God's nature had substance. And for the first time in His eternal existence, God now had a nature that was capable of dying! So the stage is now set for a transaction of eternal redemption to be made. God is on earth as a man, with a mortal human nature — something awfully big is in the making! The vital ingredients of a coming Calvary are now in place.

C. S. Lewis, the British scholar and Christian, wrote these helpful words: "Did you ever think, when you were a child, what fun it would be if your toys could come to life? Well, suppose you could really have brought them to life. Imagine turning a tin soldier into a real little man. It would involve turning the tin into flesh. And suppose the tin soldier did not like it. He is not interested in flesh; all he sees is that the tin is being spoilt. He thinks you are killing him. He will do everything he can to prevent you. He will not be made into a man if he can help it. What you would have done about that tin soldier I do not know. But what God did about us was this. The Second Person in God, the Son, became human Himself; was born into the world as an actual man — a real man of a particular height, with hair of a particular color, speaking a particular language, weighing so many pounds. The Eternal Being, who knows everything and who created the whole universe, became not only a man but a babe, and before that a fetus inside a woman's body. If you want to get the hang of it, think how you would like to become a snail or a crab."

Think of it! The great *Creator* has become a *creature* in His own *creation* — in order to *recreate* both the sin-tainted creation and the sin-infected creature, man. The glorious Son of God voluntarily forsook the splendor of His pre-existent state in Heaven and became as genuinely human as we ourselves are — *and all for our sake.*

Some years ago, I read with great pleasure Ernest Gordon's partial autobiography entitled <u>Miracle On the River Kwai</u>. Gordon was a British Highland soldier captured by the Japanese during World War II. He was kept in a POW camp in a Burmese jungle. The prisoners of war were forced to build a railroad for the Japanese in the jungle. Gordon nearly starved along with the other prisoners, and became the victim of numerous tropical diseases. He was not a Christian when he was placed in the death house and left to die. However, a fellow prisoner took Gordon out, shared his meager food rations with him, and nursed him back to health. This friend also introduced Gordon to Christ.

The story is the remarkable story of faith's triumph over the many obstacles that stood against it, or the story of *Christ's triumph* among His helpless people. Years later, when Ernest Gordon was chaplain at Princeton University, he wrote that Jesus Christ "came into our Death House, to lead us out and deliver us to full spiritual health." But before He could come "into our Death House," He first had to become a man. When Jesus came to the earth, He might have said, "I *am* what I *was* — **God.** I was *not* what I *am* — **man.** *I am now both* — **God and man.**" The Son of God became also the Son of Man. He who was totally God became truly man.

Movement Number Two: *He who was the Greatest Somebody in the universe became the least nobody in the universe.*

The King James Version explains it by saying, "He made Himself of no reputation," and "He humbled Himself." The Amplified Bible says, "He stripped Himself (of all privileges and rightful dignity)." The Williams translation says, "He laid it aside," and "He humiliated Himself." The New English Bible says, "He made Himself nothing." Jesus Himself said that He was "set at nought" (Mark 9:12). All of these statements are attempts to explain one of the biggest words in the Bible. The root word is "kenosis," and refers to the self-emptying of Jesus in coming to the earth. But what did Jesus strip from Himself, or empty Himself of, in coming to the earth? P. T. Forsyth used an extraordinary term for it; he called it Christ's "self-disglorification." What did Jesus strip Himself of in Heaven before coming to this earth? This is a delicate and difficult question, and requires suitable thought and effort to answer.

John Milton, one of the greatest of Christian poets, wrote:
"That glorious Form, that Light insufferable
He laid aside: and here with us to be,
Forsook the courts of everlasting day,
And chose with us a darksome house of mortal clay."

But just exactly what did Jesus "lay aside" in Heaven? Did He lay aside His Godhood, His Deity, His *Divine Nature*? Certainly not! Indeed, He *could not* lay aside His very "nature." He was just as much God when He walked the streets of Nazareth as when He trod the courts of Heaven. Did He strip Himself of His *sinlessness*? Certainly not! He was just as surely sinless and perfectly pure on earth as He had always been from eternity. He was as sinless and holy while on earth as a man as He had been when He was only God and in Heaven. He stripped Himself of the outward expression of His Deity, of the outward manifestation of His Heavenly glory. Be very careful here. Jesus stripped Himself only of the *expression* of His Deity; He did not give up the *possession* of His Deity. He was always fully God, even when His Godhood was veiled in human flesh. He stripped Himself of the independent use of His Divine rights and powers. He laid aside the glory, privileges and majesty that had always been His.

Notice the emphasis in all of these phrases on the *voluntary nature* of Christ's actions. He was coerced only by His love for us. "*He made Himself* of no reputation." "*He took upon Him* the form of a servant." "*He humbled Himself.*" "*He stripped Himself.*" "*He became* obedient unto death."

There is an incredible illustration of all of the movements of this text in the great foot-washing episode in John thirteen. In that story, Jesus did seven things, and those seven things reveal "Jesus From Eternity to Eternity." Each of them has an exact counterpart in our text. Read John 13: 1-13, and note the seven actions of Jesus: (1) He stood up; (2) He put something off; (3) He put something on; (4) He poured something out; (5) He washed His followers with that which He poured out — and "wiped them with the towel," suggesting a finished work; (6) He returned to His original position and reassumed His original garments; and (7) He sat down again. Can anyone miss that sequence? This is the eternal history of Jesus. One awful but glorious day in Heaven, *He stood up — and prepared to go to Bethlehem* **and Calvary....**

Many people will remember the English Duke of Windsor as the man who was at one time the King of England, but who abdicated his throne and stripped himself of the royal vesture of his rightful office in order to marry Wallace Simpson, the woman he loved. Even so, Jesus abandoned the eternal throne of Heaven that was His by right, in order to fully identify Himself with you and me, whom He loved. For a moment, return to the human illustration I have just shared, and put yourself "into the shoes" of the lady in the story. When Mrs. Simpson was on the point of marrying the King of

England, the newspapers at home and abroad had some very unkind things to say about her. They told the world how she had already wrecked two marriages. They indicated that she would marry the King whether she loved him or not, for his position and his wealth. All in all, they made her out a rather cheap woman. We will probably never know just what her reactions were to all this. But if she was a sensitive woman, she must have agonized over the reactions. But even if she felt unspeakably unworthy, she could have said something like this: "The King of the greatest empire on earth has loved me enough to uncrown himself for me." Christian, *the King of Heaven has loved you enough to uncrown Himself for you.* What should your response be, personally and practically?

But there is still more that must be said before we leave this movement. Not only did He leave the throne and lay aside His glory; it wasn't even known by most people where He walked that He had ever *occupied a throne* or had *possessed any glory.* "He was in the world, and the world was made by Him, but *the world knew Him not*" (John 1:10). He Himself once said, "There is one among you whom ye know not." He not only was God *incarnate*; He was also God *incognito.*

John D. Rockefeller, Jr., used to walk around Rockefeller Center when the skyscraper was in the process of construction. He would stand on the sidewalk and watch the advancing construction for a few minutes every day. One day, a watchman accosted him. "Move along, buddy," he growled. "You can't stand loafing here." He quietly withdrew, unrecognized. Jesus often told people whom He helped to "tell no one." Most people would have accelerated their publicity machine into high gear, but Jesus was content to be an unknown.

Suppose that a general of the United States Army walked into the soldiers' common barracks. The moment he enters, the men snap to attention and salute, because they recognize the uniform and the insignia of his rank. They continue at attention until he says, "At ease." If he sits down to talk with them, their restraint is obvious. He is a general, they are enlisted men, and they are conscious of the difference in rank and position. However, if he should enter the barracks without the emblems of his rank and *incognito*, there would be quite a different atmosphere. The men would take him to be one of themselves, would talk more freely with him, and might be flippantly familiar with him. Even so, when Jesus "made Himself of no reputation," *He merely took off His insignia. His rank had not changed, though the outward signs of it were somewhat hidden.* The people who were near Him received Him as a man. Furthermore, He put Himself at the mercy of friends and enemies alike.

I spent five years of my life in Fort Worth, Texas, where I attended seminary. The name of Dutch Meyer was a familiar name in the Fort Worth area. Dutch Meyer was the longtime, legendary, revered former Texas Christian University football coach. The Daniel-Meyer Coliseum on the TCU campus was named for him. One day some years ago an older gentleman dressed in old, rumpled clothes came into the coliseum offices with an armload of newspapers. He placed the papers on the floor, said, "Here are some newspapers," and started toward the door. The secretary stopped him. When she questioned him he said that he had read in the newspaper that they were collecting used newspapers and that he had brought some in. The secretary told him to remove the papers; he couldn't leave them there. But this idea did not appeal to the old gentleman.

When the young TCU athletic director came out to see the cause of the disturbance, he, too, suggested that the man remove the papers. When he refused, they asked him to leave the office. He refused to do that, too. Then the athletic director went to the phone and called campus security requesting that this man be removed from the office. When the veteran campus security officer arrived and was told the situation, he said to the younger office staff, "I beg you to reconsider your request. This man is Dutch Meyer. You're about to have him thrown out of his own building!" "Jesus was in the world, and the world was made by Him, and the world knew Him not. He came unto His own (world), and His own (people) received Him not." A blind and arrogant world *threw the Son of God out of His own building,* and He hardly defended or explained Himself! He was far greater than a five-star general in Heaven, but He came to earth without His insignia showing. The Greatest Somebody in the universe became the least nobody in the universe — voluntarily.

Movement Number Three: *He who was Master of all became the slave of all.* "He took upon Him the form of a servant" (verse 7). "I am among you as he who serves," Jesus said. He who was eternally and rightfully accustomed to *giving orders* voluntarily placed himself in the subordinate position of *taking orders.* The word "form" in verse seven is the same word that is used in verse six. The same Jesus that was in His very nature and essence, *God,* took on the nature and essence of a slave. He submitted Himself to authentic servanthood, always considering others before Himself (verse 4). In fact, He declared that this was one of the primary reasons for His coming: "The Son of Man did not come to be served, but to serve, and to give His life a ransom for many" (Matthew 20:28). Remember that a slave has no rights of his own, no will of his own, no property of his own, and no schedule of his own. During his teenage years, He served as an apprentice carpenter to his foster father, Joseph. He is now making yokes for cattle, but before He came, *He was making worlds.* It is simply part of the "incarnational package" that the Lord of the universe became a lowly servant among men.

Movement Number Four: *He who was Life DIED!* The text says that Jesus "emptied Himself," and this speaks of His incarnation. Then it says that He "humbled Himself," and this speaks of His crucifixion. So His voluntary condescension was in two successive stages: first, to the earth, and then on the earth. The first stage was a humiliation to humanity, and the second was a humiliation in humanity. He "became obedient unto death — even the death of the Cross!" "He went even to the extent of dying, and the death that He died was the death of a common criminal" (Phillips). "He carried His obedience to the extreme death, even the death of the cross" (Amplified). Note carefully the giant word, "obedience," and remember that Jesus' obedience to His Father was total and perfect. "I do always those things that please Him," He declared. "One man's disobedience" had to be undone "by the obedience of One" (Romans 5:19). Adam's obedience would have been unto life, but instead, he disobeyed — unto death. So Jesus, the last Adam, must now obey unto death, that His obedience unto death might bring life unto us, the disobedient ones. What a Gospel!

During some turbulent days in ancient Rome, a slave heard that his master's name was on the death list. He quickly put on his master's cloak and quietly awaited the arrival of the political killers. When they found the slave dressed in his master's clothing, they killed him, supposing him to be the master. In the same manner, the Master of the universe, the Lord Jesus Christ, took on Himself the cloak of our humanity — and died. The death He endured was the death we deserved.

The kind of death Jesus died — the death of the cross — was the very symbol of disgrace, agony, and shame. And the reality was far, far worse than the mere symbol! When Paul said, "*even* the death of the cross," you can feel Paul recoiling from this terrible thought. You see, the mere death of Christ was not enough. If His death was all that was called for, then He could have been killed by Herod while yet in His infancy and the world would have been saved. The death of Jesus acquires its redemptive quality from two things: (1) The life of perfect obedience which lay behind it, and (2) The kind of death it was -- "even the death *of the cross."* It is amazing that Jesus *could* die. It is more amazing that He *would* die. It is more amazing yet that He *should* die. It is still more amazing that He *did* die. But the most amazing thing of all is that He died *"even the death of the cross!"* As if crucifixion were not terrible enough in itself, to compound both the horror and the amazement, the law of Moses attached a curse to anyone who suffered this mode of death (Deuteronomy 21:23). But again, wonder of wonders, our loving Father turned this around to make a *Gospel* out of it. "Christ hath redeemed us from the curse of the law, being made a curse for us" (Galatians 3:13). Everything the world and the devil means to be evil to us, God turns it into good! Hallelujah! And Paul uses all of this to appeal for our humility and unity!

"When I survey the wondrous cross, On which the Prince of Glory died, *My richest gain I count but loss, And pour contempt on all my pride."*

Gladys Aylward, the missionary to China, about whose life the Hollywood film, "The Inn of the Sixth Happiness," was made, said in an address to Christian college students, "Are you thinking of going to the mission field for thrilling and romantic experiences? If so, don't come! They aren't there. Instead, it is following Jesus, step by step, from the graveyard of selfish ambitions into the life of God." But this is not only the standard for a missionary. It is the daily standard for every Christian. The Christian life is *following Jesus, step by step, from the graveyard of selfish ambitions into the life of God.*

HIS HEAVENLY EXALTATION

The second large movement in the text concerns *the heavenly exaltation* of Christ *after* His human emptying and humiliation. This passage is equally as great in pointing out the exaltation of Jesus as it is in pointing out the humiliation of Jesus. Note the dimensions of His exaltation.

First, it is a *deserved* exaltation. This is indicated by the word, "wherefore." The exaltation of Christ follows reasonably and inevitably on the heels of His humiliation. The masculine pronoun "him" is used twice in verse nine, and the human name, "Jesus" is used in verse ten. So the person who is exalted in verses nine through eleven is the same person who "emptied Himself" and "humbled Himself" in the preceding verses. In the Greek text, the word "Himself" in all these phrases comes before the verb, emphasizing that the self-emptying was of Christ's own free will. It was a totally voluntary act. At the beginning of the redeeming process *He stripped Himself* in Heaven of the insignia of royalty, glory, majesty, and honor, and came into humanity by a miraculous supernatural act. At the end of the redeeming process *He humbled Himself* and *gave Himself up* to die.

Give much thought to these next sentences. It was not because of His essential glory as the Eternal Christ that He was recrowned with supernal glory. No! The exaltation declared in Philippians 2:9-11 is given in exact proportion to His voluntary humiliation. How deep was His humiliation? You may answer that question by measuring the height of His exaltation. How high is His exaltation? You may answer that question by placing a measuring line alongside His humiliation as presented in Philippians 2:6-8. His ascent to the throne of glory was only His descent *reversed*. **His "up-rising" in verses nine through eleven is an outcome of His "down-stooping" and "down-stepping" in verses six through**

eight. Considering His Divine Personhood, any exaltation that followed these acts of self-giving was certainly a deserved exaltation. The exaltation corresponds to the humiliation. The exaltation was not arbitrary, but reasonable. The outcome did not depend on the thoughtless whim of a Divine dictator, but on the reasonable heart of a Heavenly Father. The reasons for His exaltation may be seen by studying the Epistles of the New Testament. For example, in Hebrews, it is His Personal *superiority* that merits His exaltation. In Colossians, it is His Personal *supremacy* in creation (both the old material creation, and the new spiritual creation, the Church) that merits His exaltation. In our text in Philippians, it is His Personal *sufficiency* in self-emptying and redemption that merits His exaltation. So His exaltation is fully deserved.

Second, His exaltation was a *Divine* exaltation. "Wherefore *God* hath also highly exalted Him." Do you see the contrast: Jesus humbled *Himself*, but *God* exalted Him. This is a law in the realm of grace: "He that exalteth himself shall be humbled, but he that humbleth himself shall be exalted." Note that the initiative in this exaltation belongs solely and exclusively to God. It is a rule that **God initiates only what He appreciates.** God acts within the limits of His own approval. God sets the standard for His own actions. No other cause except the pleasure of God would ever draw the approval of God. God exalted Jesus because it was perfectly suitable to His nature to do so.

Third, it was a *defined* exaltation. We are left in no doubt about the degree or kind of this exaltation. "God has highly exalted Him, and given Him a name which is above every name." The verb, "highly exalted," is used only in this one instance, and is here applied only to Jesus. It literally means that "God has *super*-exalted Him," or that God has elevated Him in a transcendentally glorious manner. The word that is used indicates double-barreled exaltation. It would help us to appreciate this statement if we brought in a great supportive passage from Paul's exalted letter to the Ephesians. Ephesians 1:19-23, where Paul speaks of "the exceeding greatness of God's power toward us who believe, according to the working of His mighty power, Which He wrought in Christ, when He raised Him from the dead, and set Him at His own right hand in the heavenly places, Far above all principality, and power, and might, and dominion, and every name that is named, not only in this world, but also in that which is to come: And hath put all things under His feet, and gave Him to be the head over all things to the church, Which is His body, the fulness of Him that filleth all in all."

Furthermore, God has "given Him a name which is above every name." Remember that this bestowal follows His self-emptying. In His humiliation, He was given the name "Jesus," so it is likely that the name given Him in His exaltation is the name, "Lord."

Fourth, it is a *demanding* exaltation. "At the name of Jesus every knee should bow, of things in heaven, and things in earth, and things under the earth; And that every tongue should confess that Jesus Christ is Lord, to the glory of God the Father." One day there is going to take place a universal acknowledgment of the Lordship of Christ over all creation and over every created intelligence. There will be no exemption, no exception, and no exclusion. That day will be marked by a conscious reversal of man's previous judgment about Jesus. When he was on earth, man said, "He is worthy of death, even the death of the Cross." But now, *God* speaks, and tells us the total, unconditional, undeniable and undebatable truth about Jesus. How shocking that day will be to sinful human beings who tragically over-estimated their ability to evaluate such a Person as Jesus!

One of Hans Christian Anderson's fairy tales tells of an emperor who wanted to see how his people behaved in his absence. So he dressed as a beggar and visited the city. The people promptly threw him out! A few days later, when he came in triumph in his golden carriage, everybody bowed low as it passed. However, when they looked into the carriage to see the emperor, they were astonished to see the face of the very beggar they had treated so badly. While they thought he was a beggar, and treated him as such, he was actually the Emperor of the Realm!

Two thousand years ago, the Emperor of the Realm disrobed Himself in His throne room of His royal robes and dressed Himself in the lowly garb of our frail and poor humanity. He came to this earth and lived as a man among men. Man's rejection of Him was shocking, and it has continued for two thousand years. He has been "despised and rejected of men" for a long, long time now. They have glibly and impudently rejected Him without investigation or consideration, without intelligence or integrity, declaring Him to be a "mere man," or merely a "good man," one who has no claim on their lives or their allegiance. But like the citizens in the fairy story, they will see and acknowledge that the "beggar" is in fact the Emperor of the Realm. They will recognize and declare with tongue and knee that the man of Galilee is the King of Kings and Lords of Lords.

This acknowledgment of Jesus will involve universal *worship*. "Every knee will bow" before Christ. *Every* knee — the proud Pharisee's knee, the arrogant rebel's knee, the atheist's knee, the cynic's knee, the stubborn and unbent knee, *my knee and yours* — shall bow before Christ. And it will involve universal *witness*. "And every tongue shall confess that Jesus Christ is Lord, to the glory of God the Father." *Every* tongue — the idler's tongue, the pagan's tongue, the heathen's tongue, the unbeliever's tongue, the gossiping tongue, the boasting tongue, the cursing tongue, the criticizing tongue, the blaspheming tongue, etc. — these will suddenly be transformed into *confessing* tongues! The sinner's tongue that always *disagreed* with God when the subject was Jesus, will now *totally agree* with God's full assessment of His Son. And the saint's tongue, which has already humbly agreed with God about Jesus in order to be saved (Romans 10:9-10), will now happily agree with God about Jesus in this great universal acknowledgment of His Lordship.

Let these words come home to your heart, dear Christian. Let them bring both conviction and invitation to you. How bent is your knee to Christ — on His terms — today? How loose is your tongue in confessing Him among men? Is the bending of your knee merely a polite and convenient courtesy? Is the use of your tongue for Him a mere stammer instead of a clear and uncompromising statement? Before you answer too quickly, be sure that you reexamine His terms as they are stated in Philippians 2:3-4.

HIS HOLY EXAMPLE

Before we leave this glorious text, let's remind ourselves of the setting, or the context, of this passage. We must remember the background of these great words. The passage is used to encourage us to follow the holy example of Jesus in emptying Himself. Read verses three and four again. "Let nothing be done through strife or vainglory; but in lowliness of mind let each esteem other better than themselves. Look not every man on his own things, but every man also on the things of others." Verses three and four provide the subject, and verses five through eleven should give us our *education*. What is the highest ideal of human character? Is it (as the world thinks) human power, clout, and macho muscle? Is it intellectual prowess, such as that of the scientist or philosopher? Is it wealth and riches? "I went into the sanctuary of God; then I understood" (Psalm 73:17). The answer is to be found in the heart of God. It is reflected in His Word in such passages as our text.

Here is Heaven's supreme conception of character. This is what eternity enthrones. The nature that stoops, cares, loves, forgives, and saves *others*; this is the ideal type. In order to see this, we must attend the School of Calvary and see Jesus modeling the ultimate lesson. Our education as Christians begins and ends at Calvary. What do we learn at the cross? At the cross, we receive the explanation for Jesus' self-emptying. You see, it is tragically easy to think that humility is the end in itself. We think, "If I can just achieve and maintain humility, I would reach the ultimate goal of being a Christian." But read the text carefully. "Jesus humbled Himself." For what purpose? To become obedient. To what end? "Obedient unto death, even the death of the cross." And for what purpose did He die that death? *To save others!* The object of all of His redeeming activity was **others.** The ideal Christian character is reached when a Christian lives for *others* and their highest welfare — on Christ's terms.

Then, we find the Supreme Example of this ultimate lesson in the Person and history of Jesus. These verses comprise a fabulous Christology, but they are presented to give an example of how important it is to live and die for others. While everybody else is living for "vainglory" (verse 3), Jesus laid aside true glory, the glory He had had with the Father "before the world was." To save others! If we have our wits about us at all, we will see that we are only truly Christian when we humble ourselves and pour out our lives to save and build others — like Jesus did. But now another problem arises. How can we be expected to imitate His act of self-renunciation and ministry to others. Who are we? What glory do we have to lay aside? None at all, nothing but empty vain-glory, only a thing of sin and shame. Yet, each of us may "have the same mind;" each of us may let the mind of Christ be in us, that mind which led Him to leave "His own things" for the sake of "the things of others."

Take a final look at Jesus. While He was revealing the ultimate extreme of self-giving, His enemies unwittingly gave Him the greatest compliment ever paid Him. They said, "He saved others; Himself He cannot save" (Mark 15:31; Matthew 27:42). They were better theologians than they knew. Their words reveal the master principle of human redemption and the master lesson of Christian discipleship. If I am to be used of God, I cannot save myself. "He who would save His life shall lose it, but whoso would lose His life for My sake and the Gospel's, shall save it." If Christ had saved Himself from the Cross, He could not have saved us from sin. To save us, Himself He could not save.

"He saved others." He didn't save money, He didn't save His own skin, He saved *others.* This is a message that should produce delight in the hearts of sinners. All sinners need to be saved, and if Jesus saved others, then why shouldn't He save me? This is a message that should stimulate dedication in the hearts of saints. I should be doing the same thing that Jesus did, giving my life for the sake of others. But tragically, this is a message that will produce final despair in the hearts of some. He save others, but He didn't save me!

If His enemies had only realized it, even as they were sarcastically admitting that He had saved others, His very dying at that moment was to save *them!* But those hard-hearted men, by their own use of that word, *"others,"* placed themselves outside the reach of His saving grace. When they said, "He saved *others,"* they were necessarily saying, "He has not saved us." By that word, *"others,"* they excluded themselves. And it is still true that the only ones who are excluded from His salvation are the ones who are self-excluded. The only ones who *cannot* be saved are those who *will* not be saved.

"Others, Lord, yes, others, Let this my motto be,
And as I live for others, Let me live for Thee."

THE BIBLE AND DISCIPLE-MAKING

II Timothy 3:10-17:

"But you followed my teaching, conduct, purpose, faith, patience, love, perseverance, persecutions, and sufferings, such as happened to me at Antioch, at Iconium and at Lystra; what persecutions I endured, and out of them all the Lord delivered me! And indeed, all who desire to live godly in Christ Jesus will be persecuted. But evil men and impostors will proceed from bad to worse, deceiving and being deceived. You, however, continue in the things you have learned and become convinced of, knowing from whom you have learned them; and that from childhood you have known the sacred writings which are able to give you the wisdom that leads to salvation through faith which is in Christ Jesus. All Scripture is inspired by God and profitable for teaching, for reproof, for correction, for training in righteousness; that the man of God may be adequate, equipped for every good work" (NASV)

When Bible students mention Paul and Timothy, everyone recognizes that Timothy is Paul's disciple. This text and other passages in First and Second Timothy tell us what this means. These two letters are replete with lessons about disciple-making (as indeed, are all of Paul's letters). I would like to draw a one-line diagram that pictures a succession which shows how this process worked with Paul and Timothy.

PAUL ➡ 2 Tim. 3:14 and 2 Tim. 1:13 ➡ TIMOTHY

You will note that at the extremes of this line are the names of a discipler, Paul, and his disciple, Timothy. These two form one of the most dynamic duos of disciple-making to be found in the Bible. But what did disciple-making involve for the two of them? This is the topic of this study.

Let me explore the above one-line diagram more fully. Paul came into Timothy's life in Timothy's home town of Lystra (Acts 16:1). Because of their common interest in the Old Testament, Paul and Timothy's family came into instant rapport. "The jury is still out" with regard to the question of whether Paul led Timothy to Christ or not. Regardless of our conclusion, a discipler-disciple relationship was quickly established between them. This relationship is a great tribute to the Apostle Paul in showing how flexible he was in bridging an age gap and a personality gap between himself and Timothy. It is also a tribute to Timothy in that he consumed the butterflies in his stomach when Paul invited him on a mission trip and became one of the revered names of the New Testament's heroes of faith.

The one-line diagram shows the essential connection that must take place between discipler and disciple if Jesus' command to "turn people into disciples" (Matthew 28:19) is to be obeyed. Let me repeat that in a personal way: In the Great Commission, Jesus commanded every believer to "turn people into disciples." Look carefully at the two verses that are installed between Paul and Timothy in the diagram. II Timothy 3:14, a part of our text, says, "You, however, continue in the things you have learned and become convinced of, knowing from whom you have learned them." Several commanding grammatical features in this verse will enable us to understand it more fully. The word "you" near the head of the sentence bears major emphasis in the original (Greek) text. Actually, the text says, *su de*, which is "you but," which shows that the word "you" bears major emphasis. Paul has just been describing the corrupt climate, the evil environment that prevailed in the world at that time. Then he abruptly says, "But *you.*" Timothy, in the very nature of your relationship with Jesus, I am expecting a distinctive difference between you and others. Why? What made Timothy different? Jesus, to be sure, but not Jesus in a vacuum. Jesus manifested through relationships.

"*You*", however, continue in the things you have learned and become convinced of." The word translated "continue" is the same word Jesus used in the great "vine and branch" passage (John 15:1-8), where it is translated "abide." In our verse, it is a present active imperative, which means that it is an activity Timothy is to participate in by choice and commitment, and it is a command. Then note the word "learned," a word which occurs twice in the verse, and strategically, dominates the verse. The original word is *emathes*. An informed New Testament student should know that this is a form of the word *mathetes*, which is the Greek word which means "disciple." In our text the verb is an aorist active indicative, and it could be translated "you actively participated in the disciple-making process in a decisive way" and thus "became convinced of" the truths that were communicated to you. The same word occurs again at the end of the verse. Paul also mentions the disciplers who engaged Timothy in the process—"knowing from whom you have received your discipling." The word "knowing" is a form of *oida*, which means to "know by seeing," indicating that the discipling Timothy had received had been close-up and personal. Indeed, it was done by Lois his grandmother, Eunice his mother (see II Timothy 1:5 and 3:15a) and the Apostle Paul, and in each case, many congenial hours had been spent by each of them in personally discipling Timothy. Read II Timothy 3:14 again, and then we will go to the second verse listed in the one-line diagram.

The second verse installed between Paul and Timothy is II Timothy 1:13, which says, "Retain the standard of sound words which you have heard from me in the faith and love which are in Christ Jesus." The word translated "retain," or "hold fast" is a present imperative, which in effect means "take hold of and never let go." It pictures the tenacity in seeking and mastering truth in the life of every true disciple. "If ye continue in My words, then are ye My disciples indeed." Note also the word "standard" in this verse. It is the Greek word *hupotuposin*, a compound Greek word made up of a preposition (*hupo*) which means "underneath" and the word *tupos*, which means "type" or "pattern." The word "tupos" means "an exact impress," or a "form" or a "pattern." One Greek lexicon says that it means "a sketch for imitation." So Paul the disciple-maker has communicated to Timothy his disciple an "exact form of sound words," and he expects him to master and grasp it in the same form in which he communicated it. I have emphasized these words because this is the precise formula for making disciples.

Paul reminds Timothy that he had "heard these sound words from me (Paul)." In this sentence, three terms are given stress in the text. One is the word "standard," which bears *major* emphasis. Then the preposition term, "of sound words," bears *minor* emphasis. Later in the verse, the prepositional phrase, "from me," also bears *major* emphasis. These are gigantic ideas, and the study of the verse is not yet complete. The word "from" ("from me") is the word *para*, from which we get such words as "parallel" and "parable." It invariably refers to something nearby, expressing a relationship of immediate vicinity or proximity. It literally means, "by the side of," or "alongside." Could anything be clearer? Paul's discipling of Timothy did not take place essentially in a crowd or through platform communication (from a pulpit or teacher's podium). It took place "along the way" as Paul and Timothy lived and moved near each other. On those occasions, Paul often took Timothy alongside and "explained the way and the truth of the Lord more fully" to him. This is disciple-making. The verse closes with another prepositional phrase, "in the faith and love which are in Christ Jesus," indicating the sphere in which all of this discipling took place.

What a model for me as a disciple-maker! It is incumbent upon me by the command of Jesus to "turn people into disciples." I must linger in such Scriptural scenery as this until I am captured by the counsel it gives. If I were to place my name at the beginning of the one-line diagram, could I add at the other end the name of a disciple whom God has used me to build? Can I see the same results in my disciple as Paul saw in Timothy? Did the process I followed include the things clearly indicated in the two verses in the middle of the diagram? "Consider what I say, and the Lord give you understanding in all things" (II Timothy 2:7).

These introductory ideas form an excellent background for Paul's great statement at the end of the chapter concerning the inspiration and intended function of the Word of God. We have already seen that it is not possible to make New Testament disciples without a deliberate, steady personal transfer of Biblical truth from the discipler to the disciple (cf. JESUS!!!). Now, let's investigate more fully the role of the Bible in this process.

I. The Perfect ORIGIN of Scripture, 16a

First, Paul makes a classic statement about the *perfect origin* of Scripture. In II Timothy 3:16a, he says that "all Scripture is inspired by God." The phrase "inspired by God" is the translation of just one word in the Greek language. The word is *theopneustos*, which literally means "God-breathed." "All (every) Scripture is God-breathed." Nothing could be of greater importance than this claim. If it is not true, Christianity collapses at the point of authority. If it is true, Christianity stands in its total body of Biblical truth and is thus the determinant of each man's eternal destiny.

The Scriptures (the writings of the Bible) were breathed out by God Himself. That is, the Bible is the product of the breath of God. It is the claim of the Bible itself that the breath of God produced each Scripture, just as my breath produces my words, making them the vehicle of my thought.

Let me make three quick points about the origin of Scripture. First, the Scriptures were produced with the cooperation of the human writer. The Holy Spirit did not override the personality of any Biblical writer, though he might have overruled the writer on any number of occasions. When John writes, he sounds like John; when Peter writes, he sounds like Peter, etc. Second, the words of Scripture were chosen without consultation with the human writer. God chose, supervised, and guarded the very words of the text in order to insure that His Word was the product, not the words of a mere man. Third, the Scriptures were produced by a process that often left the human writer without full comprehension of the content of the text. If this is a question, I suggest that you study I Peter 1:10-12 with great care.

If you wish to pursue this truth further, let me encourage you to write for our other study on this theme entitled, "The Closer the Look, the Greater the Book." Meantime, we will hurry to our next point in this study.

II. The Plain OBJECTIVES of Scripture, 15, 17

Second, Paul indicates the *plain objectives* of Scripture. That is, he tells us the purposes for which God gave us the Bible. Let me mention the three purposes that are either stated or suggested in our text.

First, God gave us the Bible *for the evangelizing of sinners to bring them to salvation.* In his great letter to the Romans, Paul said, "Faith comes by hearing, and hearing by the Word of God" (Romans 10:17). In this text, he makes a great statement about the place of the Bible in the Christian life of his disciple, Timothy. In verse 15, he said, "From childhood (the word for infancy) you have known (again, 'known by seeing,' which suggests that someone modeled the Scripture and mouthed the Scripture to him close-up from his earliest life on earth) the sacred writings which are able to give you the wisdom that leads to salvation through faith which is in Christ Jesus." Note that Paul does not say that the Bible saves anyone, but that it makes sinners wise unto salvation by their exposure to its truth.

There is a great example of this use of the Bible in the story of Philip and the Ethiopian eunuch recorded in Acts 8:26-39. When Philip joined the eunuch on his chariot in Gaza, south of Jerusalem, as he traveled back toward his home in Ethiopia, he found the African man reading from the book of the prophet Isaiah (we know the text today as Isaiah 53, perhaps the greatest single prophecy of the coming Cross and Death of Christ in the entire Old Testament). Philip asked the eunuch, "Do you understand what you are reading?" The eunuch answered candidly, "How can I, except some man should guide me?" Then the eunuch added, "I ask you, of whom is the prophet speaking? Of himself, or of some other man?" Then the text strategically says, "Then Philip opened his mouth and preached unto him Jesus." The word translated "preached" comes from the same root word that gives us our word "Gospel." So it says that Philip opened his mouth and "good-newsed" this man to Jesus, or "good-newsed" Jesus to this man. "The rest of the story" informs us that the eunuch received and trusted Christ, was baptized in His Name, and "went on his way rejoicing." Here is an example of man's use of the Bible according to the Divine intention—to evangelize sinners to bring them to salvation.

Second, the Bible is *effective in the edifying of saints to advance their sanctification.* The four specified uses of the Bible mentioned in verse 16 all advance the sanctification of the saints of God. It is the Bible that challenges the disciple with a Divine standard of life and then the Holy Spirit (the author and interpreter and implementer of the Bible) changes him progressively so that his lifestyle is conformed to the Biblical standard. If the disciple has regular exposure to the content of Scripture, he is given opportunity to be more and more like Christ. When the Bible is known and believed, the believing Christian is progressively "set apart" for God's purpose to be fulfilled in his life. He will learn in first-hand relationship the meaning of the words, "beholding as in the mirror of the Word of God the glory of the Lord Jesus, you will go on being transformed into the image of Christ from one stage of glory to another, even as by the Spirit of the Lord" (II Corinthians 3:18).

Third, the Bible is to be used for *the equipping of the saints to bring them to service.* Paul says that by the proper use of Scripture, "the man of God may be adequate, equipped for every good work" (verse 17). Note the progression of the three key words. *Salvation* must lead to *sanctification,* and the saved/sanctified saint should be involved in a *service* that is clearly defined by Scripture (majoring on the making of disciples). I will discuss verse 17 at the end of this study, so I will only mention it here.

Salvation—sanctification—service. These three words cover the Divine intention for the entire life on earth of every human being. It is God's clearly declared and defined will that sinners be saved, and that the saved be sanctified, and that the saved/sanctified believers be mightily productive in their service for Jesus Christ. None of these crucial things can occur in the life of a human being independently of the Bible. No wonder Paul was so firm in insisting that there be a solid transfer of Biblical truth from himself to his disciple, and equally insisted that the disciple further transfer the received truth into the lives of many other disciples.

III. The Practical OPERATION of Scripture, 16b

Third, Paul reveals the *practical operation* of Scripture in the lives of God's people. He says that "all Scripture is profitable (valuable, beneficial, worthwhile) for teaching, for reproof, for correction, for training in righteousness." Of course, he is referring to God's intention for the use of the Bible in the lives of His children on earth. He mentions four practical purposes.

One, the Bible is profitable for *revelation.* "Profitable for teaching"—these are his exact words. Here again, we will see the "profit" of the Bible by engaging in a careful word study. Remember that Jesus said, "We live by every word that proceeds out of the mouth of God." I want to give you several exact quotes taken from a lexicon of Biblical words. The word translated "teaching" points us to four closely related words, and each of them is a gold mine as we think of disciple-making. The Greek word for teaching is the word *didache.* The lexicon says, "when this word is used in an active sense it means the art of teaching, instructing, tutoring. When used in a passive sense, it refers to the teaching which is presented, that which anyone teaches." A second closely related word is the Greek word *didasko*, which is the verb form meaning "I teach." Give careful attention to this exact quote from the lexicon: "*Didasko* has inherent in it the goal of the increase in understanding of the pupil and the adaptation of his character and conduct to what is being taught. Its counterparts are *akouo*, to hear for the purpose of understanding, and *manthano*, to learn, from which *mathetes*, learner, pupil, disciple, is derived. The one teaches and the other learns and assimilates the truth as part of himself. *Kerusso*, to preach, proclaim, does not inherently have the same expectation of learning and assimilation as *didasko* does. The thing aimed at when teaching is the shaping of the will, the life and the conduct of the pupil." Dear Christian, read and study this long paragraph carefully. It is loaded with echoes and implications of the Biblical concept of disciple-making.

 Let me continue in exploring the several Greek words that derive from the Greek word *didache*. Again, I am presenting literal quotes from a Greek lexicon. The third related word to consider is the word used in our text when Paul says that Scripture is "profitable for teaching." The word translated "teaching" in our text is the Greek word *didaskalia*. The lexicon defines this word as "that which belongs to a teacher; that which is taught, the teaching, the instruction. This is the word for doctrine. *Didaskalia* occurs fifteen times in Paul's three Pastoral Epistles—First and Second Timothy and Titus."

 When a believer understands the Biblical mandate to "make disciples," he will also understand why this word was so prominently used by the Apostle Paul. Teaching for the transfer of Divine truth is mandatory in disciple-making. Paul

THE BIBLE AND DISCIPLE-MAKING

says in our text that Scripture is profitable to give the discipler the body of doctrine, the teaching material, that he is to teach to a disciple. The discipler is not to "invent" new things to teach; he is simply to carefully and faithfully teach the revealed truths, the "doctrines," of the Bible.

Two, the Bible is profitable for *refutation*, or *reproof*, or *rebuke*. Christians often fail, they (far too) often sin, often become careless, often drift, often lose their focus on Jesus and His purpose, and when they do, they need reproof. To be exposed to the truth of the Bible is like placing a perfect plumb line beside a crooked wall. The crookedness is a good picture of the distortions that so easily occur in a believer's life. The plumb line is the perfect truth of the Word of God. When the Christian is so measured, the Word of God rebukes his iniquity. The usual course followed then is conviction, followed by confession, which leads in turn to cleansing and correction of the sin. Thus, the Word of God is profitable to correct him and advance his sanctification. "Correction" is the third profitable use of the Bible which Paul indicates.

Three, the Bible is profitable for *restoration*, or "correction." The Greek word used here is another loaded word. It is the word *epanorphosis*, which is a triple compound made up of the word *epi*, which means "to," the word, *ana*, which means "up," and the word *ortho*, which means "right" or "straight." So the word means "to restore to an upright state." This is the profit of the Bible when its truth is presented to an errant Christian and he accepts and believes it. He is set back on his feet in an upright state and it is now possible for him to move forward again in the purpose of Christ.

Finally, the Bible is profitable for *regulation*, or for "instruction in righteousness." Again, the word that is used is gigantic in its meaning. The word translated "instruction" is *paideian*. The root of this word is the Greek word for "child," and the word means "child-training." This is the same word that is used in the classic passage in Hebrews 12 about the chastisement or chastening of God's children. Most of our interpretations have done a terrible disservice to the doctrine of chastisement. We have presented it as a punitive practice on God's part, that is, as a punishment administered by God upon his sinning children. However, Biblically, chastisement is not for the purpose of punishment. The Christian's punishment for sin was totally absorbed by Jesus in his death on the Cross. God fully "settled up" with our sins when His Son died for them. So the discipline which God administers to each of His children is not for the purpose of punishment, but is remedial and corrective when they have sinned, and is for sanctification when administered otherwise. "Whom the Lord loves, He chastens." The word itself means "child-training." Because the word is based on the Greek word for a "child," and yet is often used as well for the same process in an adult believer's life, this word entails lifetime education, lifetime training. This is a very significant ingredient in the life of a disciple and a disciple-maker. You see, training is a big part of God's daily activity in our lives, and is to be a big part of our agenda with our disciples. These are the Biblically stated purposes for the practical operation of the Bible in a disciple's life.

IV. The Personal OUTCOME of the Proper Use of Scripture, 17

Finally, Paul points out the *personal outcome* that may be expected from the proper use of Scripture in a believer's life. The proper use of Scripture in a disciple's life has a purpose. Verse 17 is a long purpose statement. "In order that the man of God may be adequate, equipped for every good work." Again, the grammar of the verse is very important.

The term "the man of God" may either refer to the ordained pastor, preacher or evangelist, or it may generically refer to every Christian. I hold the conviction that it refers to every Christian. Every rule suggested here applies to every believer, not merely to officially ordained Christians. What happens when the principles of verses 15 and 16 are implemented in a believer's life?

First, there is an individual outcome, a result in the believer's *person*. When the Bible is properly used in his life, the believer is made "perfect" (KJV) or "adequate" (NASV). The Greek word is *artios*, which means "complete." It pictures a person or a thing that by its construction is able to meet all demands that are placed upon it. Note the word "construction." This is an excellent definitive word for disciple-making. Disciple-making should build believers, using the Bible and every other appointed means, to make the believer "complete." He should be made capable of performing any expected service, and this capability should be instilled primarily by the teaching and proper use of Scripture.

Then there is a vocational outcome, a result in the believer's *performance*. That the man of God may be adequate, equipped for every good work." Again, there are two terms of major emphasis in this closing verse. One is the word "adequate" or "complete." Dear Christian, God wants you to tackle every project He desires for you, fulfill every mandate He gives, assume every assignment He places upon you—and be adequate in accomplishing it. This is one reason why the regular intake of the Word of God and the intelligent implementation and teaching of it are mandatory in your life.

The other emphatic term (in this case, minor emphasis) is the term, "every good work." Note the comprehensiveness of God's expectation. And note, too, that this is an active assignment, involving "good works," not merely an institutional faithfulness. Each of us must honestly examine ourselves to see if God's expectation is being honored and fulfilled in our lives.

THE INFINITE IMPORTANCE OF ILLUMINATION

Ephesians 1:15-23:

"Wherefore I also, after I heard of your faith in the Lord Jesus, and love unto all the saints, Cease not to give thanks for you, making mention of you in my prayers; That the God of our Lord Jesus Christ, the Father of glory, may give unto you the spirit of wisdom and revelation in the knowledge of him: The eyes of your understanding being enlightened; that ye may know what is the hope of his calling, and what the riches of the glory of his inheritance in the saints, And what is the exceeding greatness of his power to usward who believe, according to the working of his mighty power, Which he wrought in Christ, when he raised him from the dead, and set him at his own right hand in the heavenly places, Far above all principality, and power, and might, and dominion, and every name that is named, not only in this world, but also in that which is to come: And hath put all things under his feet, and gave him to be the head over all things to the church, Which is his body, the fullness of him that fills all in all."

    The publishers of my Bible have added editorial paragraph summaries to the text of Scripture, attempting to help the reader discern the theme of the coming paragraph in each instance. Just before the text recorded above, they added the explanatory words, "A Prayer for Knowledge and Understanding." This assessment is reasonably accurate. I believe these words to contain the most important single prayer that any human being can pray for any other human being at any time. I simply do not believe that it is possible to pray a more important prayer for yourself or for any other human being.

Notice the mood that Paul was in when he prayed this prayer. The word "wherefore" (verse 15) indicates that he was in a very *thoughtful* mood. The word "wherefore" is a connecting word. When we read such a word in a text of Scripture, we should ask, "What is the *wherefore there for?* " In this case, the answer is absolutely overwhelming. When we inquire about the preceding thoughts and words, we discover that the Apostle Paul has just written the greatest single sentence ever written. It is an incredibly long sentence. So long, in fact, that it probably would not pass any grammatical structure test in any classroom on earth. But remember, Paul is not interested in grammar; he is only interested in grace! As far as I know and have been able to research, this is the longest sentence ever recorded in literature. The sentence is twelve verses long in the Biblical text, and some of the verses are lengthy by themselves! Paul has just written a celebration, a kind of hymn, of the Christian understanding of the grace of God. He has just verbally celebrated grace as the source, the reason, the cause, the producer, of our salvation.

The written celebration (verses 3-14) is divided obviously into three parts. The first part is made up of verses three through six, and ends with the refrain, "To the praise of the glory of His grace." The second "stanza" is made of verses seven through twelve, and ends with the chorus, "That we should be to the praise of His glory." And the third stanza is

THE INFINITE IMPORTANCE OF ILLUMINATION

comprised of verses thirteen and fourteen, and ends with the refrain, "Unto the praise of His glory." So the hymn has three stanzas, and they all end with essentially the same chorus.

The respective themes of the three stanzas are a delight to explore. The subject of the first stanza is the work *of God the Father* in accomplishing our redemption. And the "smaller" subjects in this stanza are fathomless. Paul writes of such things as "the heavenly places," "election," "holiness," "justification," "the love of God," "predestination," "adoption," and "the will and pleasure of God." No wonder his mind is soaring when he comes to our text. But he goes higher yet before he records the prayer of our text.

The subject of the second stanza is the work of *Jesus the Son of God* in securing our salvation. Such terms as "redemption," "his blood," "the forgiveness of sins," "the riches of His grace," His abounding wisdom and prudence, and the inheritance we have in Christ, comprise the themes of this second stanza. Paul's soul seems to soar right out of prose into spiritual poetry! He ascends the ladder of the stars as his spirit explodes in celebration, yet he is solid and deliberate in his verbal expression of these great treasures.

Stanza three presents the work of *the Holy Spirit of God* in securing our redemption. After Paul has given the order of the "saving steps," he writes about the Holy Spirit as a "seal" and an "earnest" in applying and protecting our salvation. He says, "you heard the word of truth, the Gospel of your salvation," and "you believed and trusted in Him," and then you were "sealed with the Holy Spirit of promise," and given "the earnest of our inheritance until the redemption of the purchased possession." And remember, the truths of these three packed stanzas form one single sentence. I say again: It is the greatest single sentence ever written! Paul ponders these great things, and then writes them down. No wonder he is in a thoughtful mood, and no wonder it leads him to pray this prayer for spiritual understanding. It is possible even to hear and read about such truths as this and be absolutely sterile of understanding. But Paul is mystical and meditative in heart and thoughtful in mind as he ponders and presents these great truths.

Then, Paul is in a *thrilled* mood, also. He says to the Ephesians Christians, "I heard of your faith in the Lord Jesus, and love unto all the saints." What a testimony! What a tribute to the Ephesian Christians! There is no pastor on earth who would not be absolutely ecstatic with joy and celebration if he could see these two things proliferating among his people "faith in the Lord Jesus, and love unto all the saints." Note several things. Note the word, "Lord," in referring to Jesus. The Ephesian Christians did not fragment Jesus into parts which could be dealt with separately. They had received a whole Christ to match their whole need. They did not think of dealing with Jesus as Savior at one time, and as Lord at another. They had "faith in the Lord Jesus."

And note the order of the two features of Christian experience which are mentioned. "Faith in the Lord Jesus" preceded "love unto all the saints." These two features have a cause and effect relationship in the Christian life. They are mutually inclusive and mutually exclusive in the Christian life. If one is present, they both will be. If one is absent, they both will be. Only the person who is rightly related to the Lord by faith will be rightly related to others in love. Faith in the Lord Jesus always leads to love unto all the saints. The presence of one indicates the presence of the other. Faith is the vertical relationship of the Christian life, and love is the horizontal relationship of it. So Paul is thrilled as he celebrates with the Ephesians the abundance of these things in their lives.

And Paul is in a *thankful* mood, also. He writes, "I cease not to give thanks for you, making mention of you in my prayers." The Greek word translated, "I give thanks" ("eucharisteo") is used twenty-three times by Paul, and only 14 times in the rest of the New Testament. What a statistic! Here is one of the gigantic secrets of Paul's incredible Christian life and influence. While everybody else thought, planned, prayed, and lived the Christian life for themselves, Paul's constant thought and conduct was "for you." While they lived "outside in," Paul lived "inside out," always toward someone else. He was constantly praying and thanking God for others.

What an introduction to the greatest of all possible prayers! Paul was in a thoughtful, thrilled, and thankful mood.

1. THE SEQUENCE OF THE REQUEST – 1:14

First, we will look at the *sequence*, or spiritual progression, which is climaxed by this great prayer. Note again the "wherefore" of verse 15. What is the "wherefore" *there for?* Paul has been straining at the leash of language, piling words on top of words, and all superlatives, to tell us that all that God is as Father, Son, and Holy Spirit is totally implicated in our total salvation. So the great truth of the Trinity is on high profile in verses three through fourteen. The doctrine of the Trinity is a high and holy mystery, just like God is. But it is a vital and indispensable mystery. The idea of the Trinity is far more relevant than we can imagine.

A book like Great Expectations, for example, may be regarded as a trinity. First, there was the essential idea in the mind of Charles Dickens. Nobody else knew the ideas at the beginning, apart from perhaps friends with whom he might share some of his ideas. Great Expectations thus existed as concept. But then, the book was published, and you could hold a copy in your hand and say, "This is Great Expectations." Now you have a manifestation or a concrete expression of the concept that continues to exist in the author's mind. Thus, you now have *two* <u>Great Expectations</u>, each of them distinct from the other, but both of them may be described as being <u>Great Expectations</u>. Finally, people read the book, grasp the concept, and may seek to put it into practice. Now, you have a *third* <u>Great Expectations</u>, this time in practice. The concept still exists, the book still exists, but now the concept manifested in the book finds realization. I bear personal testimony at this point. When I read Dickens' great novel, I saw that all fleshly and selfish expectations must be refined into gentleness and unselfishness, and that this likely takes place only through a process of suffering. So the author's idea, published in a book, became a means of insight and change in my life. Notice that all three have to exist – the book in *conception*, the book in *publication*, and the book in *action*. Any two would be insufficient by themselves. You must have a trinity.

A trinity is found in everything. In everything, there is a hidden inner nature (the *inner essence*), an exterior form (the *outward expression*), and a result (the *ongoing effect*). Suppose that I hold in my hand a fountain pen; suppose that you also hold (your own) fountain pen in your hand. Suppose that mine is a Parker and yours is a Schaeffer. They have the same *inner essence* in that they both are fountain pens. But they have a different *outward expression* in that each has the distinctive manufacturers form and trademark. And they both have an *ongoing effect*. You can write or mark with them. In fact, I could use my pen to sign my name on a piece of paper, mail the paper to central Africa, and the pen might still be held in my hand in Memphis, Tennessee. Understanding the limits of any finite illustration in addressing infinite truth, the inner essence of God is *God the Father;* the outward expression of God is *God*

THE INFINITE IMPORTANCE OF ILLUMINATION

the Son, and the ongoing effect of God is the work of *God the Holy Spirit.*

Salvation has been called "the house that Grace built." The *Architect* who provided the blueprint was God the Father; the *Contractor* who has purchased and supplied all the materials is God the Son; and the *Carpenter and Builder, the Constructor* who makes all applications to "materialize" the Finished Product, is the Holy Spirit.

Horace Bushnell was a teacher at Yale University before he became a famous preacher. Later he wrote, "When the preacher touches the mystery of the Divine Trinity and logic shatters it all to pieces, I'm glad I have a heart as well as a head. My heart wants the Father; my heart wants the Son; my heart wants the Holy Spirit and one just as much as the other. The Bible has a Divine Trinity for me; my heart says that I need that Trinity and I mean to hold by my heart." Give careful attention to the word "heart" in this statement. I have just completed the reading of a book by Peter Kreeft entitled, Heaven, the Heart's Deepest Longing. In his book, the author says, "Our desires go far deeper than our imagination or our thought; the heart is deeper than the mind." Blaise Pascal, the French philosophical genius, said, "The heart has reasons that reason knows not of." We must learn to trust the innate, natural, God-implanted instincts of the heart. When these are taught by Scripture, we find the deepest needs within us addressed and met through the truth and work of the Divine Trinity.

So the Apostle Paul has just celebrated the truth of the Trinity, and has shown us his mood as he ponders it and the Ephesian Christians. Now, he will record the prayer he prays for them in light of this great celebration. Remember the marginal title: "A Prayer for Knowledge and Understanding." Actually, it is a prayer for spiritual illumination. And what an incredible prayer it is.

II. THE SIGNIFICANCE OF ILLUMINATION, –1: 18

Next, we will attempt to see the *significance* of spiritual illumination, which is the subject of this great prayer. The effectiveness of any truth in our lives depends on our apprehension or understanding of it. If a truth only "sits there neatly arranged on the shelf," it won't move us very far.

Television has a "Discovery Channel," but the Bible is the greatest "discovery channel" in the world. But just as a TV set must be turned on, tuned in, and flooded with light for us to appreciate what the Discovery Channel reveals, so it is in our relationship with the Bible. It is not possible for the unaided human mind, regardless of its natural brilliance, to understand the mind of God in Scripture without the miracle of Divine illumination. Note this carefully; it is an absolute dogma. There is no understanding of the mind of God at any time without the miracle of illumination!

A family was entertaining another family of friends in their home for an evening of food and fellowship. After a good meal, they were all seated in the family den, visiting. The little four year old was playing quietly with toys in the floor. There was a lull in the conversation, and the four year old spoke into the silence, repeated something he had heard his older brother say as he was reciting his arithmetic assignment. "Two times two is four," the little boy said thoughtlessly. Suddenly, everyone gasped when they heard this erudite recitation from a four year old. The mother just knew that they had a child genius! She said proudly, "What did you say, dear? Say it again." The little boy, surprised at the attention he was receiving, said, "Two times two is four." And the two families expressed their amazement that a child so young could know so much. But suddenly, while they were discussing his brilliance, he interrupted and said, "Mommy, what's a two? "

THE INFINITE IMPORTANCE OF ILLUMINATION

You see, he had information without illumination, and this is precisely the problem with most of us.

Many of the sophisticated cameras of today have two shutters. One covers the lens, the other covers the film. To open one is to prepare the camera for use. To open the other is to snap the immediate picture. The one corresponds to the new birth, the other to illumination. The new birth is only the beginning. It gives the spiritual eyes, and prepares them for use. Thereafter, we need accurate understanding of every "immediate picture" that God brings before us. And this ongoing understanding comes to the individual exactly the same way the new birth comes by a miracle of Almighty God produced in the heart of the person. John Calvin said, "Illumination is like a pair of spectacles. Without it, our visions may be blurred, but with it, we can see clearly."

The Psalmist said, "In Thy light shall we see light." Go into a great cathedral at night. You can't see the astounding beauty of the windows because of the absence of the light. Go again at noon. The light makes the windows show their splendor. You had the power of sight before, but no light. What the sun is to those windows, the Holy Spirit is to the student of the Word of God. To see, we must have both sight and light. If we have sight but no light, we cannot see. But if we have light but no sight, we still cannot see. Both sight and light are indispensable for us to see.

A policeman saw a man crawling around on his hands and knees under a street light, searching with his hands through the grass. The policeman approached, spoke to the man, and discovered that he was drunk. "What are you looking for?" the policeman asked. "I lost my wallet," the drunk man replied. The policeman joined the pitiful drunk and began searching with him. After a considerable time of fruitless search, the discouraged policeman asked, "Sir, are you sure you lost the wallet here?" "Why, of course not," mumbled the drunk. "I lost it back down the street." "What!" exclaimed the policeman, "Then why are you looking for it here?" "Because there ain't no light back there!" the drunk sighed. Whatever his folly, his reasoning was accurate. You need light as well as sight in order to see. At the new birth, God issues to his newborn child a "new set of eyes." Then, at each occurrence of illumination, he turns on the light so those eyes can see clearly. So this prayer of Paul is crucial if we are to understand the things of God.

Only God can reveal God! There are three indispensable factors in God's Divine disclosure of Himself: 1. Revelation (some call it "manifestation"), in which God discloses Himself; 2. Inspiration, the *recording* of revelation; and 3. Illumination. Revelation and Inspiration are objective; Illumination is subjective.

Unaided intelligence gives you your point of view; illumination gives you God's point of view.

III. THE SOURCE OF ILLUMINATION – 1:17a, b.

Next, Paul identifies the nature and *source* of illumination. Verse eighteen uses the word "heart." The King James Bible translates it "understanding," but the Greek word is "kardia," from which we get our word, "cardiac." This does not merely refer to man's intellectual understanding. It refers to "the eyes of the heart." Misguided by our everyday use of the word, we have forgotten that in the Bible, "heart" means every area and function of the personality.

Paul uses a remarkable phrase in Ephesians 1:18: "the eyes of your *heart.*" So every believer has two pairs of eyes. One pair is in his head, and the other pair is in his heart. He received the eyes in his head at physical birth, and he received the eyes of his heart at spiritual birth. But just as the eyes of his head must be trained and developed after birth for proper use, the eyes of the heart must be trained and developed after the new birth. Our hearts have eyes by which we are to see (all things) from the depths of our personality. But this "seeing" requires spiritual illumination.

Paul reveals the *source* of this illumination of the heart in verse 17. He tells the Ephesians that he is praying for them, "That the God of our Lord Jesus Christ, the Father of glory, may give unto you the spirit of wisdom and revelation." "Wisdom" is the understanding and appropriation of Divine truth. "Revelation" is the disclosure, the "unveiling," of God and His truth. Note the order of these words in the text. Why this order? You might expect that revelation would be mentioned first, then wisdom, but such is not the case. In Genesis one, God created light before He created the material universe. Why? Because, no matter how many worlds He created, no matter how many eyes He made, there would have been no sight without light. The same is true in spiritual experience. He gives wisdom with which to understand (the *means* to see), then He begins to bring His revelation (the *thing* to see) before us.

IV. THE SUBJECT OF ILLUMINATION – 1:17c

The *subject* of this illumination is "the knowledge of Him." There are three kinds of knowledge: 1. "I – it" knowledge, which we may call *scientific* knowledge; 2. "I – you" knowledge, which we may call *social* knowledge; and 3. "I –Thou" knowledge, which we may call *spiritual* knowledge. The basic, ultimate, eternal knowledge is relational knowledge, one's knowledge of God, himself, and others. This is reflected in the "great commandment," the duty to "love God with all your heart, mind, soul, and strength," and the second great commandment, which is to "love your neighbor as yourself."

The greatest knowledge of all is the knowledge of God through His Son, Jesus Christ. In fact, Jesus said, "This is life eternal, that they may know Thee, the only true God, and Jesus Christ, Whom Thou hast sent" (John 17:3). To know God *personally* is salvation; to know God *progressively* is sanctification; and to know God *perfectly* is glorification.

"Ready information is everywhere;
Relation insight is all too rare."

V. THE SUBSTANCE OF ILLUMINATION – 1:18b, 23

Now we come to the most incredible part of the prayer. Now we will see why this matter of illumination is so vital and urgent. Verse 18 says that the purpose of this illumination, or "heart seeing," is "that you may know." The word "know" is "oida," which is distinctively not the word for intellectual or academic knowing, the knowing you do by the use of your mind, your brain, your reason, your intelligence. The word "oida" means "to know by seeing." This is the intuitive spiritual seeing of the heart, and requires that the eyes of the heart be opened and flooded with Divine light, a miracle of the Holy Spirit. When this occurs, a blind person can accurately say, "Oh, I see!" Helen Keller was likely referring to this when she said, "I would rather be blind the way I am blind, and see the way I see, than to see the way many people do, and be blind the way they are blind." Think over these words carefully. A reporter asked Miss Keller, "Is there anything worse than to be without organic sight?" She quickly replied, "Oh, yes, there is one thing much worse, and that is to have sight without vision." But remember, true vision is an absolute miracle of God!

And what does the illumined person "know by seeing"? Verses 18 and 19 have been called "the prayer of the three `whats.'" When the eyes of my heart are opened by a miracle of God, I discover that: 1. I don't have to *protect* myself because God has provided perfect *security* for me; 2. I don't have to *prove* myself because God has provided perfect *significance* for me; and 3. I don't have to *provide* for myself because God has supplied perfect *sufficiency* for me. These insights are conveyed through the three "what" clauses of verses 18 and 19. We will now attempt to examine and explain the content of these three "what" clauses. These three "whats," these three objects of the prayer for illumination are the greatest and most vital areas of human life, and the answer to this prayer solves the three greatest problems in a believer's life.

A man is lost in a forest. He is in darkness and danger. A storm shatters the silence, and the lightning illumines the darkness. The fool will look at the lightning; the wise man will look at the road that lies illuminated before him. The quest for illumination has its own peculiar and massive dangers, the dangers of egocentricity and superiority, the dangers of diabolical pride. Psalm 119:130 says, "The entrance of Thy words giveth light; it giveth understanding to the simple." So we must ask God for this "simplicity" of heart and spirit, and for the proper "entrance of His words" into our minds and hearts, and for the light that will enable us to see and appreciate these three incredible "whats."

The telescope was "accidentally" discovered by a Dutch spectacle maker. Spectacle making involves handling lenses which need to be checked and this involves looking through them. It was during such an examination that the spectacle maker found himself looking through not one, but two lenses. To his surprise the magnification of the lens combination was much greater than that of a single lens. In placing the two lenses at opposite ends of a tube, the telescope was invented. Again, the "accident" "happened" to a careful and diligent researcher (!!). In spiritual matters, the "serendipities," or "happy surprises" ("accidents"?!), happen to the diligent researchers, also. The two indispensable ingredients are *heart-hunger* and humility. John Baillie wisely said, "I am sure that the bit of the road that most requires to be illuminated is the point where it forks." Much damage is done in the community of believers because we rush ahead roughly and crudely, without illumination, at the forks of the road, the forks of dispositional differences, doctrinal differences, etc. So we must approach this great territory boldly, but humbly.

First, Paul prays that God may open the eyes of the heart and flood them with light, so that the Christian may know by seeing "what is the hope of his calling. " At first glance, these words sound so very innocent. They evoke a yawn and a "Ho, hum." But once you examine them thoroughly and carefully, you see why the reader needs illumination. This is a vast treasure, but it appears at first glance to be of little worth. There are two words which require attention and definition and interpretation. One is the word "hope," the other is the word "calling." In both cases, these words do not mean in the New Testament what we mean when we use them in everyday conversation today. For example, consider the word, "calling." Today, a "calling" is an inviting, or a vocation. But in the New Testament, the word "calling" is the all-inclusive word for Divine salvation. So we see immediately that this first "what" is infinitely bigger than it first appeared to be.

Then consider the word, "hope." Again, the word is vastly bigger and more meaningful than even our big word "hope." To us, hope is wish-projection, or wishful thinking. It is the desire for something projected into the future. But in the New Testament, the word "hope" has another dimension to it. It is identified in the New Testament as "a sure and certain hope." So there is no degree of uncertainty in the New Testament use of the word, "hope." But uncertainty is a very

THE INFINITE IMPORTANCE OF ILLUMINATION

significant part of our modern word "hope." So the New Testament word would be accurately translated, "guarantee," or "assurance." Eureka! What a serendipity this is!

So the prayer of Paul is that the eyes of the believer's heart will be opened up and flooded with light, in order that He may "know by seeing" how absolutely guaranteed his salvation is. Think of this: It is God's intention that every believer have absolute, unconditional, perfect assurance of His salvation. Do you see now why I earlier said that the believer no longer has to prove himself, because God has provided perfect, inviolable, invulnerable, invincible security for him! The reason for this is vital. Only secure people will ever serve God. Insecure people cannot serve God; they must serve themselves, seeking the security that eludes them outside of Christ.

Every person outside of Christ is a nobody seeking to make of himself a somebody, but every person in Christ (though many don't know it) is everything to the most important Person in the universe; thus, he can easily volunteer to be nothing, because he cannot lose what he has in Christ. Once he is truly in Christ, he is perfectly secure! So this prayer is a petition that each Christian will realize His *perfect security* in Christ. But look around you. It is easy to see that most Christians (yes, truly born again people) act regularly out of insecurity instead of security. Why? Because the first "what" has never been deeply and richly illuminated to the eyes of their hearts. Is this an important prayer or what?

Now, look at the second "what" in this prayer. Paul prays that the eyes of your heart may be flooded with light, that ye may "know by seeing what are the riches of the glory of his inheritance in the saints. " Again, careful consideration must be given to the words, and Divine illumination must disclose their meaning to our hearts (see II Timothy 2:7).

Question: what "inheritance" is being considered here? Be very careful. Our first tendency would be to answer: The believer's inheritance in Christ, or what I received when I became a Christian. But that is not what the verse says! In fact, the believer's inheritance in Christ has already been discussed in the preceding verses of Ephesians one (verse eleven). No, the inheritance here is God's inheritance in the saints! You see, Christ and His estate are the believer's inheritance, but the Christian is God's inheritance. Study the Old Testament, and note how many, many times His people are identified as God's "portion," God's "lot," God's "treasure," God's "inheritance." This is the idea here. Christians are God's inheritance, God's treasure. From God's viewpoint, He came into possession of something extremely valuable when He saved you.

So what did God get when He got you? Can you believe it? He says that He got rich! Paul speaks of the "riches of the glory of His inheritance in the saints." You, dear Christian, are God's precious treasure. Now, the Christian who looks at himself and thinks only with his own mind will say, "You gotta be kidding! I am the most worthless creature in the universe. The God who would become rich by getting me must not have much of an inventory!" But again, we must put on the lenses of Heaven. We must think with the mind of God. We must see with the eyes of Christ.

Just how much is a Christian really worth, anyway? Are you ready to get blown clean away? Every Christian on earth is exactly equivalent in value to Jesus Christ Himself in God's eyes! How do we know that? Because that is exactly what God paid for me – Jesus Christ Himself! Now, none of us could make the claim that we are inherently as valuable as Jesus is. And if we made such a claim, nobody would believe us. But this is the whole point. The value referred to here *is conferred value,* not mere inherent value.

THE INFINITE IMPORTANCE OF ILLUMINATION

Suppose that I am very, very rich. I assure you, that is a supposition! Then suppose that you own a grocery store. That, also, is likely a supposition. Then suppose that I walk into your store today and say to you, "I have come in to buy a Classic Coke and I am prepared to pay twelve million dollars for it." What should you do? Certainly! Ask me if I would be interested in a six-pack of Cokes at the same rate, or an entire case of Cokes! As stupid as the illustration is, it enables us to consider a vital truth. The value of an article is not determined by the price tag that appears on it on the shelf; it is determined by the willingness and capability of the purchaser. When God showed Himself willing and able to pay Jesus Christ to purchase me to Himself, He conferred upon me an unbelievable value. Ephesians 1:14 refers to the believer as God's "purchased possession," and verse seven tells us that the price of purchase was the life, yes, the death, the blood, of Jesus Christ Himself. So God has conferred on every Christian the exact value of Jesus Himself.

Several years ago a painting entitled *Irises* by Vincent van Gogh sold for $53.9 million. Now the canvas and paint were barely worth $10 by today's standards, yet Alan Bond, an Australian financier, was willing to pay an incredible sum for this work of art. Yes, incredible!

At another auction, Pablo Picasso's *Acrobat and Young Harlequin* was bought for $38.46 million. It was purchased by a Japanese buyer who became quite emotional over the acquisition. Well, I would have gotten emotional, too, but for an altogether different reason! The buyer was so excited to have this wonderful masterpiece that he paid that vast price without questioning it.

Would you think any differently of yourself if someone very famous and important regarded you as a treasure of incalculable value, like a great work of art, a masterpiece? Dear

Christian, that is the you God sees! Ephesians 2:10 says, "You are God's workmanship." The word is "poiema," a work of art, a masterpiece!

But wait a minute! Isn't God looking through blind eyes when He confers such worth on someone like me? Is God realistic when He buys me at the cost of Jesus? Remember, dear friend, that this is conferred worth. By the transaction of purchase, God confers on you the value of Jesus. But God is certainly not stupid. He knows that you are not inherently as valuable as Jesus. So He confers on you the value of Jesus by the purchase of Calvary and then, in order to justify His investment, He sets out immediately after you come into His possession to make you like Jesus! What a *Gospel* this is!

Suppose you inherit a gold mine. You're absolutely elated. You love that gold mine. But the first time you go out to inspect your new treasure, the gold says to you, "How can you possibly love me? I'm all dirty. I'm all mixed up with that awful iron ore, and I have that filthy clay all over me. I'm contaminated with all kinds of alloys and mineral deposits. I'm ugly and worthless." "Oh, but I do love you," you reply to the gold. "You see, I understand what you can become. I know you have all these imperfections, but I have plans for you. I am not going to leave you the way you are now. I am going to purify you. I am going to get rid of all that other stuff. I see your real worth, though it only appears now as potential. I know that the alloys and mineral deposits are not the true you you are just temporarily mixed up with them. I warn you, it won't be easy. You will go through a lot of heat and pressure. But look at this piece of gold jewelry. Isn't it beautiful? That's what you are. Left to yourself, you would remain in this dark place, buried in the dirty ore. But I know how to change you from what you are now to what you can be. I will make you beautiful, and you will make me rich! " Now, dear Christian,

THE INFINITE IMPORTANCE OF ILLUMINATION

read the second "what" again, being sure to put on the "God-glasses" of illumination first.

Do you see why I earlier said that 1 don't have to prove myself any longer, because God has provided me with perfect significance? I am His cherished treasure! So this prayer is a petition that each Christian will realize his *personal significance* in Christ.

Now, we come at last to the final "what" of Paul's prayer. "I pray that the eyes of your heart might be flooded with light, that you may know by seeing what is the exceeding greatness of God's power toward us who believe. " So the third "what" of this prayer has to do with *personal sufficiency*. It has to do with "God's power" in our lives. Paul shows that this power is *defined* power (verse 19) and *demonstrated* power (verses 2023). In defining God's power that is to be operable in our daily lives, Paul uses four words in verse nineteen. He speaks of "the exceeding greatness (the word means to "throw immeasurably beyond," a picture of great magnitude) of God's power toward us who believe, according to the working of God's mighty power." One word for power in this verse is the Greek word, "dunamis", from which we get our English word "dynamic." This word essentially means capability or potential A second is the word "energeia," which gives us our words "energy" and "energize." This word means effective or operational power. A third word is "kratos," which refers to power that is exercised in resistance or control. And the final word is "ischuos," which indicates inherent, vital power. So again, Paul strains at the leash of vocabulary to show us how great is the character dynamic that is available to the believer in Christ.

But Paul doesn't stop with mere words which define God's power. He also points to certain events which *demonstrate God's* power. You see, when the Bible wants to impress us with the *love* of God, it points us to the Cross of Christ. When it wants to impress us with the *power* of God, it points us to the Resurrection and Exaltation of Christ. So Paul says that God's power was "wrought in Christ" when God *enlivened Him from the dead* and *exalted Him in glory.* In his words, this power was wrought in Christ "when God raised Him from the dead, and set Him at His own right hand in the heavenly places, far above all principality, and power, and might, and dominion, and every name that is named, not only in this world, but also in that which is to come, and has put all things under His feet, and made Him to be head over all things to the church, which is His Body, the fullness of Him that fills all in all." So He declares that the same power which elevated Jesus to a position of glory is available to elevate us to a life of Divine sufficiency. I emphasize again that this power is available to us for the sake of building our own character and exerting character impact upon others.

Do you see why I said earlier that I don't have to *provide* for myself because God has supplied perfect *sufficiency* for me? So this prayer is a petition that each Christian will realize his *powerful sufficiency* in Christ. However, again we must sadly admit that these expressions of power are foreign to the experience of most Christians. And we must again guess that one of the primary causes for the dearth of power is a lack of illumination. Most Christians are sadly blind to the great character power that is available to them.

Dr. C. I. Scoffield related an illustrative story from his preaching ministry. He was in a Bible Conference in the city of Staunton, Virginia, many years ago. The week had been especially busy, with two services daily and a round of other activities. On Friday night, a kind layman invited Dr. Scoffield to visit his workplace on Saturday in order to have a little relief from the press of people and the pressure of communication.

THE INFINITE IMPORTANCE OF ILLUMINATION

He accepted the invitation and went with the man the next morning. He discovered that he was being taken to a mental institution which the layman managed. They casually toured the grounds, visiting along the way, then they entered the main building. As they walked down the long central hallway through the building, a heavily muscled man came toward them, though he was walking with the shuffling gait of a mental patient. As he came near, Dr. Scoffield stepped aside to let him pass, marveling at the muscled strength of his body. When he was out of earshot, Dr. Scoffield said to his host, "Man, you must have a real problem when *he* gets angry and goes on a rampage! It has been a long time since I have seen such a strong man." But the manager's answer surprised the preacher. "Oh, no, Doctor Scoffield," he replied, "that man is no problem at all. You see, as strong as he is, he is in this institution because he has the illusion of weakness. He thinks that he is so weak that he can't even lift a spoon full of food or a glass of water to his lips. Someone else must do it for him." Later that day, the Holy Spirit spoke to the preacher about the visual parable he had seen that morning. "My child, you have just seen a picture of the typical Christian of today, and the typical church. While the great power of God is perfectly available to those who believe, instead *they struggle under an illusion of weakness.* " Friends, the primary difference between the Christian suffering under the illusion of weakness and the Christian functioning in the efficiency of God's power is the *miracle of illumination.*

Christian, what you see is what you will be within the limits of God's revealed truth. What you behold is what you will become. I repeat, this is the most important prayer that any Christian can pray for another, and when this prayer is answered in a Christian's life, he has just become the recipient of the first great blessing toward total victory in Christ. By means of the miracle of illumination, the problems of *insecurity, insignificance, and insufficiency* are solved for the believer.

The Psalmist said to God, "In Thy light shall we see light." "The entrance of Thy words giveth light; it giveth understanding to the simple" (Psalm 119:30). As God gives us grace to see, His story becomes ours, His vision becomes ours, His concerns become ours, and His vocation becomes ours. So illumination is a continual necessity in disciple-making. Lord, you have given sufficient light; now, give us sufficient sight.

THE CHURCH, THE BODY OF CHRIST

I Corinthians 12:12-27:

"Now you are the body of Christ and individually members of it. And God has appointed in the church first apostles, second prophets, third teachers, then miracles, then gifts of healing, helping, administrating, and various kinds of tongues. Are all apostles? Are all prophets? Are all teachers? Do all work miracles? Do all possess gifts of healing? Do all speak with tongues? Do all interpret? But earnestly desire the higher gifts. And I will show you a still more excellent way."

The New Testament employs several meaningful figures of speech when it speaks of the relationship that prevails between Christ and His Church. For example, it speaks of that relationship in terms of a "building," with Christ being the foundation and chief cornerstone and believers the "living stones" in the building. Again, it speaks (some say it only *suggests* this picture) of the church as the "Bride" of Christ. But no symbol is so familiar and so forceful as the figure of the "body." "So we, though many, are one body in Christ, and individually members one of another" (Romans 12:5). Note that the Bible does not say that the church is "like" a body. There is more intended here than an apt illustration. It is plainly indicated in the New Testament that the church is not an organization but an *organism*, not a society formed by men but a body created and indwelt by the Spirit of God and composed of living souls united by faith to a living Lord.

The Church of Jesus Christ has been brought into being and its growth has been secured by the power of the Holy Spirit. On the day of Pentecost the followers of Christ were united into one body by the Holy Spirit. To this body, by the influence of the same Spirit, 3000 souls were added, and ever since that day all who accept Christ as Lord and Master are brought by His Spirit into membership with His body. "By one Spirit are we all baptized into one body." As we look at the verses of our text, some of the glory of the church as the body of Christ begins to unfold.

I. THE VARIETY AND DIVERSITY WITHIN THE BODY

First, our text tells us something of the *variety and diversity within the body*. "There are diversities of gifts . . . there are differences of administrations . . . there are diversities of operations" within the body of Christ. "The body is one, and hath many members." "The body is not one member, but many." "Now ye are the body of Christ and members in particular." The church is like the human body, which has eye, ear, tongue, foot, hand, heart and many other different members. The multiplicity and variety of the members make for enrichment and growth. No one organ of the body can do the work of the whole body. All of the parts are different. They are different in what they do and where they are and the honor they receive; yet all of their differences emphasize their essential oneness, because they thus *complement each other* and *complete the whole*.

THE CHURCH, THE BODY OF CHRIST

A backward look to the long ago will show how long God has been doing business like that. Go to the backside of the desert, even into the mountain of God, Mt. Horeb. God had a job that He wanted done, so He gave Moses the gift of prayer and intimate fellowship with Himself, but to Aaron He gave the gift of speech. Together they formed the "body" of leadership for the children of Israel. One was the head, the other was the mouth. Each working in his own realm fulfilled the purpose of God and achieved His will.

Many years and thirteen chapters later in Exodus, we find another story illustrating one "body" with many members. Joshua, the young leader, was given the gift of military leadership. He was the fighter. There he was down on the plains, leading his troops in the dust and heat of battle. High on the mountainside overlooking the battlefield was Moses—now an old man, but still with the gift of prayer. There he was praying, while Moses fought. Standing behind Moses were Aaron and Hur. Perhaps they were not much when it came to prayer, but they *could* stand close and hold up the old man's hands. All together, they won a battle that day; Joshua fighting, Moses praying, and Aaron and Hur holding up his hands. Even so, within the church there are all varieties of service, of function, all varieties of people. "We have a God of infinite variety." It has been sheer tragedy that the Church has gone on so often, through the centuries, as though these words were never written. Many followers of Christ have gone on trying to put God's people into one mold, one type. Joseph Parker once complained, "The church has been a great brick maker." It has often worked perversely to press people into the same mold and size. The church is the body of Christ, and like the human body, the members are different and perform different functions. There is great variety within the body of Christ.

II. THE UNITY OF THE BODY OF CHRIST

Then our text tells of something of the *unity of the body of Christ*. The body of Christ is unified by "the same Spirit . . . the same Lord . . . the same God" (verses 4-6). "As the body is one, and hath many members, and all the members of that one body, being many, are one body: so also is Christ" (verse 12). "And whether one member suffer, all the members suffer with it; or one member be honored, all the members rejoice with it."

The unity of the body of Christ is derived by the union between the members of the body and the Head of the body, Jesus Himself. If the church is the "body of Christ," then the self-giving, crucified, risen Christ can never be far from the center of the church's life. The word "body" suggests something which is vital and alive. The physiologist tells of the millions of cells in the human body. We are like those cells, many in number, diverse in function, yet united in the life which animates the body. The body lives in relation to the head. A body without a head is without life. A head without a body is without action and expression. We have tried to think of the church as just another organization. We have often divorced it from Christ. But the head cannot work without the body. The body cannot function without the head. Only as the body responds to the direction, the wooing, of the head can there be any effective action. There must be co-ordination between head and body. And just as the members in the natural body are one because they are nourished by the same blood, so the true bond of Christian unity lies in the common participation in the life of the one Lord Jesus Christ. It is important to see that the Bible never writes about a body of Christians; it is the body of Christ.

It is not only the *life* of the body, but also the *usefulness* of the body, that derives from Christ the Head of the body. In the human body much depends upon the afferent and the efferent nerves. The efferent nerves are the "out-going" nerves connecting the brain to outward appendages of the body; the afferent nerves are the "in-coming" nerves connecting the appendages with the brain. Let a pin prick touch our body and at once a message is sent to the head by the afferent nerve and immediately a response comes back to the member through the efferent nerve. In this light we can understand that when anything touches the Christian at any point of the church, Christ, the Head, is aware of it and responds immediately. The sensitivity of the Head to everything which affects His body is clear.

When there is *mutual cooperation* between the Head and the members of the body, the church is the *working* body of Christ. In Ephesians 4, provision is made for different ministries within the working body of Christ, but no provision is made for non-working members. Christ dwelt within the body and life of Jesus of Nazareth. His desire now is to live within the life of the members of His body. The body of Jesus of Nazareth once did the work and will of Christ. Now His disciples are His body and must do His work and will. And the purpose of this "re-incarnation" of Jesus in His body today is *that Christ Himself may be seen* just as He was seen in His body 2000 year ago. A good stained-glass window is made up of thousands of tiny pieces of colored glass held together by some cementing agent. Each Christian is like a piece of colored glass in a total picture depicting Christ. The church, the communion of saints, is the body of Christ. The cementing agent holding the saints together is the Holy Spirit. Created by union with the Head and the penetrating energy of His Spirit, there is unity within the body of Christ.

There is one implication of this unity which needs to be recognized and explored in practice in every local body of

Christ. If we are members of the same body, then we are members of one another. Several nights ago, I got up in the middle of the night to get a drink of water. As I walked into the dark kitchen, I ran into a carton of cokes that had been used as a doorstop during the day. The timing was perfect. I struck the carton hard on the little toe of my left foot. Immediately my whole body reacted! My lips cried out, my eyes swam with tears, my hands grabbed and massaged the injured spot, and the other foot suddenly took on the weight of the whole body—in fact, the whole body suffered! The same is true (or should be) when a member of the body of Christ is damaged, offended, or is out of fellowship with the other members! "If one member suffers, all the members suffer with it; or if one member is honored, all the members rejoice with it." When the body is healthy, there is marvelous unity within it.

III. THE DIGNITY AND RESPONSIBILITY OF EACH MEMBER OF THE BODY

Finally, our text tells us some important things about *the dignity and responsibility* of each individual member in the body. In verses 15 through 24, the Apostle Paul explores some of the members of the body to show that each member has its own distinctive dignity and its own individual responsibility. "Members in particular" indicates that the place and the function of each is ordained of God. Each member has offices to discharge for the benefit of each other member. In the Christian community, as in the organism of the body, the active co-operation of all the parts is the condition of health.

One of the famous Aesop's fables graphically illustrates the function and importance of each member of the body. "In former days there was a quarrel among the members of the human body. Each part professed itself indignant at being obliged to work for the stomach, which remained idle and enjoyed the fruits of their labor. They one and all resolved to rebel and grant it supplies no longer, but to let it shift for itself as well as it could. The hands protested that they would not lift a finger to keep it from starving. The mouth wished it might never speak again if it took the least bit of nourishment for the stomach as long as it lived. The teeth refused to chew for it so much as a morsel for the future. The solemn covenant was kept as long as anything of that kind can be kept, which was till each of the rebel members pined away to skin and bone and could hold out no longer. Then they found there was no doing without the stomach and that, as idle and insignificant as it seemed, it contributed as much to the maintenance and welfare of all the other parts as they did to its welfare." Each member in the body has its own respective dignity and responsibility.

The Apostle Paul reveals this in the most graphic way in our text. In verses 15-20, he deals with the supposed "inferior" members and functions of the body. Then, in verses 21-24, he deals with the supposed "superior" members and functions of the body. In verses 15-20, Paul speaks of the *"foot,"* the *"hand,"* the *"ear,"* and the *"eye."* He also suggests the *nose* by a reference to "smelling." The "foot" stands for the *pedal* work of the body; the "hand" stands for the *manual* work of the body; the "ear" stands for the *aural* work of the body; the "eye" stands for the *optical (visual)* work of the body; the nose stands for the *nasal* work of the body. If you are a Christian, you perform one of these functions, or a similar one, in the body of Christ. I pray that none of us will become paralyzed limbs, but that each of us will be quick to respond to the dictates of the Head. May all members of the body be motivated and moved by the Head!

We must be careful to understand the message of our text. In verses 15 and 16, Paul supposes a theoretical case in which the foot and the ear, which are *inferior* to the hand and the eye, declare that they do not need these members in the body. However, *all* members are necessary and essential to the healthy functioning of the total body. The body cannot "go" without the feet. The body cannot "serve" or "do" without the hand. The body cannot "hear" without the ear. The body cannot "see" without the eye. The "inferior" foot and ear cannot spurn the "superior" hand and eye without injuring *themselves*. Then, in verse 21, the eye and the head, which are *superior* to the hand and the feet, declare that they do not need these members of the body. However, the "superior" eye and head cannot spurn the "inferior" hand and feet without injuring *themselves*. "God hath tempered the body together" (verse 24), and every member has dignity and responsibility.

Look closely for a moment at the functions Paul mentions, and seek to locate *your own* dignity and responsibility.

First, he mentions the "foot" (verse 15), the "feet" (verse 21). The feet represent the mobility of the body. How important are the "feet" in the body of Christ! They enable the body to fulfill the first mandate of the Great Commission, "Go!" How many there are who seem to be in the body, but never *go*, and don't seem to sympathize with those who do!

Second, Paul mentions the "hand" (verses 15 and 21). The hand represents the manual work of the body. "Do with your might what your hand finds to do."

This thought was beautifully expressed in an incident that happened in a little village in France after the war. A detachment of soldiers had been left as occupational troops to keep order in the town. Time hung heavy on their hands. One day they decided to help the villagers restore their bombed homes and city. They started on the church. It was a big job, for the church had received a direct hit. They worked joyously

THE CHURCH, THE BODY OF CHRIST

and cheerfully, cleaning up debris, putting back the windows, and rebuilding the pews. Amid the debris they found a marble statue of Christ. It was badly broken, but they managed to cement it together and set it up in its niche in the wall. But search as they would, they could not find the *hands* for the statue of Christ. And so when they had finished arranging the statue in its place, a moment of inspiration came to one of them. He made a placard and hung it on the statue. These simple words were printed on it. "He has no hands but yours." There is plenty of manual work that needs to be done day by day and week by week. Could this be *your* function?

Third, Paul mentions the "ear" (verse 16). There is a crucial need for hearing in today's church. We live in a noisy world. The din has dulled our sense of hearing. How important it is that the body of Christ "lend an ear" to God and to man! We do not read of Jesus ever talking to His disciples on how to speak. He talked much about how to hear. He said, "Take heed how you hear." Does the church need a hearing aid? Perhaps, but most of all, it needs functioning ears! Could this be *your* function in the body?

Fourth, Paul mentions the "eye" (verses 16 and 21). The eye is the symbol of spiritual vision. The church needs open eyes and unimpeded vision! "Where there is no vision, the people perish." Could this be *your* function?

Finally, Paul mentions the "smelling," or the nose (verse 17). Paul seems to shrink from naming some Christians as nasal men, but he does imply their existence (and their necessity) in the phrase, "If the whole body were hearing, where were the smelling?" Let it be freely acknowledged that, in the course of the centuries, the church has had reason to be grateful for her spiritual noses—men like Athanasius and Luther. The ability to smell represents a sensitiveness to wrong. Which one of us has never experienced an offended olfactory nerve and cried out, "What *is* that I *smell*?" Admittedly, compared with the *other* senses, smell is in dishonor. People boast of 20-20 vision, but no one takes a bow on being told that he has a 50-50 power of scent, or whatever figures as a good average for a bloodhound. But the church needs its "nose" today! In fact, one of the great problems of today is that the church has a badly stopped-up nasal passage, and often can't recognize foulness—of doctrine and practice! Could this be *your* function in the body of Christ?

You see, the "eye" (the church's *vision*) cannot say to the "hand" (the church's *service*), "I have no need of you," or again the "head" (the church's *creative ideas*) to the "feet" (the churches *plodding, faithful going*) "I have no need of you." These words cannot be repeated too often. They make a powerful declaration that the ideas of the mind and the vision of the eye need the hands and the feet to give them value. Many self-sufficient heads in the body of Christ have said to the hand, "I have no need of you." They feel that the idea itself is enough. Or the eye says to the hand, "I have no need of you." A lovely vision is enough. Of course, all of these organs, and their functions, are essential—if the body is to be healthy. The thinking of the head, the smelling of the nose, and the functioning of all the other members—all are imperative! Effective Christianity is always an operating conspiracy of eye, mind, hands, feet, nose, etc.—getting orders and energy from Jesus the Head of the body.

Let's conclude with a critical reminder and an urgent question. *The reminder*: any one Christian by inconsistency and unfaithfulness can weaken the life of the church, and the spiritual power of the entire body can never exceed that which is possessed by its combined membership. And *the question*: what if the body of Jesus of Nazareth had served the Son of God no better than you and I are serving Him? What if, that day when Jesus stood beneath the sycamore tree and looking up, saw little Zacchaeus, His marvelous *voice* had refused to vocalize saying, "No, the man is a sinner! a despised tax gatherer; I shall not speak to him"? What if, when they brought the poor wretch of a woman and threw her at His feet, the *heart* of Jesus had become hard and cruel, saying, "I refuse to open to this woman in loving forgiveness. No! Condemn her!" But none of these things happened. The body of Jesus responded to the great heart of the unique Son of God.

If you are not in His body, receive Christ today, and let His Spirit insert you into His body, as a member in particular. If you are in His body, receive and pursue His directive with every step you take, and "abide in Him" that His Life may "abide in you," and that you may "bear much fruit" for His glory. May God grant it!

WHAT DOES A GENUINE SALVATION EXPERIENCE LOOK LIKE?

Acts 16:11-34

Two extremely important (crucial) things happened at the seaside city of Troas. Those two things would effect the history of Christian missions and the history of the western world (including the United States) forever. First, The missionary team of Paul, Silas, and Timothy was joined by the brilliant Dr. Luke at Troas. Probably locally caused by the fact that Paul had developed a serious eye problem in his travels through Asia Minor, and aided by the likelihood that Paul led Dr. Luke to Christ (possibly in his doctor's office in Troas), this addition to the team proved extremely eventful for the future of the Christian movement. Dr. Luke became the brilliant writer of two historical documents of Christian apologetics, one a story of Christ which we know as the Gospel of Luke, the other the history of missions in the early church. Second, Paul received in a night of uneasy rest "the Macedonian call," or the vision of "a man of Macedonia" (Acts 16:9), standing before Paul and pleading with him, saying, "Come over to Macedonia and help us." Remember that Paul's team had just traveled a southeast to northwest corridor through Asia Minor, and twice had tried to turn to mission fields to preach the Gospel and begin the Christian movement in these fields, but "they were forbidden by the Holy Spirit to preach the word in (the province of) Asia. After they had come to Mysia, they tried to go into Bithynia, but the Spirit did not permit them." Remember, also, that Paul was following "a heavenly vision" in mapping out his itinerary, and these prohibitions of the Spirit must have been extremely challenging, even discouraging, to him and his team. Why would the same God who called him to the work and to world impact through missionary work close two doors in his face? But it is always best to trust the Divine Chairman of the Missions Committee, the Holy Spirit! He had far bigger plans in mind for this team than the evangelization of two small areas. He wanted to begin the evangelization of southern Europe!

In 1620 a ship left Plymouth, England, with men of strong hearts and an intense love of liberty as passengers. In that ship were the ripe seeds of a new civilization which was to be developed under new circumstances, the seeds of life as we find it (though much distorted) in the United States today. But this departure from England, though pregnant with great destiny, is not to be compared with a departure of four men on board a ship in A.D. 52, departing from Troas and bound for Philippi. One of the men was Paul the Apostle, a strong, determined, fearless leader. Another was Silas, an earnest preacher whom I call "the trouble-shooter of the early church." The third was Dr. Luke, obviously a cultured professional man, a man of scientific training, a physician, historian and writer.

The fourth man on the trip was a "diamond in the rough", as yet uncut and unpolished, but full of astounding potential. Up to this point, Asia had led the world, but now the balance of power would begin to shift to the west—to Europe and America—and this voyage across the northern

WHAT DOES A GENUINE SALVATION EXPERIENCE LOOK LIKE?

arm of the Aegean Sea was a significant part of the beginning of the shift.

When the group arrived in Philippi, some strange and seemingly insignificant things happened quickly, and out of them the foundation of the Philippian church was solidly laid. When you read Paul's letter to the Philippians, remind yourself that the stories that make up our text reveal the strange *beginning* of the church to which he wrote this shining letter.

Our text records, in rapid succession, a trio of personal conversions to Christ. Some years ago, a Harvard psychologist wrote a book entitled, <u>Varieties of Religious Experience</u>. Professor James would have had a field day observing these three conversion occurrences in Acts 16! One was the conversion of a woman named Lydia. The other two persons are unnamed in any Biblical account. Only Lydia's name is retained in the Holy Spirit's record for future reference. We call them by a proper name and two descriptive terms—Lydia, a local slave-girl, and the Philippian jailor. In this study, we want to analyze their respective conversion experiences. This study began for me years ago, and it was a veritable eye-opener about the kinds of genuine conversions to Christ that Christians may experience.

I. The Implications of the Chapter

Acts 16 is a grand chapter on personal conversion, and provides several case studies on the Christian doctrine of salvation. We are first going to examine the implications of the Christian word, "saved," as those implications are suggested by this chapter. The word is used in the question which a shaken jailer asked two of his prisoners who had led a jailhouse "revival" in his prison, the question, "Sirs, what must I do to be *saved*?" Why did a rough Roman soldier use the word "saved"? What prompted his mind to thrust this word onto his lips? From a Christian standpoint, what implications are always conjured by the word "saved"?

The first implication in the word "saved" is that *there is a **danger** to be saved **from**.* This is clear and consistent teaching of the entire New Testament, that human beings are universally sinners, and that sin is an extremely dangerous ingredient in human experience (even the slightest, most "innocent" sin). Now, the three people whose conversions are described in our text had different degrees of *awareness* of sin and its danger, but even the fact that men are *totally blind* to their sinful and threatened condition does not reduce or lessen the threat of their condition one whit. A person laughing his way through life is likely strutting his way directly to hell! All the suave and casual Christless people you meet, perhaps daily, are moving one-minute-at-a-time, one-hour-at-a-time, one-day-at-a-time, one-week-at-a-time, one-month-at-a-time, one-year-at-a-time, one-decade-at-a-time, nearer to a serious eternal hell. This is a hateful thought to a typical sinner, but again, his blindness, ignorance and protest do not change reality. Every sin has in it the germ of *eternal damnation*, and this is the necessary, inevitable judgment of a holy, just, righteous, sovereign, ***loving*** God. What kind of parent would he be who did not deal with that which threatens to annihilate his entire family? Would he really love his family if he turned a blind eye to the killing disease when it is in fact curable and he could provide the cure, and a deaf ear to all the sounds of the misery generated by this disease?

In our text, Lydia, whose conversion to Christ is recorded first, impresses you as a decent, good, honorable, efficient, kind person—but she still has to be saved to be acceptable to God in time or in eternity. Read the story of the jailer (the third conversion account) again, and remember that he not only faced the disgrace of knowing that he had failed in his only vocational assignment if his prisoners have escaped, but that Roman law required that he forfeit his own life for this failure. However, this particular threat was resolved when he discovered that all of his prisoners were still present and accounted for, though the prison doors were opened and their chains were all loosed by the earthquake.

The jailer's consciousness was probably aroused, sharpened and intensified by what he heard concerning the charge that put Paul and Silas in his jail. Paul had precipitated a social riot among the panderers of a local slave girl when he cast a "demon of divination" out of her. Paul's action was stimulated by her cry in the street of Philippi as she followed the team of missionaries through the city, "These men are the servants of the Most High God, who proclaim to us *a way of salvation."* Her cry contained a very real truth, but she proclaimed it with a totally false spirit. Perhaps the jailer heard a recitation of the charge that brought these men to his prison. Also, he surely had noted their extremely strange behavior when, in spite of their discomfort (the beating and the stocks) "at midnight Paul and Silas were praying (he had probably heard many a prayer from a blasphemous prisoner, but surely nothing like this!) and singing hymns to God, and the prisoners were listening to them." If I had been in their place, I would have been singing, "Rescue the perishing; care for the dying," but they probably sang "How Great Thou Art!" or "My Tribute"! Anyway, this criminally hardened jailer, who had worked his way up by tough fighting in the Roman military and had been given this job as a reward, was suddenly awakened to a need for a salvation far more important even than the saving of his earthly life. By a miracle of sudden illumination, the opening up of the eyes of his heart and flooding them with light (Ephesians 1:17), he became starkly aware that there was a more desperate death than physical death, and that there was a salvation that would meet his deepest need. He knew he was perishing and needed to be saved! The same is true of every person who has never come to know Christ in the full pardon of his sins and in the reception of Christ's gift of eternal life. There is a serious danger to be totally saved from.

The second implication of the chapter is that *there is a* **destiny** *to be saved* **to**. One of the great caricatures of the western church is that salvation is basically *from* something, *from* sin, death, judgment and hell, but we have largely ignored the gigantic and boundless inventory of what the one-time-sinner, now a saint of God, has been saved *to*. The salvation of the Bible is a line of demarcation, a point of absolutely new departure, an introduction into an entirely different life-orientation, the instant of becoming heir to God's vast estate of truth, resources, life, love, joy, peace, etc, etc, etc, ad infinitum!!!!! God's salvation makes a radical difference in one's life—a day and night, life and death, Heaven and Hell difference! Tragically, many a Christian evaluates his salvation on the thoroughly inferior basis of a rescue from Hell and a pre-paid ticket to a nebulous Heaven. The real dimensions of this Heaven in which he believes he will "spend eternity" he has not even explored (what a strange inconsistency), taking his "Heavenology" from sentimental songs which magnify the pleasant temperature and the beautiful furniture of the place, but ignore the life we will know and live there and the basis for it. The salvation of the Bible involves a moment-by-moment, day-by-day, etc., destiny we are saved to—and it is far bigger than the tame life of going to church as if we were part of the pews we sit in.

The third implication of the word "saved" is that there is a **dynamic** to be **saved by.** In Romans 1:16, the Apostle Paul testified, "I am not ashamed of the Gospel of Christ, for it is the power (Greek, *dunamis*, or "dynamic") of God unto salvation to every one who believes, to the Jew first, and also to the Greek." No person is saved unless he has been inwardly revolutionized by the dynamic of God through the message of the Good News of Christ! Paul gave a slightly different twist to the same truth when he wrote to the Corinthians, "The word of the Cross is to them that are perishing foolishness, but to those who are being saved it is the power (Greek, *dunamis*, or "dynamic") of God" (I Corinthians 1:18). This dynamic of God is like a swinging wrecking ball inside a person, collapsing and destroying the pleasure of sin and its stronghold in a person's life, and like a Divine construction crew, rebuilding the life with a new meaning, a new purpose, a new loyalty, a new vocation, new goals, a new product, a new destiny,…. What I am saying is that "all things are new" when a person is suddenly transplanted by the dynamic of God out of Adam, out of sin, out of death, and into Christ (II Corinthians 5:17).

This dynamic was clearly released into the lives of the three persons in our text. In Lydia's conversion, "The Lord opened her heart," and it is the word that would be used for the silent, unobtrusive, but very beautiful opening of a rose to the early morning sun. In the case of the slave girl on the street, Paul invoked "the Name of Jesus Christ" and addressed the demon of divination in the girl, saying, "I command you to come out of her," and "he came out that very hour." In the case of the jailer, Paul specifically detailed the activation of God's dynamic in his shattered experience—"and he rejoiced…with all his household."

This is an unvarying reality: Every saved person has been absolutely transformed by an out-of-this-world dynamic, "the power of God unto salvation."

The fourth implication of the word "saved" is *there is a **dependence** to be saved **through***. Paul wrote in Ephesians 2:8, "By grace are you saved *through faith*." "Faith" is the shorthand word of the Gospel which explains the dependence through which sinners are saved. "Faith" is a *relational* word—through faith I am livingly and vitally related to God. It is a *resource* word—through faith I receive and appropriate all of the resources that are available in Christ (a veritable and vast treasure trove of resources). It is a *rescue* word—through faith I have been rescued (past tense) from every destructive factor in the universe, am now being rescued (present tense), and will yet be fully and finally rescued (future tense).

I have spent a lot of my life traveling. The nature of "the ministry I have received of the Lord" is such that it entails a lot of long-distance traveling. I have boarded many an airplane for long flights. I don't suppose I have ever boarded a plane without the awareness that I am committing myself to the plane, an instrument designed to fly, to the pilot, a person assigned to fly it, and that once the door closes behind me, my destiny is identified with the plane. I simply sit down in my seat, fasten my seat belt, and trust.

I make no contribution to the trip whatsoever while I am on board the plane, but every plane I have so trusted accomplishes the desired service. Of course, my faith is only as sound as its object, and an airplane and/or its pilot can fail! A sinner convicted of sin by the Holy Spirit does the same thing with regard to Jesus Christ the Savior of sinners. The sinner places his faith and trust in the most reliable Person in the universe, suspending his entire destiny in Christ's hands. He ceases self-trust, trust of any other thing or person (including himself), and totally trusts Christ to save him. This happens in every true Christian conversion.

In the case of Lydia, "the Lord opened her heart to heed the things spoken by Paul" (Acts 16:14). This is "the obedience of faith" of Romans 16:26. In the case of the slave girl, the control of the demon of divination was replaced by the control of the Divine indwelling Savior, creating a protest riot among her former employers. In the case of the jailer, he obeyed Paul's injunction to "believe on the Lord Jesus Christ," and he truly trusted Christ and was saved, along with the believing members of his household.

This is the dependence of faith, through which sinners are saved from sin and all of its by-products, and to Christ and all of His resources and responsibilities.

II. The Instructions of the Chapter

This chapter is loaded with significant *instructions* about the practical dimensions of God's salvation. The "salvation questions" of *who, when, where* and *how* are addressed and answered in the conversion stories told in our text.

First, we learn in these stories that *any **person** can be saved*. The early Christians, most of whom were Jews, had to learn that God is no respecter of persons. This trinity of conversion accounts confirms that truth. The extraordinary thing about Paul's missionary work in Philippi, and the Spirit's salvation work through the missionary team in Philippi, is that an amazing cross-section of the culture of the Roman colony of Philippi was impacted through this work.

Lydia was a cultured business woman who represented the top end of the social scale. She was a cultured, dignified, calm, attractive woman. Although the missionary team had been brought to Philippi by the vision of "a man of Macedonia," Paul's first convert was a woman! And this first convert in Europe was a woman from Asia, from Thyatira, in the very area where Paul had been forbidden to enter! In fact, the only people present at the prayer meeting in Philippi in which Lydia was saved were women. The Gospel of Jesus Christ entered Europe through a women's club!

The slave-girl who was saved amid the traffic of a busy downtown street in Philippi was essentially the opposite in character and culture to Lydia. The girl was more like an animal or a piece of living slave-property. She was at the bottom end of the social scale of the city. While Lydia had to be saved *in spite of* her culture and her character, the slave-girl had to be saved *because of* her personal culture and character. But they both had to be saved, and they found that the ground at the foot of the Cross is level ground, and that the life they found in Christ was the common life of every believer.

The Philippian jailer provided a worthy climax to these conversion stories. He was one of the sturdy middle class who largely made up the Roman civil service. His life had been brutalized inwardly by its history. He was a hardened customer when Paul and his team showed up in Philippi, and he already had a momentum of brutality when Paul and Silas were cast into his jail. He was simply practicing his norm when he beat Paul and Silas with rods (verse 22), one of the three such beatings Paul mentioned in II Corinthians 11:25. He added to their misery and revealed his deep-set norm of violence when "he put them into the inner prison and fastened their feet in the stocks" (verse 24). It is said that he did this because he was "commanded to keep them securely" (verse 23). This reminds me of Governor Pilate's instructions given to the temple guards when they were about to place a giant stone at the mouth of Jesus' tomb—*to guarantee that a dead man stayed dead!!!* Pilate spoke beyond his intelligence and awareness when he wryly said, "Make it as secure *as you can.*" The tomb could not finally imprison the Son of God, and the jail could not finally confine these sons of God! God the Father had a Bigger Agenda for all three sons than a grave and a jail!

Don't these stories prove that any person can be saved? To further prove this truth, I itemized some of the conversions that are recited in the New Testament. Mary Magdalene was dispossessed of seven devils when Jesus saved her! Nathaniel was rescued from his own morality when Jesus saved him! Nicodemus was saved from his "double damnation"—that of sin *and religion*—when Jesus saved him! Rich and traitorous Zacchaeus was saved from the enchantment and dependence of his own riches and wickedness when Jesus saved him! The first disciples were broken from their attachment to their fishing boats, their fishing nets and their parents when Jesus saved them! Luke was saved from the lesser vocation of a lucrative medical practice (!) into a loving ministry of missions when Jesus saved him! (Don't misunderstand the previous sentence; a medical practice is only "lesser" because if a Dr. stops with that vocation, no matter how useful and productive, he has missed the "greater" vocation of living for the glory of God). The Ethiopian eunuch was saved from another "lesser" vocation, though the prime minister of the Ethiopian empire, when the Jesus of Isaiah 53 made Himself real to the eunuch through an itinerant preacher named Philip! Jesus saved a trinity of tentmakers when He saved Saul of Tarsus and his vocational associates, Acquila and Priscilla! He also saved a quisling tax-collector named Levi (later called Matthew)! And a lawyer named Zenas in the Book of Acts!

You see, friends, Jesus Christ can save *any person*.

The second "salvation lesson" of these stories is that *any person can be saved at any* **point of time.** The Savior of sinners never slumbers or sleeps, and He is alert to save any sinner who is aroused to repentance and faith. Think of the respective times of day in which sinners were saved in the Bible. On the

Day of Pentecost, some 3,000 people were saved in the time-proximity of 9 a.m.! In John 4, a Samaritan women was saved during the noon hour at the "lunch break" of Jesus' disciples! Saul of Tarsus was saved at "midday" (Acts 26:13)! How many of you reading these words were saved between sunup and noon on your day of destiny? The thief who died on a cross beside Jesus was saved sometime between noon and 3 p.m. on the great Day of Atonement! John the beloved Apostle was saved sometime near 4 p.m.! How many of you reading these words were saved between noon and sundown on your day of destiny? Nicodemus was saved under the dark umbrella of night (John 3). How many of you reading these words were saved after darkness and before dawn of the next day on your day of destiny? You can poll an audience of saved people, and you will find a substantial representation in any part of a day—morning, afternoon, evening, night. Any person can be saved at any point of time! Now, there is a moment in which *nobody* can be saved, and that's some *other* moment than *now*, and there is *one* moment in which you *must* be saved if at all, and that's the *now* moment.

Lydia was saved in the morning; the slave-girl was saved in the late afternoon; and the jailer was saved at the strange hour of midnight. Any sinner can be saved at any point of time!

The third "salvation lesson" of this chapter is that any person can be saved at any point of time and in any place—*if he will* **trust the right Person.** In all cases mentioned, whether it be Mary Magdalene, or Nathaniel, or Nicodemus, or Zacchaeus, or the first disciples, or Dr. Luke, or the Ethiopian Prime Minister, or the three tentmakers, or Levi the despised tax collector, or Zenas the lawyer, or Lydia, or the slave-girl, or the Philippian jailer—each of them had to commonly trust Jesus Christ, the Savior of sinners, and receive Him into their lives, in order to be saved. And in all cases, the Same Person did the saving. He Himself said, "I am the way, the truth, and the life; no man comes unto the Father except by Me" (John 14:6). Sounds to me like He believed He was the only possible Savior of sinners—and my hearing is correct! In Acts 4:12, Simon Peter echoes this truth: "Neither is there salvation in any other, for there is no second name under heaven by which sinners can/must be saved" (Acts 4:12).

The right Person to save sinners is Jesus, and trust is the means of receiving Him and relating to Him.

These are the salvation lessons revealed in these conversion stories. We have just one more point to examine.

III. The Common Ingredients of Salvation

Finally, these stories show us *the common ingredients* in every genuine experience of salvation. Though salvation has no stereotype, each experience of salvation has certain common denominators.

First, in all three cases of salvation recorded in Acts 16, each sinner *heard a dynamic word from God.* With regard to Lydia, Luke says, "We sat down and spoke to the women who met there. Now a certain woman named Lydia heard us.....The Lord opened her heart to heed the things spoken by Paul" (verses 13, 14). Three times the text indicates that the Apostle Paul spoke Divine truth to the women, and Lydia heard, believed and trusted Christ to save her. In the story of the slave-girl, Paul turned and said to the spirit, "I command you in the name of Jesus Christ to come out of her," and "he came out that very hour" (verse 18). In the conversion of the jailer, Paul and Silas declared with Divine authority and authorization, "Believe on the Lord Jesus Christ, and you will be saved" (verse 31). "Faith comes by hearing, and hearing by the Word ("hrema", the living, quickening Word of God) of

God" (Romans 10:17). Every sinner must hear the Gospel with a hearing that penetrates his heart with Divine power, or he will not be saved.

Second, in all these cases, each sinner *felt a definite sense of need.* There is a life-and-death difference between a need for Christ and a *felt* need for Christ. There is a vast difference between saying, "Oh, everyone needs Christ, I guess," and "I am ruined by my sins; I need a Savior more than I need the air I breathe. What must I do to be saved?"

Third, in all three stories, *each sinner was transformed by the Divine Christ as personal Savior and Lord.* In Romans 15:7, Paul said, "Christ received each of us." He was encouraging the Roman Christians to treat each other in exactly the same way Christ has treated us. He received each of us; we should receive one another. Here is an interesting feature of Paul's statement: the word translated "received" is the Greek word, *proslambano.* This is a compound Greek word. The "lambano" part of the word means "to aggressively embrace." The prefix "pros" means "face to face with." So the word means to face the other person and aggressively embrace him. This is what God did to us. He saw us perfectly, reading us like the proverbial "open book"—and yet He aggressively embraced us anyway! That is grace! And one of the big salvation texts of the Gospel of John uses essentially the same word. John 1:12 says, "As many as *receive* Christ, to them gives He the power to become sons and daughters of God." The word "receive" is basically the same word, and it again means "to aggressively embrace" Jesus Christ. Using a two-fisted grip of faith and embracing Him "with both arms" of trust, aggressively take Him into your heart. Nobody has been saved without such a transaction between him and Christ.

Finally, in all three of these conversion stories, *each saved sinner proved his definite conversion by a changed life.* Lydia, for example, begged for the privilege of showing thoughtful Christian hospitality. After she had been baptized, "she begged us, saying, 'If you have judged me to be faithful to the Lord, come to my house and stay.'"

The slave-girl also showed evidence of her genuine conversion by forsaking her sinful business association in order to follow and serve Christ. The Philippian jailer's transformation was remarkable. Using the same hands that had earlier *inflicted* the wounds on the backs of Paul and Silas, after his encounter with Christ, he now *washed* the very wounds he had made. Could there be a finer illustration of a transformed heart than this? "Hereby we know that we have passed from death to life, because we love the brethren." (I John 3:14).

Dear friend, have you heard this dynamic word from God that has effectually called you to Christ? Have you recognized your own personal Heaven-and Hell need for Christ? Have you aggressively embraced Jesus Christ as your personal Savior and Lord? Is there the radical evidence of definite conversion in your life, the evidence of a transformed life?

A little girl, beginning to show an awakened heart, said to her mother, "Mama, how can I come to Jesus when I can't *see* Him?" The mother softly answered, "Do you remember when you asked me to get you a drink of water last night? Did you *see* me when you asked me?" "No, you were in the next bedroom, but I knew you would *hear* me and get it for me!" "Well, that's the same way you come to Jesus. You can't *see* Him, but you know that He is near and hears every word you say, and that He will give you what you need." Dear friend without Christ, Jesus will give you what you really need—**Himself!** No one goes to Hell with Christ living in his heart, and no one goes to Heaven without Him there. He said,

"Behold, I stand at the door and knock; if any man will hear My voice, and open the door, I will come into him, and will sup with him, and he with me." If there is a door between you and Jesus, and you are alone on the inside of your own heart, lost and condemned, why not open the door and receive Him at this moment? He will save you like He saved all the others in this story, and you can know His Presence, His pardon, His purpose and His power all the way to Heaven. Then, you will know and enjoy *Him and His Place* forever.

WANTED: PEOPLE WHO KNOW THE ROPES

Acts 9:23-25

"And after that many were fulfilled, the Jews took counsel to kill him: But their laying await was known of Saul. And they watched the gates day and night to kill him. Then the disciples took him by night, and let him down by the wall in a basket."

Saul of Tarsus had begun to taste his own medicine. He had been doling out large doses of suffering to Christians — and now he *is* one; and the tables are turned. "The Jews took counsel to kill him," and they tried a secret ambush to fulfill their desires. However, in the protective providence of God, someone "snitched" to Paul that they were watching the gate day and night to capture and kill him. "Then the disciples took him by night, and let him down by the wall in a basket." Get the picture. Here is the man who is to become the world's greatest Christian theologian, the world's greatest Christian philosopher, the world's greatest Christian teacher, the world's greatest Christian statesman, the world's greatest Christian missionary, the world's greatest Christian scholar — beginning his ministry as an absolute "basket case"!

Do you have any idea what an "ego blow" that basket ride was to Saul of Tarsus? He was a man of massive ego strength. With that ego strength, he had "progressed in Judaism above many my equals in my own nation, being more exceedingly zealous of the traditions of my fathers" (Galatians 1:14). With that ego strength, he had pursued a blameless religion before God (Philippians 3:4-6). With that ego strength, he had hounded Christians, both men and women, to trial and possible death (Acts 9:2), constantly "snorting out threats and violent murder against the disciples of the Lord Jesus" (Acts 9:1). And now, suddenly, he had been conscripted into a basket ride that struck a mighty blow at that ego strength.

Paul leaves us no doubt about what this basket episode meant to him. Many years later, he indicated that it was one of the greatest things that ever happened to him. II Corinthians 11 rehearsed some of "the things that happened" to him (Philippians 1:12). Beginning in verse 23 of II Corinthians 11, he said: "Are they ministers of Christ? (I speak as a fool) I am more; in labors more abundant, in stripes above measure, in prisons more frequent, in deaths oft. Of the Jews five times received I forty stripes save one. Thrice was I beaten with rods, once was I stoned, thrice I suffered shipwreck, a night and a day I have been in the deep; In journeyings often, in perils of waters, in perils of robbers, in perils by mine own countrymen, in perils by the heathen, in perils in the city, in perils in the wilderness, in perils in the sea, in perils among false brethren; In weariness and painfulness, in watchings often, in hunger and thirst, in fastings often, in cold and nakedness. Beside those things that are without, that which cometh upon me daily, the care of all the churches."

What an incredible list of sufferings! Why would anyone live like that if they could choose otherwise? Paul gives us the answer in verse 29, though it will take a hard pull to unravel the verse. "Who is weak, and I am not weak? who is offended, and I burn not?" The New International Version says, "Who is led into sin without my intense concern?" Here is a classic example of the meaning of Christian compassion. Christian compassion is a spiritual game of "musical chairs" in which, as Ezekiel said, "I sat where they sat." It means that I climb voluntarily inside the other person's skin (whoever he may be), and I look out at life through his eyes, I touch with his fingers, I feel with his feelings. This is what Jesus did for each of us! He zipped Himself up (fully God) inside a human skin and experienced what we experience.

Just this week, the home newspaper carried a Dennis the Menace cartoon which shows Dennis kneeling at his bedside in a stream of light flowing down from above, and he is saying very seriously, "So I figured You'll understand, having a boy of your own." And, great news, God does understand! He identified fully with us, becoming weak like us, and deeply wounded over our sins. When man "missed the mark" in his sins, the arrow in full flight turned aside and wounded the heart of God.

In II Corinthians 11:29, Paul practices a Christ-like compassion; he fully identifies with hurting humanity and accepts each man's hurt as his own. One little boy defined compassion as "Johnny's pain in my stomach," and he was right.

Read again the list of Paul's sufferings in II Corinthians 11:23-28. If you had a list of sufferings like that, and you had not yet reached a climax in the list, what do you suppose you would add? Listen to Paul: "In Damascus the governor under Aretas the king kept the city of the Damascenes with a garrison, desirous to apprehend me: And through a window in a basket was I let down by the wall, and escaped his hands." What an apparent anticlimax!

The basket episode looks "innocent" compared to all those other massive sufferings. What does this mean? Why so direct, so definite, so detailed an account of the basket story? Let me venture a calculated guess. In all those *other* sufferings, Paul could feel heroic and brave. "After all, I'm suffering for Jesus." And, unconsciously, credit would accrue to him for his sufferings. But in the basket story, heroism and boasting were out of the picture. The only thing he got out of that episode was abject embarrassment to his great pride.

Every child of God must suffer in one manner or another, to one degree or another, to break the hard shell of the self-life which encloses and encases the Presence of Jesus within him, and the only suffering that will accomplish God's purpose is the kind in which a sense of heroism is unthinkable and only abject embarrassment is experienced. You see, God is not out to *hurt* your *pride* - He is out to *kill* it! No man can hope for any deliverance from God that will save his pride. There is not the tiniest bit of pride in Heaven, and God will knock much of our pride out of us on the way to Heaven.

Here is an interesting feature in the story, and I will try to hang the rest of my message on something that emerges at this point. When Dr. Luke tells the story (Acts 9), he uses *one* word for a "basket," the word for a large, round, woven, wicker-work basket. However, when *Paul* tells the story in II Corinthians 11:32-33, he uses a quite different word for a basket. Paul's word means a "*rope* basket." Who was right? Well, who was in the basket? Luke wasn't concerned to tell what kind of basket it was; he just reports the story. But Paul's memory was vivid and fresh, and he noted the exact kind of basket it was.

Let's ponder Paul's technical word, a "*rope* basket." I want to introduce two strange categories of characters into our message on the basis of Paul's specific identification. You probably would not have thought of these two categories of people - but then, this is the message God has let _me_ see. It has walloped my life with spiritual reality since the first day I saw it.

I. THE ROPE-MAKER

First, I want you to think of *the rope-maker* who is necessarily in the unseen background of this story. Would you ever have thought of him? License your imagination and make a sight-seeing trip down into the craftsman's district of Damascus. Down a long narrow street, you come upon a craftsman's shop. There is a business sign over the doorway: "_____, Ropemaker." You go in the front door and there is the counter at which he does much of his bargaining in selling or trading the ropes he has made. Go down the narrow, dim hallway and you come to a small room. In that room an ordinary man sits at a work desk. He is weaving strands of fabric into a rope. He works rapidly and skillfully. As each strand of rope is completed, he stretches it across the table and tests its strength with his weight as his hands spread as far apart on the new rope as possible.

Why do I mention him? The idea was triggered in my mind years ago by a tiny devotional thought I saw entitled, "Somebody Made a Good Rope." The little paragraph that followed that title opened with the question, "What if that rope had broken?" Great question! I have stood at the spot at the foot of the wall of Damascus beneath the very high window where (our guide said) Saul of Tarsus was lowered in a basket to run like a river rat under the umbrella of night, scurrying for his very life. If that rope had broken, either Paul would have died in the fall, or the sound of the crash would have brought the two soldiers nearest him from the chain of soldiers surrounding the city (Acts 9:24; II Cor. 11:32). The Jews would have killed him (Acts 9:24b), or the soldiers would have arrested him and disposed of him (II Cor. 11:32). However it occurred, we would have never heard of Paul the Apostle (I am speaking from a strictly human standpoint here). How much it meant to the world that Paul escaped!

Do you remember the line in Longfellow's poem about Paul Revere, "The fate of a nation was riding that night"? There was far, far more than the mere fate of a nation riding in that basket that carried Paul. So much of the world's spiritual welfare was in that basket. How crucially important it was that someone made a good rope! Who the craftsman was, we do not know (and that's all the better). He had no way of knowing what a part in the world's history his everyday, ordinary rope was to play. He had no idea that God was going to suspend the survival of the greatest Christian who has ever lived in a basket of ropes which he had woven with his own hands. What did he do? He just made a good rope!

Friends, if Christians are to be heard today in this wicked American nation, they will "earn the right" to be heard. How? By the quality of work they turn out at their daily workbench! By the skill, efficiency and attitude of their rope-making.

A Catholic priest and a Baptist preacher were playing golf together. The priest was beating the preacher consistently by one or two strokes a hole. On the 15th green, the preacher noticed that the priest crossed himself before each putt. He also gave special note to the fact that the priest putted much better than he did, winning by one or two putts on each hole. "If that works for him, maybe it would work for me," he thought. So, he secretly crossed himself. But still he three-putted and lost the hole. The same happened on the 16th, 17th, and 18th holes. "I want to ask you something," he boldly said to the priest. "How is it that you cross yourself before each putt, and you one-putt or two-putt each hole? I cross myself and I still lose by one or two putts on every hole. Why?" The priest answered, "Preacher, that's an easy one. You can cross yourself all you *want* to, but you still have to be *able to putt!*"

Friends, we can go through all the religious exercises imaginable, can invoke the blessing of God upon all we do, can be religiously unimpeachable, but all of our crossing of ourselves (our religious activities) will do absolutely no good if we are less than Christian at the daily work bench. It is there we earn respect for Christ, His Gospel, and His lifestyle.

In a large eastern city there was a rope factory which manufactured docking halters for ships - the vital, giant ropes which anchored the ship to the docking place. Over the entrance to that factory a message was printed: "The Worker in This Factory Weaves His Conscience into His Work - Because Lives Are at Stake."

What kind of ropemaker am I? My ropemaker is in the minister's "trade." What kind of daily work do I do? What kind of Christian craftsmen am I helping fellow Christians to become. The pastor-teacher's "job description" is in the word "equip" in Ephesians 4:12. The pastor-teacher's job is the "equipping of the saints (all believers) that they might do the work of the ministry for the upbuilding of the Body of Christ."

The word translated "equipping" is an enlarged form of the word "artis," from which we get our word "artisan." An artisan is a skilled craftsman. So, the business of a pastor-teacher is to turn every Christian near him, as much as possible, into a skilled craftsman in the way he handles, applies, and lives the Word of God. He is to help him to become like a skilled craftsman in the efficient way he "lives in the Spirit" (Galatians 5:25), "walks in the Spirit" (Galatians 5:16), is "led of the Spirit" (Romans 8:14), is "filled with the Spirit" (Ephesians 5:18). "The best way to tell that a man is carrying a full bucket is that his feet get wet." Our daily walk will either commend Christ to men or push them away from Him.

What kind of ropemaker are you? Are you making a good rope? If God were to suspend a modern-day Apostle Paul in a basket made of your rope, would he survive or perish?

II. THE ROPEHOLDERS.

The other category of people who play an important role in this text are *the ropeholders*. They are a bit more visible than the ropemakers. "The disciples took him by night, and let him down by the wall in a basket." Let me "spiritualize" the account. That is, I will turn it into an illustration. In doing so, I want to ask — and answer — some five questions about the ropeholders.

From a spiritual perspective, *what is a ropeholder?* A ropeholder is one maturing (there is no "mature" Christian, only a maturing one) Christian who cares for, sustains, protects, encourages, teaches, rebukes, corrects, rescues, builds, and invests his life in a less mature Christian for the purpose of guaranteeing the less mature Christian a future possibility of maximum productivity for Christ. In short, a ropeholder is a Christ-centered disciple-maker.

Who were these ropeholders? Here's a good answer: we don't know! We don't have any identification except that they were "disciples." They are completely unknown by name. Scripture gives us no names; history offers no names; tradition doesn't even introduce them by name. These were anonymous people. And that is all the better! These ropes are best held by unsung, unheralded people. Recognition in the church and in the world are not necessary. The ropeholder's recognition will be in Heaven (I Cor. 4:5, "Then shall every man have praise of God").

WANTED -- PEOPLE WHO KNOW THE ROPES

Martha Mott is a faithful member of Speedway Terrace Baptist Church in Memphis, Tennessee. She is a teacher's aide in a nearby elementary school, assisting a first-grade teacher. The kids lovingly call her "Mama Mott." One day, she was on the playground with the kids at recess, and she was asking them what they wanted to be when they grew up. One first-grade boy was a brilliant student of birds and could name and describe at least one bird for every letter in the alphabet. An expert on birds is called an "ornithologist." When Martha asked him what he wanted to be, he confused his word and said boldly, "I'm going to be an ordinary-thologist!"

The fact is that each of us is an ordinary-thologist. Most ropeholders are common folks like you and me. You see, you don't have to be in <u>Who's Who</u> to know what's what in Christian service. If you have a growing edge in which you are daily and dynamically walking with Jesus, and you are willing to invite someone to go with you, you can be a world-impacting ropeholder.

There is a great illustration of this in the early history of Israel. Two men who were representatives of Jehovah God were trapped inside the fortified pagan city of Jericho. If they had been captured, it would have meant certain death for them. They were running through the streets inside the city, desperately searching for a way out. They hurried to the door of a home that was built into Jericho's outside wall, hoping against hope that the resident there might have pity on them and help them to get out. When they knocked, a woman came to the door. They frantically explained their situation, explaining that the Jericho "police" were just behind them. The woman excitedly replied, "I have just come into covenant with your God! Certainly I will help. Come in quickly!"

They entered, she close the door, and she hurried them upstairs onto the flat roof where some grain was drying. "Lie down in these piles of flax, and I will cover you!" She spread the flax evenly over them, and just in time, for there was a loud rapping again at her front door. She hurried down, composed herself, answered the door, and feigned ignorance as the magistrates questioned her. They came in, searched for the two men throughout the house, didn't find them, and hurried away to look elsewhere. When they had departed, this woman opened a window in the outside wall of the city and let these two men down outside in a basket.

The two stories sound somewhat similar, don't they? Who was this woman? She would not easily be accepted in the typical church today. She was a prostitute, and her history would disqualify her from service in many churches. But, there was one thing she could do which no human being could prevent by rules and regulations. She could hold ropes to save and secure the lives of others!

Every parent should be a spiritual ropeholder. Every pastor should be a spiritual ropeholder and not merely an institution-builder. Every Sunday School teacher should be a spiritual ropeholder, not merely a teacher of lessons. Every Christian should be a ropeholder, not merely a self-centered survivor in the Christian life. Remember that a ropeholder is a people-builder, a disciple-maker. He does not merely count people; he qualitatively builds people who count. This necessitates close-up, long-term, visionary investment in people's lives.

Who were these disciples? We don't know, but they were ropeholders — and that is enough.

When did they hold the ropes? The verse says, "Then the disciples took him *by night*, and let him down by the wall in a basket." What an illustration! If there has ever been a spiritual nighttime, it is today. If the world has ever been dark, it is today. One newspaperman said about Europe at the beginning of World War II, "It was so dark that even the cats were running into each other!" It is that dark spiritually today. If God ever needed ropeholders, He needs them right now – people who will function faithfully "in the darkness" as little bright spots of spiritual light – quiet but efficient ropeholders.

How long did they hold the ropes? The answer is simple — they held the ropes until the basket hit the ground – until the thud was heard at the foot of the wall, or the rope slackened in their hands. In other words, they held the ropes until the job was done. When a man's life is at stake — as it was in our story — people who hold ropes in spurts and spasms, by starts and stops, with irregularity and erratically, are not only worthless but actually harmful. "It is required in stewards (managing ropes, in this case) that a man be found faithful" — not fitful or flashy, but faithful.

Just as Nehemiah stayed up on the wall — against all opposition — until the last brick was laid; just as Jesus stayed up on the Cross — against all opposition — until the last necessary drop of blood was shed, we must faithfully "stay at the window and measure out the ropes" until the job is done. Only eternity will reveal what could have been done if every born-again believer had been trained (and had trained others) to be an efficient, visionary, world-impacting reproducer of other efficient, visionary, world-impacting reproducers.

A ropeholder is a Christian disciple who sees the masses through the man, and builds the man to impact the masses (through other individuals) to the ends of the earth until the end of time. As long as sin is contemporary, sinners are lost, the world remains largely unevangelized, and Christians are untrained to hold the ropes, our job is not done. We must hold the ropes until the basket hits the ground.

Who was in the basket? To them, he was just a brand-new Christian who was proving to be a trouble-making upstart.

To them, he was just a hot-hearted, hot-headed new believer who got himself in trouble with the local authorities. Many veteran Christians today would have restrained Saul by saying, "Son, when you learn a little diplomacy, God will use you! When you learn to control yourself, God will use you!" This often means, "When you backslide far enough to get in tune with us, everything will be okay." A committee of veterans might say, "He will just have to learn the hard way. He made his bed; let him lie in it! He dug his own grave; let him be buried in it. He mixed his own poison; let him drink it!"

When I ask, "Who was in the basket?," today's Christian looks smug and says, "Oh, I know the answer. Anybody should know that one! It was the Apostle Paul!" But, did *they* know that? Certainly not! They had no way whatsoever of knowing that this man would scatter Christian churches all over the Roman empire like a sower sowing seeds in a field or a housewife sprinkling salt in a salad. They had no way of knowing he would be God's appointed missionary to the Gentile world. By the way, that is one of God's jokes on Mr. Worldly Wiseman and Mr. Carnally-Minded, because Paul was conspicuously equipped by nature, background, and training to be the Apostle to the *Jews*, but God disregarded those "credentials" and sent him instead to the Gentiles. These "disciples" didn't know the potential in this man. So what did they do? They just faithfully held the ropes!

If you never hold any ropes, you will never know whom God might have "put in your basket." Let me quote a long paragraph which will illustrate the possibilities. "The night was cold and the wind was blowing up a storm. Conrad Cotta, an esteemed citizen of a little town in Germany, was playing his flute while his wife Ursula was preparing supper. Suddenly they heard a sweet but weak voice singing outside, 'Foxes to their holes have gone, every bird into its nest; but I

WANTED -- PEOPLE WHO KNOW THE ROPES

have wandered here alone, and for me there is no rest.' Hearing a light knock at their door, they opened it and saw a half-frozen, ragged lad who asked for charity in the name of Christ. 'Com in, young man,' said Mr. Cotta, 'we'll give you some food and a place to stay tonight.' Ursula immediately began to prepare a meal, but before it was ready the boy fainted from weariness and hunger. They tenderly cared for him, gave him a nourishing broth, and put him to bed. They found later that he had wandered about for a long time, singing and living on the money that people gave to him. He seemed such a worthy teenager that they prayed about the matter and decided to treat him as their own son. They sent him to school, and he later entered a monastery. There he found a Bible which he read eagerly and from which he learned the blessed way of salvation. Unable to keep the good news to himself, he spread abroad the word that 'justified by faith' we can have 'peace with God through out Lord Jesus Christ.' Little did Conrad and Ursula know, when they took that young singer into their home in the name of Christ (Matthew 25:40), that they were nourishing the great champion of the Reformation; for that poor lad was none other than Martin Luther!" But what if Conrad and Ursula Cotter had not held the ropes?

Another illustration: "The old Scots minister climbed wearily into the pulpit. Bowed and dejected, he had just faced the harsh criticism of one of his deacons. 'Sir, there is something radically wrong with your ministry. Only one person has been saved this year, and he is only a boy.' The words stung the old minister deeply, for he too felt heartbroken that so few had responded to the Gospel; yet still he trusted God for the results.

The service concluded, but the weary man of God lingered on in the church, wondering if there was any point

TAKING THE WHEEL FOR DISCIPLE-MAKING

continuing in the ministry. A young lad saw him and waited behind. 'Please, sir....' 'Yes, Robert?' 'Do you think if I worked hard for my education that I could ever become a preacher?' 'God bless you, my boy,' replied the old man with tears in his eyes. 'Yes, I think you will become a preacher!'

It was years later that an elderly missionary came back to London from Africa. He had pushed back the boundaries of geographical knowledge and brought savage chiefs under the influence of the Gospel of peace, given tribes the Bible in their own tongues; but most of all he had followed the Lord with all his heart. Robert Moffatt—'only a boy,' won to Christ and encouraged by a tired old man of God, had made a lasting mark on the world.

On one visit to England, Robert told of the need of Africa. Among those who heard him that day was a young Scottish medical student who had given his life to God for missionary service. Robert Moffatt's words pierced his heart: 'There is a vast plain to the north where I have sometimes see, in the morning sun, the smoke of a thousand villages where no missionary has ever been.' Filled with the vision of what God wanted him to do, the student asked Mr. Moffatt, 'Would I do for Africa?' The direction of David Livingstone's life had been changed.

Who can tell what impact was made through the ministry of that old discouraged Scotsman? 'Only a boy' it seemed—yet far-off generations and tribes knew the effect of it!" But what if the old pastor had not held the ropes?

One day in the year 1865 a nervous Sunday School teacher walked down a Boston street to a shoe store. He had gone to see a dynamic but uneducated young shoe clerk whose ambition it was to make a million dollars selling shoes. The Sunday School teacher nervously hesitated outside, but finally built enough courage to go into the store. He found the young clerk on lunch break in the back of the store; and after stumbling through a greeting and mumbling a few introductory words, he faltered his way through a Gospel witness to the young clerk. The young man was like ripe fruit. He fell to the teacher's nervous touch, opened his heart to Christ, and was saved that day in the back of that shoe store. Few people ever remember the name of Edward Kimball, the Sunday School teacher; but every studious Christian has heard many, many times of Dwight L. Moody, perhaps the greatest evangelist up to that time in the history of the church. What if Edward Kimball had not held the ropes?

An old-fashioned, fighting, whiskey-bottle smashing evangelist named Mordecai Ham put up a tent in Charlotte, North Carolina, and held an evangelistic crusade. One night, a tall, gangling teenage boy and his short, heavy sidekick came stumbling "down the sawdust trail," fell into the altar, and gave their hearts to Christ. Not too many people remember Mordecai Ham today, but hardly a person in the civilized world doesn't recognize the face and the name of Billy Graham. Every time he preaches on TV, he preaches to an average audience of 90 million people. But what if Mordecai Ham hadn't held the ropes?

A young Jewish doctor was converted to Jesus Christ in a Siberian prison as a result of his own disillusionment with the Soviet socialist system and the Christian witness of a well-educated and kind fellow prisoner who spoke to him of a Jewish Messiah who had come to keep God's promises to Israel. We don't know this man's name, but his testimony was used of the Holy Spirit to guide the young Jewish doctor to Christ and to eternal life. As the doctor progressively grew in the freedom of his new life, he opposed the brutality and inhumanity of many events in the prison. He also shared his own testimony with the few who would listen. One day, he met and treated a patient who had just had surgery for cancer of the intestines. The doctor's soul was stirred toward this patient, and he began to tell boldly what had happened to him. Though the patient was shaking with fever, he was captured by the doctor's testimony of conversion and freedom in Christ. The encounter lasted from afternoon until very late that night. The patient listened raptly to the doctor's incredible confession. Finally, he fell asleep.

The doctor never knew the response of his patient. That night, the doctor's head was smacked in by eight blows on the head with a plasterer's hammer. The deed was apparently done by some men who were angry that he was fighting against the Soviet system. But, his testimony and influence did not die with him. The patient pondered the doctor's last, dramatic, impassioned words about the miracle of new birth in Jesus Christ. As a result, he too became a Christian.

Today, very few people know the doctor's name (or the name of the one who led him to Christ). The name of Boris Kornfeld, the Jewish Christian doctor, will never be entered in the annals of history. According to the world's estimation, he was a failure, but "they that be wise shall shine as the brightness of the firmament; and they that turn many to righteousness as the stars for ever and ever" (Daniel 12:3). You see, Kornfeld's cancer patient not only survived that Siberian prison; he became one of the greatest Christian thinkers and spokesmen of the 20th Century — Alexander Solzhenitsyn. But what if Boris Kornfeld – and the lesser known believer who brought him to Christ — had not held the ropes?

Dawson Trotman was founder of the international Navigators, a Christian organization that majors on rope-holding, or disciple-making. "Daws" had worn himself out at 50 years of age, building disciples, training and dispatching men, and heading up Billy Graham's crusade follow-up efforts.

He went to Word of Life's Schroon Lake Christian Camp to lead the East Coast Navigators Conference in 1956. While there, he and Jack Wyrtzen, the camp owner, went out on the lake to ride and to water ski. On one ride around the lake, they filled the boat with conferees and started a roaring ride around the lake. When Dawson discovered one girl couldn't swim, he locked arms with the riders on either side of her for security. Suddenly, the boat made a fast turn and simultaneously smacked a big wave. The combined effect threw the girl who couldn't swim off the boat, and Dawson was thrown into the water with her. Dawson was an expert swimmer, and he assisted her until the boat returned. The others pulled her into the boat, but it had taken all of Dawson's depleted strength just to keep her head above water; and when they turned to retrieve him from the water, they couldn't find him in the darkness. He had sunk in sheer exhaustion and drowned.

Dawson Trotman's impact on people was amazing. The next issue of Time magazine after Dawson's death carried an article about his life and work. With his picture, they ran the caption, "Dawson Trotman: Always Holding Somebody Up." Daws Trotman was one of the world's great rope-holders.

One night, a man named Robert Newell ran out of gas on a lonely road. A friendly traveler came along, took a rope from the trunk of his car, and towed the stalled car almost thirty miles to the nearest garage. When Newell insisted that the man accept pay, he refused. He also rejected Newell's offer to fill his gas tank. When Newell protested that he must be allowed to do something to return the kindness shown, the stranger said, "Well, if you really want to show your gratitude, buy a rope and always carry it in your car."

Friends, are you "holding the ropes" for anybody? Do you have anyone in your basket? Isn't it time to "know the ropes" and hold the ropes for someone else? Will you close your hands around some ropes today? Will you willingly get rope-burns in your palms if somebody else can be saved and secured for Jesus and His purpose? Will you ask God to put somebody in your basket today and hold the ropes until the basket hits the ground? Who knows? Maybe God will let you recruit and train a Twenty-first Century version of the Apostle Paul!

THE CHRISTIAN RACE

Hebrews 12:1-3:

"Wherefore, seeing we also are compassed about with so great a cloud of witnesses, let us lay aside every weight, and the sin which doth so easily beset us, and let us run with patience the race that is set before us, Looking unto Jesus the author and finisher of our faith; who for the joy that was set before him endured the cross, despising the shame, and is set down at the right hand of the throne of God. For consider him that endured such contradiction of sinners against himself, lest ye be wearied and faint in your minds."

The eleventh chapter of Hebrews contains what someone has called "God's Westminster Abbey," the Hall of Fame of the great heroes of faith from history past. To read this chapter is much like traveling through a "Divine mausoleum," and reading the names and epitaphs of the great champions of faith, men of whom God was not ashamed. In that chapter, we come across the names of great men such as Abel, Enoch, Noah, Abraham, Moses, Joshua, and others. And now, in the opening verses of chapter twelve, by a single touch, these saintly souls are pictured as having passed from the arena of faith, having finished their course, and now, they have taken their places in the crowded grandstand, and form a "great cloud of witnesses" who surround us as we run the race which they have already run.

So, at the very beginning of the twelfth chapter of Hebrews, we are alerted with a dramatic announcement—that as we live the Christian life and run the Christian race, we are being encouraged by those who have victoriously finished the course. Then, the writer takes us into the very heart of what it means to be a Christian. Join me in examining his words.

I. THE ILLUSTRATION

First, he sets before us a beautiful *illustration* of the Christian life. He says that the Christian life is like a "race." "Let us run with patience the *race* that is set before us." Paul frequently dips into his knowledge of the world of athletics to find an illustration of spiritual truth. Here, he takes us to a track meet. Every true believer in Jesus Christ is in a race. The illustration reveals some important truths about the Christian life.

First, it shows us that the Christian life is an *appointed, assigned* life. It is a "race that is *set before us.*" We do not select the course ourselves. We do not follow a route of our own choosing. The course is set before us by our Heavenly Father. The Christian is not a wayfarer along the byways of life. He is not a tourist taking a scenic tour. If he takes off on his own, he is on a course to ruin.

Many children of my generation read the story of the little train engine that became weary of following the same old track all the time. "I want to cross the fields and climb the mountains," it said, "and I don't have the freedom to do the things that I want to do." So one day, the little engine jumped from its track and started off on its own. However, it soon found itself bogged down in the sand or the swamp, bumping into rocks and trees, and its progress was totally stopped. Then, it saw that it was only free to fulfil the destiny for which it was made—to travel on the appointed track.

I recently read this story. "The morning sun shimmered brightly on the choppy waves of the bay as a small motor boat moved slowly over the water. Perhaps 200 yards away, 14 swimmers plied through the chilly waters. Twenty men and women had begun the race that morning, but six had been pulled from the water into one of the many boats that lined the course. Exhaustion, muscle cramps, or some other malady had taken them from the race even before the swimmers had reached the mid-way point.

"Just now the swimmers were bunched more closely than they had been for some time. As the far shore came into sight the competitors appeared to reach into their resources and pull with greater power and precision. Between them and the beach lay their greatest test, an area of swift-moving currents that had carried many a swimmer far toward the sea before he had been rescued or finally had given up and drowned.

"Of the 14 swimmers in the water, 13 had swum the bay before. They knew from experience the dangers of the currents. Although those who watched from the boats kept an eye on the veterans, it was the one rookie swimmer they watched most closely. Just now he was in the lead, several hundred yards ahead of the pack.

"Would he heed the warnings and follow the instructions he had been given to swim up the coast a little way before attempting to cross the swift-moving channel? If he did, he would win the race easily. If he did not, thinking that he didn't want to waste the time to swim parallel to the shore, or that he was strong enough to meet the currents head on, they were ready to move quickly to rescue him. All watched anxiously to see what he would do.

"As the rookie neared the buoys that marked the swift-running water, it appeared for a moment that he would stay within the marked course and swim upstream. He had not moved more than 20 yards, however, when he turned and swam directly toward the shore. Instantly, motors sprang to life and two boats sped across the water to the now-struggling swimmer. There were Coast Guard boats manned by experienced rescuers.

"Later that afternoon when all the swimmers had reached the beach—including the rookie, who had been brought in by a Coast Guard cutter—the winner of the race approached the young man who had nearly drowned, 'Why did you change your mind?' he asked. 'The officials told me that you started to follow the path marked out for us, but then you suddenly veered toward the shore.'

"'Those 20 yards that I swam upstream against the current were so easy that I thought all the fuss about that channel was just so much hype. So I decided to cut through it to win the race by a large margin. I soon realized that not only wouldn't I win the race, I wouldn't even finish it. For an instant I felt so dumb for throwing away the race, but then I realized that I had jeopardized my life as well. I'll never try this again.'

"'Oh, I think you should enter the race again next year,' said the veteran racer. 'You're a magnificent distance swimmer. Just follow the rules the next time and you'll find that the crossing point determined by the race organizers is challenging, but not life-threatening. Each year that point is different because the currents constantly change, so we all have to follow the prescribed course. One year we didn't race at all because the officials couldn't find a safe place to cross the channel. I wanted to talk them into sponsoring the race anyway, but I knew that would be foolish. Most likely no one would have finished anyway. Well, I hope to see you next year. It's about time someone beat me. For a while I thought this would be the year.'"

What a sad story! Although the rookie swimmer had the ability to beat the veteran, he lost the race, and nearly lost his life, because he wilfully chose to leave the assigned course and follow a convenient course of his own choosing.

Instead, the Christian is a runner engaged in a race that God has appointed for him. This is an "invitational" race. The one invited may reject, ignore, or accept the invitation. If he accepts the invitation, he also accepts the prescribed course. And each runner is assigned a specific lane on the race track, and expected to stay in that lane. All *opportunities* are previously determined, and all *obstacles* as well. It must be clearly fixed in the Christian's mind that God sets before each of us a clearly defined race, an appointed course.

Then, this illustration shows us that the Christian life is an *active, aggressive life*. "Let us *run*," the text says. It is God's job to set the course of the Christian life, and He has done that quite precisely. Now, it is our job to run the course He has set. We are not to sit still to be carried by the prevailing currents or winds. We are not to loiter or linger. We are not even to *walk* as men with measured step. We are to *run!* Sometimes the life of faith is presented as if it were completely passive. It is true that we are to "not try, but trust," and that the Christian life is "not I, but Christ." However, this does not mean that we are carried dreamily to heaven on an air-foam cushion. The Christian life is a life of concentration, discipline, and energetic effort. In fact, the Greek word that is translated "race" in this verse is the word, *agona*, from which we derive our English word, "agony," and it pictures strong and powerful exertion of energy. In order to live the Christian life, we must "run."

Several years ago, one of the leading international diplomats of our nation was Mr. Averill Harriman. He was the United States representative at many European conferences. One day a reporter asked him the question, "How is your French?" He replied, "My French is excellent, all except the verbs." What a commentary on the life of the average Christian. It often happens that our Christianity is excellent—all except the verbs! The verbs are the *action* words. The Christian vocabulary has wonderful *nouns*—such as "Master, Savior, Redeemer, Lord, repentance, faith, forgiveness," etc. It also have inspiring *adjectives*, such as "excellent, wonderful, unsearchable, unspeakable." But the *verbs* are often missing. There are no verbs—there is no *action*—which corresponds to the wonderful nouns and adjectives of our faith. The *propositions* of the Christian faith are magnificent, but the *practice* of the Christian faith is often deficient. Yet the verbs are the very heart of the Gospel, great verbs such as "come, go, follow, serve, give, love, share, make disciples." The true Christian life is an active, aggressive life. There is no room for idleness, slackness, negligence, indifference. This is powerfully illustrated by the picture of a race.

II. THE INSTRUCTIONS

Then, the writer records the *instructions* for running the Christian race. A runner who does not discipline himself *before* a race, and follow a plan *during* the race, is not likely to *win* the race.

Twice, the author uses the words, "let us." And each time he follows with instructions for running the race. What must we do to win this race?

THE CHRISTIAN RACE

First, we must *listen to the witnesses who encompass us.* "We are compassed about with so great a cloud of witnesses," the writer says. The word "witnesses" that is used here does not include in its meaning the idea of a person looking at someone or something. These witnesses have already seen something, and now are testifying to us of what they have seen. These witnesses are not spectators who are watching you, but "speakers" who are silently witnessing to you. Rather than their looking at us, we are to look at them and listen to them. Note especially the word about Abel in Hebrews 11:4, "He being dead yet speaketh.

The very success of each of these heroes of faith recorded in Hebrews eleven is a witness to us. When the Emperor Napoleon was leading his French army in the great Egyptian campaign, they came one day to the neighborhood of the famous Pyramids. Napoleon called his army together, raised both his arms toward the nearby ancient monuments of Egyptian culture, and cried out, "Men, forty centuries are looking down on you today!" This is the message of Hebrews 12:1—not in the sense that former runners actually see our performance today, but that their trophies of victory encourage us to excel in the same race of faith. Any athlete will tell you how inspiring it is to read of the examples of great athletes in his field.

Some years ago, a great film was made about the post-war trial of Nazi war criminals. It was entitled, *Judgment at Nuremberg.* The courtroom scenes are packed with drama and emotion. Spencer Tracey played the judge. He listens to the prosecuting attorney build his case, piece by piece, film by film, fact by fact, against the Nazi officers on trial. Then he listens to the defense attorney as he presents them in a different light. After a particularly tense part of the courtroom trial, the judge calls for a recess in the courtroom procedure. During the recess, the judge leaves the courtroom and takes a walk.

As the judge walks the streets of Nuremberg, he comes to a vast arena where there are no people. There are just seats in a stadium. He walks onto the race track in the floor of the stadium, and he begins to hear in his imagination the sounds of a great cloud of witnesses. Though they are imaginary sounds, they make a deep impression on the judge. Director Stanley Kramer brings to life the imaginary picture of a man—a madman—Adolf Hitler, screaming his shouts and empty promises and hopes. You hear the people shouting back from the stands, screaming in almost antiphonal voices their words of allegiance and confidence in him. It's a powerful scene. Well, this is precisely the way we are to receive the idea of Hebrews 12:1. We are at this moment "surrounded by a great cloud of witnesses," and their testimony to us is powerful and overwhelming.

One of the renowned leaders of the Salvation Army was a "Colonel" named Samuel Logan Brengle. Late in Brengle's life, when speaking engagements had to be canceled because of the gathering darkness at the end, he wrote, "I have sweet fellowship at times in my own room. The saints of all the ages congregate there. Moses is present and gives his testimony, and declares that the eternal God is his refuge. Joshua arises, and declares, 'As for me and my house, we will serve the Lord.' Samuel and David, my dear friends Isaiah, Jeremiah, and Daniel, Paul and John and James, and deeply humbled and beloved Peter, each testify to the abounding grace of God. Luther and Wesley and the Founder (General William Booth) and Finney, and Spurgeon and Moody, and unnumbered multitudes all testify. Blind old Fanny Crosby cries out, 'Blessed Assurance, Jesus is mine!' So, you see, I am not alone. Indeed, I can gather these saints together for a jubilant prayer and praise meeting almost any hour of the day or night. Hallelujah forever, and glory to God!" In the same imaginative way, the writer of Hebrews asks us to hear the loud and clear testimony of silent witnesses from the past.

Each of these former victors of Hebrews eleven is a *silent spokesman,* and each has a testimony to give to us concerning the necessity, the nature, and the power of faith. Kenneth Wuest says, "The word is *martus,* one who testifies, or can testify, to what he has seen or heard or knows by any other means." So we must listen to these witnesses that encompass us as they say to us, "It is gloriously true that the just shall live by faith. You are on the right track. Be faithful to Christ. God did not mock our faith, and He will not mock yours." So, as we live the Christian life and run the Christian race, we are being encouraged by those who have victoriously finished the course.

Second, we must *lay aside the weights which encumber us.* "Let us lay aside every weight," the writer says. The word translated "weight" is *ogkon,* which means "bulk," or "mass," or "excess, superfluous flesh." To follow the analogy of the text, "weights" were training devices for an athlete. He would train with heavy weights attached to his lower leg or ankle. This would strengthen his legs, and the removal of these weights before the race would make the runner light-footed and eager. No athlete would think of competing in a race while wearing these weights. In fact, the athlete will give up things that are perfectly legal and innocent in order to excel in athletics. The track coach would say, "If you would win, you must run light." Anything which puts a drag on your feet in following Christ is a "weight."

What a message there is here for Christians! One of the greatest failures of the average Christian is that his loyalty is divided, his life is fragmented by countless preoccupations.

Each reader will remember the children's fable which we heard many times as children. It is entitled, *Little Red Riding Hood*. The little girl in the story was on an assigned mission of mercy to visit and care for her ailing grandmother, but she was distracted by the flowers on the way and stopped in the woods and did not reach her grandmother's house in time. She ran into serious danger, both to herself and those she loved, because of this distraction. In our Christian lives, we often run into serious danger because of the "weights" that slow us down or turn us aside from our assigned race. The weights may appear innocent, but they prevent our victory in the race of life.

> *Some men perish from shrapnel, Other lives go down in flames,*
> *But most men perish inch by inch, Playing at little games."*

These preoccupations, these "little games," may be completely legal and innocent in themselves, but if we realize the true nature of the Christian race, we will put them aside so we can run to obtain the prize. The Moffatt translation says, "Let us lay aside every handicap."

In the Christian community, we have often failed to distinguish between sins and weights. The word here does not refer to sin, but rather to needless baggage, excess weight. I have read of mountain hikers that they even trim the one-inch margin from the maps they carry to get rid of any unnecessary weight! They are far wiser than most Christians, who never realize the handicap that "innocent" weights are to them.

This will make sense when we emphasize the picture of running in a race. Simply stated, 350-pound people don't win races! (Each of us needs to hear and heed the implications of this last sentence) A Christian must apply a different standard than the standards others use. He can't merely ask, "Is it *wrong*?" He must also ask, "Does it hinder me?" Arthur

THE CHRISTIAN RACE

Pink said it vividly: "In a race, a bag of gold is as great a handicap as a bag of lead." In his devotional commentary on Hebrews entitled *The Way Into the Holiest*, F. B. Meyer wrote, "Thousands of Christians are like waterlogged vessels. They cannot sink, yet they are saturated with so many inconsistencies, worldlinesses and little permitted evils that they can only be towed with difficulty into the celestial port."

In running the Christian race, this rule must not be forgotten: All that does not help hinders. When we stand still, innocent things don't feel burdensome. But when we try to run, we learn what encumbrances "innocent" things may be. We begin to feel entangled and weighted down. In fact, the best way to discover what hinders us is to begin to run this race. When we're taking life easy, we can be covered up with burdens and hardly know it. But when we enter this race, we begin to recognize many of the trappings of our comfortable lives as burdens. Every believer must decide what his own "weights" are—and we must not judge one another on these.

Pastor and author Hoover Roopert told of a *Washington Post* reporter's account of the maiden voyage of a cruise ship on the Potomac. The ship was built to carry passengers from Mount Vernon to Washington, D. C. All kinds of Washington dignitaries gathered for the trip, including Congressmen and Senators and Cabinet officials. The ship steamed out into the river on a very hot, humid, muggy day.

One Congressman sitting by the rail took off his shoes and socks. Suddenly someone running down the deck knocked one of his socks over the rail and into the water. "Now," said the reporter, "this Congressman did a very impressive thing." Without hesitation he picked up the other sock and dropped it over the rail too. The reporter found that impressive because he knew exactly what he would have done. He would have taken the remaining sock home and kept it in his drawer for a year until he could figure out what to do with it. Yet, how much more sensible it is to just say good-bye to the useless sock, as the Congressman did.

The aspiring Christian must say good-bye to some good things he has gotten used to in order to say hello to a lot of Best Things he has not yet experienced. He must have the courage to let go of "that old sock"! "Let us lay aside every weight."

Third, we must *leave the wickedness that entangles us.* "Let us lay aside . . . the sin which doth so easily beset us," the writer says. The word translated "beset" occurs nowhere else in the New Testament. It comes from a root word which means to "surround." The phrase could be translated, "the easily-clinging-around-us sin." Just as no runner could hope to outstrip his opponent if he has not first stripped himself of the close-clinging oriental robes he wore previously, so the Christian must strip from himself "the sin which so easily entangles him."

What is this sin? In the context of the book of Hebrews, he is not referring generally to "besetting sins," but to one particular sin which is always dogging the steps of Christians and threatening to entangle them. There is one primary and deadly sin in the book of Hebrews, and it is the sin of unbelief. The greatest chapter of this book is chapter eleven, *the faith chapter,* and the greatest sin of this book is *unbelief.* The mother sin, the father sin, the parent sin, of all sins is the sin of unbelief. Unbelief is not merely a weakness, as we so often regard it; it is a deadly sin. Unbelief is a sin which needs our repentance and God's forgiveness. What heavy garments would be to an athlete approaching the starting line of a crucial race, the sin of unbelief is to a Christian. What that athlete does to those garments, the Christian should do to the sin of unbelief—he should strip it off, and lay it aside. You see, weights slow us down, but sins trip us up. "Let us lay aside . . . the sin which doth so closely cling to us."

Fourth, we must *last through the weariness which exhausts us*. "Let us run with patience the race that is set before us." Verse 3 warns us of the danger of "being wearied and fainting in our minds." Verse 12 says, "Lift up the hands which hang down, and the feeble knees." Apparently, discouragement, weariness, and exhaustion are real dangers as we run this race. Our own personal experiences allow us to know just how real these dangers are.

The word translated "patience" in our text means "steadfast endurance." Moffatt translates it "determination." The Christian life is not a wind-sprint, such as a 100-yard dash. It is rather a long-distance race, a marathon, an endurance contest. Many Christians would easily manage the Christian life if it were just a brief span of concentrated energy. It was to spiritual sprinters that Paul wrote in Galatians 5:7, "You did run well; who did hinder you?" They started well, but had little endurance. The track coach would use the word "stamina," and this is a good word for Christians. Faith is not to be a mere momentary burst of emotion, but a settled habit of the soul which carries us through the tenth lap as well as the first. These are the instructions—"let us lay aside every weight, and the sin which doth so easily beset us, and let us run with patience the race that is set before us."

III. THE INSPIRATION

Finally, the writer sets before us the *inspiration* for the running of the race. Where do we find our example, our motivation, our inspiration for running this race? The text answers, "Looking unto Jesus, the Author and the Finisher of our faith." Every word of this phrase is important. Here we find the supreme inspiration for the running of the race of faith.

We are to *"look unto Jesus."* The word translated "looking" in this verse is found nowhere else in the Bible. It is the Greek word "aphorao." It literally means to "look *away* to" Jesus. It includes a deliberate turning from all possible distractions and a deliberate focusing on one object. It describes the complete capture of the attention by the single object, Jesus. We are to look away from sin, from self, from the future, from the past, from failure, from people, from circumstance, from our own ignorance, from our own learning, from our own helplessness, from our own merits, from our own efforts and struggles, from our own self-righteousness, from our own works, from our own faith. We are to look **away from everything else**, and **to Jesus**.

I can remember hearing the saints I met in my early Christian life state it over and over again as a rule for victory in the Christian life that the believer must "keep his eyes on the Lord." No greater counsel can be given or received. For years, I played the game of golf with a mixture of enjoyment and embarrassment. There are many (many!) important things to remember in the game of golf, such as correct grip, right stance, coil of body, use of legs, smooth back swing, complete follow-through, *ad infinitum, ad nauseum,* but most important of all is *the keeping of the eyes on the ball* (and being sure you are not standing too close to it *after you hit it!*). All the other lessons are of little value if the golfer does not learn to keep his eye on the ball. In the Christian life, also, the other lessons are mere religious regulations if the believer does not keep the eye of faith fixed on the Person of Christ.

Englishman Roger Bannister and Australian John Landy were the first men to be timed in less than four minutes in the one-mile race. A highly publicized match between them was held in Vancouver, British Columbia, and the hype of the match turned it into one of the great sports events of modern

THE CHRISTIAN RACE

times. In fact, the race was billed as "the Mile of the Century" by sports writers. The race was decided in the stretch run just a few yards from the finish line. Landy was leading by perhaps two steps when he turned to look over his left shoulder to see where Bannister was. The distraction was fatal to the Australian's hopes for victory. At precisely the second that Landy glanced over his left shoulder to check the position of his opponent, Bannister was making a move on the outside, to Landy's right, and the split-second break in pace allowed Bannister to pass Landy. The record books of the game of track and field will forever hold Bannister's name as the winner of "the Mile of the Century," the race that set the four-minute standard as the target for all future runners—because John Landy became distracted from his goal and looked to his opponent instead of the finish line. I repeat: we are to look away from everything else, and unto Jesus.

Also, this verb is a present participle, which means *continually* looking away to Jesus. We are not merely to look now and then, but we are to acquire the habit of looking always. We are to see the other witnesses who surround us, but we are to see another vision which will turn our eyes away from them. We may see the distractions—the weights and the sin which cling closely to us— but this vision calls our attention even from them. This vision, when once seen, will make the soul forget all else. If your faith is growing weak, and your feet are growing weary, and you are not running as you should in the race, I call upon you to "look unto Jesus." In the Christian race, we are found all too often looking at ourselves or others. This may look innocent, but it is fatal to the successful running of the appointed race. Our sole safety, our constant inspiration is to be found in keeping our eyes off of self and others, and keeping them unswervingly "looking unto Jesus."

To "look away unto Jesus" means to keep the mind and heart firmly and unwaveringly fixed on Jesus Christ. The first chapter of Hebrews tells us that Jesus Himself is the exact representation (the "image") of God (Heb. 1:1-3). Human beings are so constructed that it is normal for some mental image (imagination) to fill their minds. The Christian should always hold before the eyes of his soul the image of the glorious Son of God. He should meditate on the mysteries of God revealed in Christ's holy birth, in His sacrificial life on earth, in His redemptive passion and death, in His death-shattering resurrection, in His ascension to heaven and in His age-long session at God's right hand. And the Christian should always remember that this risen and glorified Jesus is in him.

Turn your eyes upon Jesus,
Look full in His wonderful face,
And the things of earth will grow strangely dim,
In the light of His glory and grace.

We are to "look unto Jesus" in a certain character. "Looking unto Jesus, the Author and Finisher of faith." In an ordinary race, there is a starter, a pace-setter, and a judge at the finish. Jesus is all of these to the believer in the Christian race.

He is the "Author," or *starter*. It is He who sets us off on the race of faith. It is by faith in Him that we are *in* the race at all. The Bible says in Galatians 3:26, "Ye are the children of God by faith in Jesus Christ." If you are not in the race, look unto Jesus at this very moment for your salvation and your start.

If you have become aware while reading these words that you are not really in the race the text describes, I am going to ask you to do a daring, crucial, revolutionary thing. I am going to ask you to break with your past self-centered lifestyle (this break is called "repentance" in the Bible), and re-center your life around the Person of Jesus Christ by a crisis act of trust (this act is called "faith" in the Bible). Let me take a moment and explain the negative act of repentance and the positive act of faith.

Several years ago, a well-known 77-year-old United States Senator named John Glenn went back into space on a United States NASA rocket. This was a return trip for Glenn, one of America's early astronauts. When a rocket ship is fired into space, there are two vital matters to know. One has to do with what NASA calls "escape velocity," which is the force of thrust that is necessary to overcome the present gravitational pull that holds the space ship down on the earth. It is a proven fact that more of a rocket's fuel is necessary for the first two minutes of the flight than for any other part. If there is not enough escape velocity generated in the first part of the flight, the entire trip is aborted. The escape velocity that is necessary to begin the Christian life is called repentance. Repentance in the sinner's life must be of such a kind and quality that it breaks him loose from the former gravitational pull of sin and selfishness—no small task! So even his repentance is a miracle of God.

NASA also knows that, once the space ship is moving away from the earth's gravitational pull, it can use the increasing gravitational pull of its new destination—the moon, for example—to supply force for its flight. The nearer it gets to its new destination, the greater is the pull of that object. The Bible defines the "flip-sides" of the salvation experience as "repentance toward God, and faith toward our Lord Jesus Christ" (Acts 20-21). Repentance provides the escape velocity that frees us from the gravitational field of sin and selfishness, and faith in Jesus Christ provides the force which "shifts the center of gravity" from self to God. Jesus becomes the new Center of a believer's life.

If you have not repented of your sin and trusted in Jesus Christ to save you, let me suggest a prayer for you to pray. While your heart is alerted to sin and to God by His Truth and by His Spirit, pray this prayer directly to Jesus Christ: "Jesus, I am a sinner, and I am lost. I cannot help or save myself. If I continue to depend on myself, I will remain selfish, sinful and lost. But you have told me in your Word that You love me, and that You want to save me. I know that You died on an awful Cross for me and my sins, and I thank You for loving me that much. You also tell me that if I will repent of my sins and trust You, You will save me. Right now, in my deepest heart, I repent of my sins and trust You and You alone. Please come into my life, forgive my sins, give me Your gift of Eternal Life, and become the very center of my life. As I trust You, take my life and make me what You want me to be. Help me to express my love and gratitude to You by walking with You and serving You the rest of my life. I thank You for saving me. In Your Name I pray. Amen."

In the moment of your salvation, you entered a great romance. You have been "married unto Another, even to Him who is raised from the dead" (Romans 7:3). The potential joys and relational victories of your new life are limitless. However, you have also entered a great war. When you enter into peace with God, you are immediately at war with the devil. The picture used in our text is that of a long-distance race. Read this message again, and ask God to make it practical to your daily life. Prepare yourself accordingly, and begin to run the race today.

Then, Jesus is the *pace-setter* in the race of faith. The word "Author" means File-leader. This means that Jesus leads the long procession of those who believe. He is just ahead of us all the way, setting the pace, drawing out our speed, and keeping up our spirits until we cross the finish-line.

Finally, Jesus is the *judge*, the "Finisher" of our faith. This picture comes from the Isthmian games, in which the judge sits behind the goal, awaiting the runners as they come in. Behind the goal sits Jesus, watching the race and awaiting the runners as they cross the goal. The runner may be pictured crossing the goal victoriously, and falling exhausted into the arms of Christ.

Hebrews 12:3 says, "For consider Him who endured such contradiction of sinners against Himself, lest you be wearied and faint in your minds." The word translated "consider" is the Greek word *analogizomai*, from which we derive our English word "analogy." The dictionary defines this word as "an agreement, likeness, or correspondence between the relations of things to one another." The shorter dictionary definition of an analogy is "an agreement or a similarity." To "consider Jesus," then, is to "draw an analogy between ourselves and Him." It means to make a comparison between ourselves and Him, to take a lesson from Him with the intent of achieving similarity between ourselves and Him. We are to give full attention to Him—His character, His conflicts, His conquests. We are to be constantly occupied with His Person (12:2a), His Passion (12:2b), and His Position (12:2c)—and with His Model always before us, we are to keep running the race!

Are you in the race of faith? If not, why not enter today? Receive Christ as your own Savior and let Him enter your name among the names of those who believe. And if you are in the race, are you running according to instructions?

ADDENDUM

HOW TO DEVELOP TEACHING SKILLS

Any adherent (*disciple*, one glued to Jesus like adhesive tape) of Christ will discover soon after His beginning in The Walk that verbal communication of his faith, his testimony, and the Gospel are a vital and inherent part of the disciple's life. He can never *be* a disciple or *build* disciples without declaring his faith on a regular basis. Furthermore, he will soon find that he is under the Master's mandate to *teach* "the faith once delivered to the saints" to as many others as will receive it. In fact, a disciple is simply a teacher-in-training. The command to "turn people into disciples" is supported by the phrase, "*teaching* them to obey all that I have commanded."

When the Apostle Paul capsulated The Process of Disciple-making into the packed statement of II Timothy 2:2, he told Timothy to "deposit the things you received from me into the lives of faithful men, who will be enabled to teachers others, also." So one of the tasks of the disciple-maker is to "enable" his disciple to teach. Do not misunderstand this strategy. A believer does not require the "gift of teaching" to teach any more than he requires "the gift of giving" to tithe. The gifts refer to extraordinary abilities, but the activity is still to be practiced by each believer. Of course, wisdom must be used to not force a person who obviously has *no* communicating skills to occupy a teaching position. I will include a few closing remarks about that disciple.

Let me suggest a few practical steps which may be taken by most disciples and disciple-makers to assure that the disciple will be "enabled" to teach (a necessary step for passing on the truths that are foundational to the process).

First, do everything possible to assist him in establishing and maintaining a vital, powerful, practical daily walk with God. This becomes the launching pad and the "power base" for anyone's presentation of the Gospel. "A cannon must be one hundred times bigger than the shell it shoots." This adage may be used to show the importance of the daily quiet time in empowering and enforcing every activity a Christian is supposed to perform. I have never in my awareness met a powerful, effective, productive Christian who did not have a meaningful and powerful "morning watch" with God. No believer could validly claim that he could be a hundred times "bigger" than the Gospel he believes and proclaims, but the adage is still accurate.

Our lives must "adorn the Gospel" which we believe and proclaim, and without a relational quiet time every day, this will not occur. The mechanics of the quiet time will be the subject of other vignettes, but this must be kept before both the disciple and the discipler. Is your present walk with God, highlighted by a daily quiet time, vital and alive?

Second, the teacher-of-teachers (the disciple-maker) and the disciple (a teacher-in-training) must have some way to get usable curriculum, or to create and develop his own materials. I personally write all of the materials I use in The Process, and hundreds of the sessions are in print and available to disciples and disciple-makers. I try to make it clear that these are not to be relatively wasted by a one-time proclamation (teaching a Sunday class, preaching a one-time sermon, teaching a group Bible study, etc.). Rather, these are strategy materials to be used as curriculum, and thus they must be strategically mastered for repeated presentation and multiplication through many generations. This strategy has literally exploded through trained disciples so that these sessions are emerging in the underground church in Asia, in many nations in the continent of Africa, in Central and South America, etc. I wish I could take the time and space to document the testimonies of both disciple-makers and disciples in distant places who are using these curriculum studies to "sustain the chain" of disciples through an enlarging network of multipliers.

I have often said to disciples in hundreds of settings, "Get or create your own curriculum materials if you can and will, but if you do not have other material, you are welcome to use mine. Furthermore, if you find better studies than mine, please send them to me, because I do not want to live and die using inferior materials when better ones were available." The crucial thing is that every study be solidly based on the Word of God, and that each be as full an exposure as possible of all the truths in the given text you are using. I must frankly say at this point that most studies I hear, including many sermons, do not reach this standard. This is a dangerous oversight of the incredible riches of the Word of God.

Two farmers were talking on a street corner at the end of harvest season. One said to the other, "How'd your 'taters turn our this year?" The other retorted rather indignantly, "Mr., they didn't *turn* out; I had to *dig 'em out!*" The rich truths of the Word of God don't 'turn out' to casual readers and handlers, they must be dug out by lengthy, calculated, spiritual searching of the words, phrases and sentences of the Word.

An old magazine used to carry a regular monthly feature entitled, "Enlarge Your Word Power." It was merely an examination of English vocabulary words. Every Christian should daily 'enlarge his Word power' by deep, rich study of the Word of God.

I want to say very candidly and very firmly, out of much experience, that the presented (perhaps printed) study session which the discipler passes to the disciple must be systematized in an evident and progressive way, so that the teacher-in-training can easily follow the progression of the lesson. A study without an outline may require 30 minutes for the teacher to present (after all, it is his material), but without an outline and the necessity of incremental teaching (one unit at a time progressively presented), the teacher-in-training will repeat *the idea* and will require only *five minutes* to tell it. Thus, both the discipler and his disciple may become very frustrated.

Third, the teacher-in-training must be afforded a teaching platform (at least occasionally) to develop, test and critique his effort. He must be allowed to teach the group of disciples in which he regularly meets, knowing that he is in a friendly atmosphere and will be evaluated lovingly and constructively. The teacher-in-training must look for and use every possible opportunity to express the teaching—in Sunday School class, in cell groups or small group settings, through testimony in groups, and in enlarging settings as he develops capability, confidence and wisdom in presenting the disciple-making sessions. He must submit his effort to the evaluation and critique of loving disciple-makers for improvement, and he must take their evaluation seriously. You see, a true self-worth in Christ, a full power-base of relationship with

ADDENDUM

Him, and a free fellowship with God's people are necessary to implement this process. All of these matters, and many more, are addressed and dealt with (extensively) in the disciple-making process.

Fourth, the growing teacher should develop, or accumulate, and keep, some four categorical studies on hand at all times, ready for immediate use. One should be an *evangelistic* message or study, a second should be a *Christian growth* message or study, the third should be a *disciple-making strategy* message or study, and the final should be a general *Bible study*. He should always have devotional thoughts in all of these areas available and ready for presentation. Also, he should have one great "lifetime" (this is my title) illustration available under each of these categories. (I would sneak in the idea that he should also have ready humor available, if possible, because humor is the universal disarmer, de-fuser, and relationship builder)

The Apostle Peter wrote, "Sanctify (give proper place to) the Lord God in your hearts, and be ready always to give an answer (Greek, *apologia*, apologetic, defence) to any man who asks you a reason for the hope that is within you with meekness and godly fear" (I Peter 3: 15). We need a gigantic (gigantic, colossal, mammoth) army of well-trained disciples who can answer that call! However, this army is like all other armies—the capability, efficiency and victory of the army will be proportionate to the quality and kind of training each soldier has had.

As usual, a word of caution is necessary in concluding this vignette. I mentioned the person "who obviously has *no* teaching skills to occupy a teaching position." Is he to be dismissed from the disciple-making process? Is he to be sidelined with no role to play in disciple-making, reproduction and multiplication? NO! A THOUSAND TIMES, NO.

He may play what will finally prove to be the most vital role of all—the "support" role, the "supply" role, the intercessory role. No wartime effort can be successful on the battlefield if the thousands and thousands of factory workers, munitions makers, doctors and nurses, etc., fail to fully and faithfully function at home or just behind the battle lines. This principle is stated clearly in a verse in I Samuel 30 (verse 24, *Amplified Bible*): "As is the share of him who *goes into the battle*, so shall his share be who *stays by the baggage. They shall share alike.*" Ponder this verse, memorize it, master it, and remind yourself and your disciples of it constantly. Note the two features, the *battle* and the *baggage*. Obviously, battles must be fought before wars can be won, but no warring battalion of soldiers can function powerfully and victoriously unless the *baggage* is secure. If the baggage is vulnerable, the enemy will attack at this weak point. The "baggage" includes all of the necessary equipment to engage in battle. In our analogy, the prayer barrage must be maintained to soften up the enemy and to make the soldiers strong, the curriculum munitions must be prepared and dispersed, and attention must be given to the "mop-up operation" (the follow-up) when the battle is over (and the analogy includes many more activities than these). These who "stay by the baggage" should be recruited and trained as thoroughly and strategically as those who "go into the battle." Thus, a regiment of disciples should be thinking (strategizing about) prayer, availability of curriculum, follow-up, etc., even before the battle begins. Everyone is to be a team player, thinking, living, acting, performing his own role, but in relationship with, and total support of, every other player on the team.